WE ALWAYS HAD BEER

An Autobiography

ANGELA "RED" WRIGHT

CONTENTS

INTRODUCTION

"A lot of things broke my heart but fixed my vision."
~Unknown

I sat in my car driving familiar streets, talking out loud to no one, asking questions to no one, relaying information to no one. I do that often and as senseless as it might sound, that fantasy friend saved me many times in my life. The peace that that friend has always brought me may just be what I needed to make large and small decisions. Each of them life changing.

I never thought about that friend as being someone or something that was ridiculous or meaningless, she was who she was and when I needed or need her, she is there.

I think that's the thing that keeps her around. She never judges, she is there no matter when I need her, or why and she has never once abandoned me. She never laughs at the wrong time, and she always cries when it is called for. She has been the one constant. When I age, she ages with me, when I am sick, she is the comfort that pats me on the head. When I cry or question, when I am angry or happy. She is all those things with me.

When young children have imaginary friends, I never thought that was odd. I understood what it was like to need that one friend that would never ever leave you. Never judge you. And she would never die.

I never had to say goodbye or miss her, because she has literally always been a part of me.

Even today, but not as often, I find myself asking her out loud if I should do something, if I should make a certain decision or if I should just let something go.

And though it seems as if I am talking to someone else, I am not. I am really just relying on myself but in a different manner. In a more transformed and oddly silly way. It is comforting to have that other piece of me, the one that as I have gotten older, keeps me from losing my shit with most people, most days.

My fantasy friend also never tells me that I am not worthy of something.

When you grow up never believing you are worth anything, you need that one part of you to say, you are worthy. Or you know, fuck those people.

In the 5 to 10 years before my mother's death I remember more times than I can count she would say to me, why do you have this or that, what makes you worthy? Why do you get to own this or that, what makes you worthy of something like this? Why do you get to travel? Why do you get to eat or drink the last of something in the house? What makes YOU worthy???

It was not just those years; I was raised in a household where everyone was more worthy than I. More worthy of love, food, attention, things.

But I was also raised that way in church. That every one of us was never worthy *enough* of god's love. We could never be good enough, do enough, beg or pray enough. Nothing we did was ever going to bring us the kind of love that we were told we needed to survive the great destructive deadly fire and brimstone Armageddon that would be coming any day now.

Not worthy, uneducated, controlled, a daily slog of depression, waiting for the great day of Armageddon when god would kill every single person that did not worship the way we did.

Every day getting out of bed wondering will today be my last day on earth. Am I worthy enough for god to save in his great rage from the sky?

I tell my story because I know there are people out there like me. Those who are or were lost. Those who cannot see a better future. Those who cannot see that they literally hold the key to the chains that bind them.

Whether those chains keep them from getting educated or get them out of a troubled marriage or relationship or keep them from being their true selves. Maybe you are gay, bi, transgender. Maybe you want to be educated, read, write, travel, sing, dance.

Maybe just one day is the one thing that will change your life. One decision, one friend. One small leap into the unknown.

It is scary for sure, but it will be worth it. And it might not feel like it today. But each moment that goes by will give you the freedom to clear your mind and make your path.

Life is short and you only get one.

YOU are worthy and I trust that my story might help you understand that no one has the right to tell you what your worth is.

No one has the right to tell you who you can and cannot be. And no one, no church, no parent, no partner, no political figure, has the right to tell you how to live your life. You owe nothing to anyone but yourself.

If you want to leap, leap. I promise there will be someone there to catch you.

I have added some newspaper articles, certificates, letters, photos, etc. to this book because while writing I have gotten a few messages from people calling me a liar and saying that most of my stories are false, made up, just a way for me to get attention. Unverifiable was also a word used. So, to prove to whoever the reader is that my stories are in fact, truthful to the extent that I had access to the knowledge and details and things I needed to prove and write this part of my life, then I have them added them so that you can see that I did not in fact, embellish or lie. My memory on a few things is a bitch sketchy, but I will also relate that to you as you read. It has taken me 10 years to put this book together and I have put in as many facts, factors, humans, dates, times, places as I can and can remember. Though I am sure there are still a few things I may have gotten wrong, the intent was to use my memory to the best of my ability to give you, my story. Especially when one's life was for many years filled with abuse and lies. Others will say "this is not how I remember it." But you do not need to remember it the same way for my story to be valid. Most names have been changed not to protect anyone but honestly, so I do not get threatening or rude messages later about how they were written. Or tell me that the secrets I kept, I should have kept. But when you read this, you will know who you are in the book. So, pour some wine, and enjoy the mess.

THE CRASH AND THE CULT

"Sometimes life takes an unexpected turn in the right direction."

~Unknown

On a sweltering summer night in August of 1968, 4 young people, leaving a party, were in a violent drunk driving accident that killed 2 people. Leaving another nearly dead and another seriously injured.

The car was destroyed beyond recognition. The driver and passenger, both dead.

Two children, each now left without a father. One father to death, one father who would live with his injures until the day he died many years later.

One mother who would now live with severe PTSD, survivors' guilt, and depression, until the day she died in 2010.

A mother who would now make one unwise decision after another, including joining an emotionally abusive cult, that eventually would be the end of her.

Families torn apart in an instant. Families demanding answers to questions for over 50 years. Answers that will never come.

Families were also torn apart by a cult that came at a time of deep tragedy.

Two children 55 years later have lived their lives in two separate states on the other side of the country from each other. Not knowing how the other was or was not affected by this tragedy.

A mother who entered a cult because she was lost, not seeing that that cult would eventually be the end of her and in the end, it would ruin and divide her family, her children.

It reminds us that in the blink of an eye life moves, changes, sometimes ends.

One wrong decision. One good decision. One decision never made.

This is the story of how that crash, that cult and the decisions that followed, would change the life of this writer.

JEHOVAH'S WITNESSES

"It is hard to imagine a more stupid or more dangerous way of making decisions than by putting those decisions in the hands of people who pay no price for being wrong."

~ *Thomas Sowell*

If you were asked to define or describe the word cult, what would you say? I want you to really think about that for a moment. A word you may just pass over in conversation or make fun of or never even use in a sentence.

And some religions, that you may think you are familiar with, would never even consider themselves a cult. Perhaps they think they are mainstream, but taking a deeper look, you will recognize the behaviors of a cult.

Think about its detrimental effects on people, what people do for a cult, how do they get involved in one, how people are trapped, or misguided, how they change their lives to bend to the demands, and how some take their lives, for this word.

We see it not only as religious but recently we have seen it deeply touch the politics of America and all around the world.

You have probably understood what you thought the word cult meant. And in your lifetime, you have most likely been aware of some, especially ones that enthusiastically made the news. Or maybe you or a family member know someone who is part of one, or you have been part of one yourself.

There are some that are incredibly famous, but not famous in a good way.

You might remember The Branch Davidians in Waco Texas, controlled by David Koresh. Ending in tragedy. April 19, 1993, 80 people lost their lives because they chose to remain brainwashed by a man who claimed to be the Prophet of God.

You may remember or have read about Jim Jones and his cult of followers, called the Peoples Temple, that also ended in tragedy. November 1978, 909 people took their own lives by drinking Cyanide, all at the behest of Jim Jones, their cult leader.

Or Marshall Applewhite and his Heaven's Gate, March 26th, 1997, where 39 people also took their own lives in a mass suicide, in anticipation of something greater. At the word of what the papers called, a mentally unstable mad man.

You might think of some cults being controlling, women being abused, men having more than one wife, young girls being married off, families being torn apart. Maybe they live in their own compounds, have their own schools. You might think of brainwashing, or people isolated from others, even their family members. Perhaps you think of rape, or incest or molesting, or perhaps you do not think much about cults at all. Perhaps a cult has never been something that affected your life. But I am here to tell you about a cult that on the outside seems caring and warm and friendly, kind, but is literally killing, raping, emotionally torturing and abusing its people every day.

Being outside it for 17 years I call it the "cult of Kindness", (though a friend of mine coined that phrase) but you have heard of them, most likely even spoken to them, and know them as Jehovah's Witnesses.

One of my sisters would begin this story differently, as she likes to do to undermine my life or memories, and she likes to pretend some of my life did not actually happen, as if our memories with a 13-year age difference will ever be similar, but because I was there, I will begin it with the facts as I know them and have put together, especially since my mother's death. Our age differences can make telling stories of our past different and even sometimes make it seem as if we were not part of the same family at all. But it diminishes neither my memories nor hers.

In 1972, a few years after the accident, my mother was once again on her own. She was divorcing my father, Gene. Custody battle for me had been taking up her time and her heart. Reeling from the loss of her husband, her friends, and having to move back in with her abusive, alcoholic, father and alcoholic stepmother, my mother needed, as I recall, something to help her find peace, to find her balance. She was still incredibly young, 24 years old, with a 4-year-old and a divorce almost under her belt. She was lost and sad.

At that time the religion, or as I am going to refer to them, the cult, Jehovah's Witnesses arrived at her door one day. Her stepmother had been studying the bible (their version of the bible) with them and had introduced them to her, but it was not until she was approached by a couple of ladies, with a book, called The Truth book, that she began to take the church seriously. There was a woman named Myrna who studied the bible with my step-grandmother, Jan, and she also studied with my mother. My mother embraced the cult, my step-grandmother just uses it to this day as an excuse to abuse people and to make excuses for her own narcissism. She left it in the 70's because she did not like something someone did. Let us be clear she never likes something someone did or does. It is a lifelong pattern of hers.

My mother was in an unbelievably bad place. Though it would not occur to me until many years later, and I cannot put too fine a point on this, *the church made my mother worse, not better.* Their empty promises and their total control of her brain and heart and her life. Every decision she made was to please the cult.

If you are not familiar with this cult let me fill you in. And emphasize that though some of my firsthand experiences in the cult may have varied from what others experienced, the foundation teachings that they push are consistent around the globe.

Jehovah's Witnesses have this disguise of being truly kind, balanced people. They say there is no greater love than their love. They pretend to be generous and devoted. You may be familiar with some of their beliefs or things they do not do, they do not celebrate holidays, or birthdays, or participate in Military service, or vote and they do not take blood transfusions. That is only a small part of it.

Jehovah's Witnesses are a (sort of) large group of "Christians." They started in the 1870's and changed over time with their name and beliefs. As of this writing they have a bit over 8 million publishers, as they call them, those active in the preaching work, going door to door, all over the world. They have over 120,000 congregations worldwide and as of this writing have once again been banned in a country, this time it is Russia. But they are restricted or banned also in Singapore, China, Vietnam, and many Muslim majority countries. Sometimes for their refusal to be part of military service sometimes because they want so badly to think they are better than others by their beliefs therefore making themselves seem superior in their teachings and dismissing or ignoring governments and or laws. Russia told them that they must follow the laws of the land, they did not like that, so banned they are. Norway has just restricted them because of their abusive shunning policies. Policies that are so abusive that people even take their own lives over it.

You may have met them at your door when they have come to preach to you, to show you god's good news, you might have seen them on a street corner peddling their literature, or you may have gone to school with one, you may work with one, or you might even have one in your own family.

What you might know about them you think is small and harmless but what I am about to tell you is far from that. It is neither small nor harmless.

My mother came into the cult to save herself. She felt that she needed to bring some peace into her life and the cult happened to get to her at the most vulnerable time.

She became so obsessed with the cult, with its teachings, with its belief in a Paradise on Earth, a new world, the resurrection of the dead, that she did not see the harm it was doing to her and her family. Her obsession led her to forget that world around her and sometimes the people around her and to focus on her and her alone and what she believed was true. No one else, nothing else seemed to matter but the hold that the cult had on her. It was as if she was possessed by ignorance and false hope. Sometimes it did seem as if she was in a trance. This cult had a deep and tight hold on my mother.

She began to easily dismiss members of her own family because Jehovah's Witness discourage you from having contact with your family members who are not part of the church. She even stopped speaking to her father and her own brother, believing that the church was her family now. Do not get me wrong, her biological family were not all worthy humans. They had their problems, Norman Rockwell paintings they were not. But dismissing them as if they do not exist is part of the control and abuse the cult has on people.

Sometimes we make those decisions because our family is toxic to us. And I agree with dismissing those things from your life and those people. But if you believe that god is so weak that he cannot allow you to speak to or be part of your family simply because your beliefs are different, than you worship a different god than the one I have studied to understand. Though I do not believe in god today, I know that there are different definitions of god for many people. And for most people, god is love, period.

This caused many years of tension between her family and herself. But she managed to banish most of them from her life. For the cult. She would banish anything if it got in the way of her salvation. Anything and anyone. Salvation that the cult dangled over us like a carrot. And there was no greater hope than this Paradise on Earth salvation. Perfection, no war, no hunger, no disease, no death. But to get this you had to succumb to all teachings of the cult, without question.

She made no friends anywhere outside the church, only those inside the church were worthy of her friendship and vice versa. She frowned upon even meeting with those she worked with for coffee, tea, dinner, etc. For fear that they might sway her thinking when it came to the cult.

My husband says my mother had subjects, not friends. Though she claimed that she had all these close friends in the cult, she loved to be worshiped, she loved to take up all the space in the room, to be revered, but I am not sure she understood true friendship, this was a deep and honest description of her.

Actually no one inside the cult understands actual friendship. Everything had conditions. All love had conditions.

This is a major teaching in the cult, no friendships outside the church. Imagine if you will, the people you encounter each day, or the people you have met in your lifetime, as a child even. The constant burden knowing that even if you like that person, have a good relationship with that person, have things in common with that person, you are never allowed to become friends with that person. No dinners, no cocktails, no phone calls, no time together, because they are a mere outsider to the teachings of the cult. A friend outside the cult is a danger to your way of thinking. What if they were to question even a small thing that you were being taught and poison your mind away from the great control the cult has over you? The cult does not like to lose members. The cult does not like to lose, period.

The cult does not encourage or in many cases allow counseling. Not for mental health reasons or for addictions like drugs or alcohol.

My mother became increasingly angry as the years went by and would say that it was because she needed to be closer to god, to Jehovah, and that he would help her get through her pain. She began to blame her anger on me. She began to take out all her anger on me in many ways.

It would not be until several years later, as an adult, who left the cult, that I began to realize that she needed significant help. Her anger was bubbling over, and it was affecting our family deeply. She needed to speak with a counselor of some kind, any kind, to help her with her childhood traumas, her pain, the pain of losing her friends in a tragic car accident, losing her husband at only 19 years old, surviving sexual and physical abuse by her father and mother. Being raped, living with alcoholics, and for her survivors' guilt, because she was the only one to fully survive the accident. I believe her PTSD was off the charts, but that was something she would never confess, and it was not something that the church allowed in casual conversation. No one spoke of mental health, yet it was obvious, especially being out of it for so long, that so many people were in desperate need of mental healthcare.

She needed serious *professional* help. I cannot begin to emphasize this enough. No amount of reading the bible, or making fake friends, or going to church three times a week was going to help her get through or even manage her emotional pain.

Let me repeat that, NO AMOUNT OF READING THE BIBLE, was going to benefit or fix her.

Her baggage was so heavy and her worries and pain so deep that no matter how many times she said it to herself, she was never going to get the peace or help she needed unless she got professional help. But since the church vehemently discouraged outside professional help, even for things like addiction, that also proved to be a challenge for her.

The church insisted that seeing a counselor would put new and different ideas in someone's head, words, or ideas outside the teachings of the church, and that that would be dangerous. Any form of teaching, reading, or conversation that contradicted anything that the church taught, was completely frowned upon. You could even be disciplined for it. Though there are some who were brought up with a more balanced view regarding reading materials. Some things that were pushed on me came more from my mother's views of the church's teachings rather than what they actually taught.

There was a lot of dysfunctions in the church, mostly produced by the controlling behavior of those in charge. And make no mistake, any church that is a cult, Mormons, Fundamentalists, Catholics, Seventh

Day Adventists, to name a few, all have a form of abusive control over its members. They lord their perceived power over every member. Always making sure the members are under man's control and that they are aware that they will have NO form of salvation without the approval of the church and those that control it. And that these men are instruments of god and you get nothing and nowhere without their say or approval. That is a cult.

There was a pyramid kind of order with Jehovah's Witnesses, the Governing Body, those that ran the entire organization from one location in NY, eight men. Always men, women were not allowed to oversee anything in the church. They are not allowed to teach from the podium or have any positions in the congregation. Except pioneering which I will cover.

And women are told to be submissive to their husbands just as they are to the church and to Christ. Women have extraordinarily little say inside the cult. Women are only tools, objects. Women are abused and many do not even know they are.

There were the Overseers, those that would come to the congregations occasionally to check on the "health" of the congregation, and to make sure there was nothing or no one stirring the pot or no one making real trouble in the congregation.

Then there were the Elders, each congregation had several, depending on the size of the congregation, it could be 3-8, give or take. Always men of a certain age, usually over 40, and always appointed by the Governing Body. These men oversaw the congregation. They were like an HR department. You could talk to them, tattle on your friends to them, get advice from them, seek help from them, get approval of something you wanted to do, but make no mistake, though these men were supposed to be there as your confidant, and protector, many of them would not be. And sometimes people found out the hard way that these men were more abusers than helpers. They did not in many cases show mercy and some of them even seem to thrive on the tragedy and sins of those in the congregations.

There were also Ministerial Servants. Just the fact that someone has the title "servant" should have made many of them run. But I remember the foolish young couples competing for a place in the congregation. You were nothing if your husband was not a Ministerial servant and you as the dutiful wife were not a pioneer of some kind. They had regular pioneers and Auxiliary pioneers. Each requiring different hours in the door-to-door ministry.

Pioneers were women, mostly, that spent all their free time out in the door to door preaching work. Some 30, 60 or 90 hours a month going door to door trying to convert people. Though the church claims that the preaching work is not a conversion work, they are lying to themselves. It is exactly that. Why do you think so many people came into the church in the 70's, like my mother, when they had such a huge campaign of people going door to door trying to bring others into the "fold" as they call it? And whenever there is some kind of natural disaster, boy do they go to town trying to convert people so they can be saved by what surely will be next, the end of the world.

Most Ministerial Servants were, as anything in the congregation, appointed positions. You were usually a young man, one who was trying to work their way up to be an elder in the church. You had to be clean shaven, have short hair, have a clean history, especially if you had grown up in the church. They do kind of a background check on you to make sure you are pure enough to be a Ministerial Servant. You had to be as clean as they come. You could not listen to corrupt music, could not have an eye-catching car, could not watch rated R or questionable movies, could not watch porn, could not masturbate, (yes masturbation or "self-abuse" as they call it, is a TOTAL no-no to Jehovah's Witnesses) They also could not be getting blow jobs from their wives, reading questionable material, or have a wife that was not submissive. Not all ministerial servants were married but because of the stance on marriage in the church, most of them were.

Yet if you were a young wife in the congregation and your husband was not working toward being a Ministerial Servant, you might as well be the worst wife in the world, not supportive enough to help him reach the goal of being a servant. Not submissive enough.

And these Ministerial servants had menial jobs in the congregation, carrying a microphone when people wanted to answer something, counting money, stacking magazines, vacuuming, cleaning toilets. Men believed that this was some form of great affection from god to have these privileges

And when I say job, mind you *none* of the positions in the church are paid positions. These men and women do everything on a volunteer basis. Which might sound fine at first until you realize that they work full time, take care of their families, and spend every other waking second of their free time, with the church. They go door to door most Saturday mornings, unless they are pioneers then that is every single day. They go to church 3-5 times a week, and if anyone questions why they are not spending more of their free time serving Jehovah, it becomes a circle of abuse of power, by telling people that they are not good enough, and until they give up all their free time serving god, he will never deem them as worthy.

The church makes it very tough to have a personal life. You are considered selfish if you take too many days for yourself, or even a vacation or sleep in on a Saturday morning. Because you need to make sure that you never question the church's teachings. And to make sure that never happens, you need to spend all your free time doing nothing but going to church, talking about church, being submissive to its values.

Because they would never be able to make it in the world outside the church, many of these men abused and abuse their powers, they would Disfellowship you (this is the word they used to use for those who are dismissed or shunned) now they call it "No longer being a Jehovah's Witness", or "mark" you or "reprove" you, all forms of abuse. Making announcements to the whole congregation as to who was being disciplined and why, and then treating them like pariahs in the church until they came crawling back and asked for forgiveness and showed they were once again worthy of god's love as well as the congregations.

I met plenty of these men that were kind, but many more that were abusive. Many of the Elders lorded their positions over the congregation, or over its members. They would make you afraid of them, and they would make you very aware that they oversaw your life, that you were nothing without their approval. This makes a lot of very hopeless people. People, many of whom are trapped inside this cult, seeing no way out.

The thought of someone being Disfellowshipped used to make my mother sick to her stomach. She could think of nothing worse than one of her children being punished or banished in that way. She used to look down on people who were disfellowshipped as if it were the worst thing that could ever happen to a family or friend.

My mother tried to follow the "rules" of the church to the best of her ability. She was a good Witness. She would read only the material that the church put out, and the bible. Again, their version of the bible. She would, as she got older, read some mystery novels, but it was rare that she would expand her mind with any other kinds of books, or news, or actual events around the world. Nothing political, no schooling, seeking no expansion of her brain.

Why did she need to, the church taught her everything she needed. And she knew that any day now, Armageddon would be here, and she would need neither knowledge, skills nor a savings account.

The witnesses teach that since Paradise on Earth will be here any day now, there is no need to have any kind of financial savings. No need for retirement, a 401K, or anything that resembles retirement. No need for emergency funds. Many of the followers are extremely poor, they have no education, work at menial jobs, and live paycheck to paycheck just waiting for Armageddon. Many of them do not own their own homes, drive broken-down cars, and live in poverty. It is almost like a symbol that you are a better Christian than the man next to you if you are poorer than him because it shows your faith is stronger.

(Though as the years went on and tech came into the picture there were plenty who worked in tech even without a college degree and did quite well for themselves. But this became a problem too as many of them had money and began to buy large homes, fancy cars, while still so many were extremely poor)

One of the most brutal teachings in the cult is that of "religious genocide." Jehovah's Witnesses teach that only Jehovah's Witnesses will survive a cataclysmic destruction of the earth. That god will destroy, burn with fire, murder, have murdered, anyone who is not a Jehovah's Witness at the time of his wrath. They teach that *only they* will walk into a paradise while walking over the dead bodies of those that their loving god has killed. And that could happen any day now. So, you live day to day in constant fear of this event. And always questioning or being questioned if you are good enough to survive this genocide.

I was raised in the church, and for 37 years I tried my best to be that perfect Christian daughter. I tried to be what I believed my mother wanted me to be. I knew early on that this cult would not be my forever belief system.

I got baptized as you were required to do, at the age of 17, some do it younger, but it is a requirement if you are to be favored. Most of my friends at the time, who were the same age, also got baptized. But the issues of being baptized were more than many people could handle. You see if you just went to church and never got baptized then if you did something "wrong" in the eyes of the church, you could never be shunned officially. But once you were baptized, if you did something that was bad in the eyes of the church, you then were on the path of almost no return. The shunning process for Jehovah's Witnesses is one of the worst, very much comparing to the Amish religion.

I wholeheartedly believe that it should be illegal to force or encourage a minor child to get baptized into this cult. It is a contract with the cult that they now own you.

The shunning process is so brutal that for me and me alone, I lost seven friends to suicide in the church, because of this abusive shunning behavior. But I can tell you with certainty that there are thousands of people today who are now dead, at their own hand because of the shunning process that Jehovah's Witnesses teach as "Love."

You see once you are disfellowshipped, or you even leave the church of your own accord, then you are no longer allowed to speak to anyone at church, or your family, or friends, and all your friends are tied up in the church. Because remember you are not allowed to have or make friends outside the church. Since the church does not allow you to have friends outside the church, now everything you know about your social life, even a simple conversation with your sister or your mother, is gone. You are to be left on your own. To fend for yourself in the world. And many people do not make it. They have no idea how to live in the world outside the church, they have no friends outside its walls. You have no contacts, no traditions, nothing.

I call this Emotional Terrorism. One of my sisters recently has been put in this position and we have had several conversations about how this "discipline" is not love. It is abuse and it is simply unacceptable in the real world. The punishment does not match the crime. They take away your entire life and social structure simply because you are human, make a mistake, or think for yourself.

Just imagine being told your whole life not to make any wrong or bad decisions because Jehovah God would no longer love you and you will be shunned by your family. Though shunning seems like an archaic punishment, it is very real inside this cult. Your life as you have known it, has literally ended. You are now alone in an exceptionally large world that the cult has not and will never prepare you for. You have been told your whole life how horrible everyone outside the church is, how they are all bad people, drug addicts, prostitutes, abusers, liars, cheaters. Now you are thrust into an emotional rollercoaster of uncertainty and loneliness.

Many countries are now recognizing that this shunning process is unacceptable because it leaves people dead, homeless, in deep depressions and they are making laws to make it illegal.

Jehovah's Witnesses do not allow children to be part of sports teams, or cheerleaders, or part of clubs or do after school activities. They teach that competition is bad, that we should all be equal, mediocrity, not stand out in any way except in our worship. That if you are part of a team or club that you will spend unnecessary time with kids who are not Jehovah's Witnesses therefore you could be influenced outside the church, and you might come to question the church's teachings. We cannot have that, they must always keep control of their members, at all costs.

Since they are taught that any child in school who is not a Jehovah's Witness, cannot be your friend. Imagine how hard that is for a child not being able to make any friends at school. Especially if there are no other Jehovah's Witnesses in the school you attend. And as you get older the only friends you have or speak to or do things with are those inside the church.

Now imagine yourself as a child, going to school and not being able to take part not only in sports, or clubs but not in any holiday or birthday celebrations, zero. Sitting in the corner or being dismissed from the classroom every time a holiday or birthday is celebrated. Imagine being told this is what god wants and that if you do not obey, he will kill you in his great day of fury. As a *child* you are told that god will kill you, if you do not obey the Governing bodies teachings, period.

So not having any social structure at all, and then being shunned, will make people do dramatic things. You either spend 6 months to a year of your life in almost total solitude, trying to be a perfect human being so the church will take you back. Or you take your own life. There is rarely an in-between. Though there are some of us who simply move on, start over, and never look back. But for many of my friends, taking their own life was the only way to proceed. Devastating.

And the cult allows this without blinking an eye. How can you sit back and watch people take their own lives and then say things like "well he just did not prove worthy" of god's love, "his faith was not strong enough," "perhaps he was mentally ill"? Mentally ill? Yet the cult does not approve of psychiatric care. It is twisted, toxic logic.

And if you commit suicide your family is not allowed to hold a funeral or memorial inside the church or Kingdom Hall as they call it, because suicide is terribly controversial. And the church has NO empathy for those that have been disciplined and did not come back to the church, begging for their lives back. They have no empathy for these people who die at their own hand, when the reality is, the church has blood on its hands. These people took their own lives because of the abuse of the church because they were left to die, and the church cared nothing about them.

They also do not salute the flag or sing any songs like in America, The National Anthem, as they are not allowed to have any views on nationalism or participate in anything that puts country over their god. When I was a child saluting the flag in school every day was required. I would have to stay seated, not put my hand on my heart, or leave the classroom during this time every morning. Which makes for incredibly angry teachers and gives the kids liberty to make fun of me all the time. It was just another brutal way for the church to control you.

You already know that Jehovah's Witnesses do not celebrate holidays. It was not until I had been out of the cult for several years that I realized the real abuse of power regarding this. You see the Witnesses say that holidays are pagan and that is why they do not celebrate them. I used to think ok, I get that. But then I was like wait a minute, of course they are pagan, every single religion and or person, knows that.

After being out of the cult for a while, and as I was making a new life for myself with real people and making devoted friends, I realized that my husband and I had zero traditions. None, not for a single holiday, or birthday. New friends we made, they all had their traditions and family time, and memories. But we had nothing. No traditions, no memories, we were literally starting from nothing. This is also a form of abuse that the church feels proud of. They do not allow you to have a single tradition so that when you do leave or are kicked out of the church, not only are you shunned by everyone you know, but you also have no way of celebrating anything with anyone, because there is no one, never has been. They hope that this loneliness without friends or family and without holidays or birthdays will be the one thing that will make you crawl back to them.

That deep loneliness alone might be the thing that makes you beg them to take you back.

They control everything about your life, inside and outside the church. The cult holds your salvation over you. One false step and you are left for dead by them and by their god.

When you leave the church, you must start your life over from scratch. As I said, you are either strong enough to do that, or you must go crawling back to these abusers, telling them how unworthy you are of their forgiveness and just hope by some mercy they let you back in. You are left to beg for that life back because you know no other life, no other way. They have ultimate control over you.

If you leave, if you can take that brave step, it takes years to rebuild your life, and I was fortunate to do it with a strong partner. Many people are left on their own. My husband and I have spent the past 17 years rebuilding our lives from the ground up. Rebuilding our community.

We joined clubs, had hobbies, and met new people; we are open to new possibilities every day. Fortunately, we both have strong personalities, and we travel the world frequently. That helped us to start finding people to pull into our new life and to be friends with. To make memories with.

One major thing that has been so freeing for me is that I am now allowed to talk about anything I want, with ANYONE I choose. Especially current events, politics, and the like. I can read what I want and discuss anything I choose. I can fill my mind with more knowledge than I ever thought possible.

Jehovah's Witnesses do not get involved in any kind of politics. Even going as far as not to vote or register to vote. They are not allowed to have an opinion on either side about any kind of politics. So why keep up on current events, why keep up on the world news, or things going on inside your own country? You are supposed to be completely neutral about all of it. They believe that only god's government, the one that will eventually take over the entire world, is the one they should be talking about, discussing. They take a few scriptures and turn it into the reason that they are to be neutral in their political views. Continued ignorance.

They are not allowed to be part of any military service. Not even volunteering in a military office to answer phones.

Being a police officer is forbidden. As is being a firefighter. Though I did know one person who was a firefighter in all my years inside the cult, and he was not allowed any "privileges" in the congregation. They said that his job did not allow him to take his life seriously and that he mocked god. Whatever.

You realize shortly after leaving the cult that you are now allowed to have an opinion. A real opinion about what is happening in the world, in your own country. And that opinion and that knowledge is important. You need to be informed about all of it. Information is key. Knowledge is key.

You are now allowed to talk about anything you want, at any time, with anyone at all. You are no longer restricted by the rules of the church. If you want to talk about a subject, do it. If you want to be informed about a subject, do it. The world is a fantastic place and in the 21st century we have access to unlimited information. Now you are allowed to use it, read it, understand it, share it. No restrictions. And now you are allowed to have any opinion you want, any belief on any subject you choose. And critical thinking skills. Something the church frowns on.

One of the hardest things for me leaving the church, besides losing my "friends" and family, was learning that you are not in charge of everyone's feelings or emotions. Inside the cult you are told that you must manage all your own thoughts and emotions and make sure that you do nothing to upset or offend others. And that if they are offended or "stumbled" as the church calls it, that you are responsible for making it different or changing their feelings. You alone are solely responsible for the feelings of others around you. And they go as far as to tell you that you could have "blood on your hands" if you do something that "stumbles" someone so severely, that they might even leave the church, or perhaps start cutting back on their attendance or door to door ministry. You are responsible for making it right with them and making sure that their relationship with god is made right.

It takes a while once you leave the church, or are forced to leave, to understand that YOU are not responsible for the emotions or feelings of others. We are each responsible for ourselves, period. I am not responsible for my friends' emotions or feelings about something. I might influence someone or something because of a belief I might have. But to take the full weight of someone else's emotions is completely insane. It is such a maddening unnecessary burden to put on people. And it is exceedingly difficult to undo once you leave the grasp of the cult.

After years of being out I have encountered thousands of people who have tried to leave or release themselves from this cult. Mostly online in Ex JW support groups. Some of their stories are heartbreaking. Many have taken to YouTube to tell their stories of sexual abuse, rape, emotional, physical, financial, any kind of abuse.

Jehovah's Witnesses do not believe in giving to charity or helping anyone but themselves. If a community is in trouble from a disaster or a neighbor needs assistance in some way, Jehovah's Witnesses will not reach out to them or help them at all. They believe in only helping themselves, or those like them or those with the same beliefs as them. They have no desire to help people who may question their faith, their cult.

They make so many excuses about why they do not give to charities or help others. They even say things like others are being lazy, that is why they are begging for food, or need material goods.

But even their own members are poor and sometimes begging for food. And it is an exceedingly rare day in the 37 years that I was in the cult that I remember them helping even one of their own out.

They also discourage their members from getting food from food banks, because many food banks are inside of actual churches. So, they keep their members poor, do not help them out and then also discourage them from getting free food. Abuse.

But the reality is that they do not want to be part of anything that does not teach or doesn't speak about their way of living, teaching, preaching. They do not want to be influenced at all by anyone or anything outside their cult. And if they are not helping others then they can spend more time preaching their way of life daily.

But there are some sad realities to this, and that is that they rarely even help each other. If you need assistance, materially or emotionally, chances are, you will not receive it from anyone inside the church. Not even those that call themselves your friend. They ignore anything that derails them from their goose stepping of kingdom preaching.

Their way of helping is to convert others to the cult. Not with food, or shelter, or gas, or grace, just conversion.

Friends inside the cult, well you quickly come to realize they are not friends at all. I define a friend as someone who knows you intimately and would do anything for you. There are no strings, no questions. They are there to build you up, to support you, to help you, guide you and sometimes grow old with you. They share similar interests, and they have deep affection for you and you them. You trust them explicitly. No strings, no tricks, no questions, friendship.

Even having disagreements that are talked about or through friendship. Not dismissing someone because they are not 100% aligned with your way of thinking.

Inside the cult friendship is vastly different. You are forced to be friends with those inside the church. You are told you must be friends with people because they are part of the church, and they have the same beliefs as you. You may spend years with these people. Growing up together, sharing all the normal things people in friendships share. But you will quickly be disheartened when you need that friend, or those friends. As soon as you really need them, especially if they feel you have done something to shame the church, they will immediately turn on you. They will throw you under the bus, going as far as to even be the one to tell on you, stab you in the back, gossip about you. You will quickly find that they are only friends to the cult, not to you. And you may have foolishly wasted years on this so-called friendship when it was false to the bone. There was not a single thing about it that defines a friend. And you will wake up one morning and have no one left if you are removed from the cult by shunning or disfellowshipping or disassociating oneself. Not even one of them will take your side over the cults. After 37 years I was painfully shown this when not a single friend contacted me ever again. That is not friendship, that is control. And it is extremely dangerous. Not just for you, the one who is being shunned. It is also dangerous for those inside, who are so conditioned to believe that friendship and love have conditions. It does not, it should not, but when you are brainwashed, you cannot be told anything. You are programed and deprogramming takes years and sometimes never comes.

I love to entertain, some of you reading this will know this because you have and are always part of it somehow. I love the feeling I get when my friends are around me sharing stories, laughing, hugging, sharing wine, sharing books that we have read, talking about the day or weeks events, perhaps we even discuss something deep that is happening in the world, politics, travel.

In the cult, and it is a deeply painful revelation, that entertaining is more of a chore than an enjoyment. Everything you do is scrutinized. You are always on the watch that you do not do something wrong or say something wrong or perhaps you have one too many glasses of wine, or said a bad word, or spoke too loudly, or your music was offensive to someone. Your home was not clean enough, or someone thinks your furniture is too expensive, or, or, or. You can never just be yourself, you must make sure, as I stated before, that nothing you do is offensive to others. And people inside the cult are so weak because they have nothing in life but the cult and its control, that they are easily offended by anything and everything. And their ignorance does not help with this.

And just imagine seeing the same people every week, the same small-minded, uneducated people who talk about nothing but the same things every single second of every single day, year after year. All they talk about is their kids, the same publications and who is getting married or who is getting punished. The gossip is so toxic that it can put you into a panic. THE SAME FUCKING conversations week in and week out for years. Nothing changes, and it is like being stuck in a time loop. You find that their minds have not improved, their education nonexistent, their life, bland, only existence, not living.

This cult is also deeply obsessed with sex. Many cults are. These are not healthy good conversations about sex, why its normal, here is how to protect yourself, here is how babies are made, etc. But a deep psychotic obsession that translates into "anything regarding sex is bad, period."

They tell you sex is a wicked thing that should never be enjoyed, certainly never discussed. That you must be so cautious about your actual sex positions or thoughts on sex because god is always watching and judging your bedroom activities. Now I do not know about you, but I wonder why is god so obsessed with sex? Or why are the ones in control of the congregations, so obsessed with telling you that god is obsessed with sex.

A dear friend of mine and I were recently having lunch and she said that the toxic obsession that the cult has with sex is all she remembers about them. Their obsession with everyone's genitals and what they are doing with them, when, how, why, who, what.

Homosexuality is banned, period. They call gay men pedophiles. They shame them, they abuse them. And one reason they are so obsessed with what kind of sex you, a heterosexual, are having in your bedroom, is because they believe that oral sex is only for gays, because they cannot have "normal" sex. So surely if you are giving or receiving oral sex then you must in some way be gay or approve of the gay lifestyle.

They teach that any sex outside of the missionary position, for men and women, is considered, GAY sex, so its perverse. They teach that blow jobs, anal sex, hand jobs, masturbation, oral sex of any kind, is all a *gateway* to homosexuality.

But this sex conversation is a normal teaching in the cult, they treat sex as if it is bad, all the time. It puts those in charge not only in charge of your salvation but of how you can and cannot use your body parts. And sex is only allowed if you are married.

It is also a way for men to control women. Make sure the woman knows her place at home and in the bedroom. Make sure the woman does not enjoy sex or enjoy pleasing her partner. But make sure the man always gets what he wants in the way of sex.

But what it really shows is the weakness of those in power, their own masculinity seems threatened by gay men and lesbian women. They are threatened by those who have normal sexual desires. If they cannot control others' sexual desires or urges, then they feel they have failed.

One of the worst parts of this cult is that they cover over sexual deviance, sex crimes, abuse of all types.

They do not believe in telling authorities if someone comes to the elders with a story of rape, of molesting, of incest, of domestic abuse. They believe in handling it inside the church, period. They say it is because they do not want people outside the cult to think they are anything like other churches. BUT the truth is they are worse than other churches or cults. They hide and cover over sex crimes and crimes of abuse. They hide people inside the church that they know are criminals and abusers. They say they want to "keep the congregations clean." Yet they allow these abusers to remain in the congregations and never make them face the legal ramifications of their crimes.

They have this "2 witness rule" inside that cult that simply says that if you claim you have been raped, for example, that if TWO other people did not witness it, then it must not have happened. Or you must be lying about something. This goes for all types of sexual crimes. Rape, molesting, sexual abuse of any kind, domestic abuse. They consider them Sexual Sin, instead of Sex crimes. Or abuse sins instead of abuse crimes.

I remember clearly as a 16-year-old girl in the cult, a friend of mine who was 14 years old. She went to the elders to tell them that her father was raping her. Though they appeared shocked by it, they did not take her seriously. She begged them to get her father out of the house, she begged them to call the police, they refused and went as far as to call her a liar. This went on for months, until she went to the elders to tell them she was pregnant with her father's child. They again called her a liar because there were not 2 Witnesses coming forward who had witnessed this incest, rape, situation. They told her that she MUST have the baby, and then and only then would they be able to prove that baby was her fathers by DNA testing and then they might be able to do something legally about it. She was discouraged from having an abortion and she was blamed for being too sexy and for somehow doing something to encourage her father to have sex with her.

Think about that statement, a 14-year-old girl was told that SHE must have done something to ENCOURAGE her FATHER to have sex with her.

Well, that day, of her giving birth, never came, because my 14-year-old friend, killed herself. And the elders said it was because she did not have enough faith in god.

I know this story because that girl was my friend and because my stepfather was one of the horrible human beings, an elder, who let this girl continue to be raped and stood by and did nothing to help her. That blood is on them, period. That blood is on my stepfather's hands as well.

My stepfather was also one of the ones who listened to a man tell them for years that he was raping his daughter. Repeatedly. And they did nothing about it. They never called the police and they just sat back and allowed this man to continue to abuse her with zero consequences. They said that they would forgive him and do not do it again and go back home and be fine with your confession.

That young girl, now an adult with children of her own, has since authored a book about her terrible experience with Jehovah's Witnesses, called; Fighting *For me; Overcoming Sexual Abuse and becoming the person I was meant to be, by Amanda Zarate.*

But these are just a couple of stories of their abuse. The thousands of stories out there about abuse, rape, molesting, incest, domestic violence, financial abuse, is simply unacceptable. They cover over crimes, many of these men in charge are committing these sex crimes these crimes of abuse, and yet the cult still moves on.

In these days of unlimited information, you can easily research how Jehovah's Witnesses are in a heap of legal trouble for the years of sexual crimes they cover up. Even just as recently as a few weeks ago in Pennsylvania arrests in the congregations because of sexual crimes and cover ups.

It seems to never end, and I hope along with the support groups helping people leave this cult that this cult will eventually be shut down all over the world before more people are hurt or take their own lives before more families are ripped apart, forced to live without a word to family or friends. How much is enough, how many victims are enough? I say ONE victim was already too many.

If a woman claims she is being beaten by her husband, or abused in other ways, financially, emotionally, the elders turn the other way and tell her she must stay with him because this is what god wants. That her faith must not be strong enough, and she must pray more. That SHE is the problem, and SHE alone must fix herself.

Instead of encouraging her to get out, to get help, to call the police, they encourage an abused woman to stay with her abuser. Many times, eventually being killed by him. And yet they say the same thing, her faith must have been weak. Always the victim's fault.

Yet you will also find that many of these men in charge are nothing but perverts who rape, molest and abuse women and young girls and boys on a regular basis. These men who are supposed to Shepard the flock are also abusers. This is not unique to Jehovah's Witnesses, sadly.

You have most likely encountered Jehovah's witnesses when they come to your door to preach to you. To convert you. The problem with it is that most of them cannot defend their beliefs when they go out to preach. They are told what to say, how to say it and what bible verse to use. It is an exceedingly rare day that you will find a Jehovah's Witness who can defend their beliefs or show you in the bible why they believe the way they do about things like, rape, holidays, shunning, Armageddon, Paradise on Earth, etc.

Jehovah's Witnesses think they are the ONLY true religion. Seeing it from the other side of the wall, I can see that most religions teach this. But it is a cult that is so brutal that it traps people inside its emotional torment, it ruins lives, separates family, takes people's dignity, keeps people trapped in stupidity and they lack any kind of life outside its walls.

Jehovah's Witnesses are NOT harmless. They will strip you of your dignity, your sense of self, sense of worth, your individualism, your youth, your life, and your education. They will prevent you from having happy and healthy relationships in marriages, friendships, and family. And if and when they have had enough of you, they will throw you away like common trash.

For those who leave it and survive it, I cannot emphasize enough how powerful that is. Because with those few that survive you will find thousands who do not.

I am sure I have not said enough about this cult, but I dedicate my writing to those we have lost in a brutal way due to shunning or abuse because this "cult of kindness" helped them take their own lives.

I also cannot emphasize enough that without this experience I would not be able to see life in such a clear beautiful way. I feel that every experience I now have, good or bad, is still better than anything "good" that happened to me inside the cult.

I blame them for taking my mother, my youth, my education, my dignity, and once I left, my family. I blame them for taking friends who I loved dearly and for allowing monsters to remain inside their walls while people take their own lives without so much as a second thought.

I can tell you that I take nothing for granted in my new chapter of life. I wasted 37 years inside a cult that could not care less about me once I was gone. Though I gave it everything I was.

I also have to say to those of you who are still stuck inside, trust me when I tell you that you are not stuck. You have the power to leave this vicious cult and move forward with your life. There is help, support, education, and now unlimited access to anything you need to make a new clean and healthy chapter for yourself and your loved one.

The world outside is not filled with rapists, and drugs and whores and murderers and terrible things. Though yes, those things exist, do not let the cult tell you how bad the world is, while they themselves allow abuse to go uncontrolled behind their own walls.

Do not let this cult take ONE more second of your life. They are abusive, toxic and they do not care about you. Period.

Reach out to any and all social media support groups to find and get the help and comfort you need to begin your real wonderful life.

And to everyone and I mean everyone who has crossed our path since we left the cult. You may have stayed with us as friends, you may not have. You may have been here since the beginning of our journey, or you have entered the middle of it.

We appreciate every single one of you. For teaching us and showing us how to build our community along the way. How to make friends, make memories and traditions. How to love, how to lose and how to maintain our dignity and our hope during this time.

You do not know how much you all mean to us. Perhaps we have disagreed, perhaps you have gone your own way. But the lessons we have learned in the past 17 years, I can say for myself, are more numerous than I ever thought possible.

And I take every lesson, every friend, every tear, every laughter as a stone onto which to step to a new day in my journey. A journey I do not take for granted.

Now, turn that page.

ONLY HAPPY WHEN SHE IS UNHAPPY

"Like most misery, it started with apparent happiness."
~ Markus Zusak

August 6th, 2017, sitting on a dive boat in Indonesia remembering the anniversary of my mother's death, trying not to shed another tear for her, looking out over this fantastic place on earth I realize I have yet to write this chapter. This is the chapter I have dreaded, deep in my soul. I abhor my mother, and love my mother, all at the same time.

I have loathed my mother for so long that it is hard to remember a time when I had unconditional love for her. Or did I? When as a child you have that, my mother is the best person in the entire world, my mother can kick your mother's ass, my mother is prettier than your mother, kind of love. I did not want to paint her as the evil, ignorant, angry, and sad bitch she was. She was not all bad, but there were many years of my life that bad was all I saw in and of her. Not to put too fine a point on it. But she was difficult, and she made much of my life dreadful.

The first few memories I have of abuse were being beaten because I accidentally spilled a glass of milk off the table at a friend's home. Being beaten across my legs with a belt, for what I cannot say. And my mother pinning me to the floor with her body weight, force feeding me dinner because it was something I refused to eat. Of course, there was more but these are the ones I remember from an incredibly early age.

My friends who have known me, particularly since I left the cult, understand how difficult and complicated my memories of my mother are and how sometimes the pain in thinking of her is almost too much for me to handle or to talk about or through. There are days when I will just weep, for no reason, thinking about how much I wanted her to hold me, to touch me, to simply love me, as I believed moms do, would, should do.

I had Normal Rockwell fantasies about growing old with her, sitting on the deck drinking wine, laughing at our memories, laughing at our faults, being two old women who felt comfortable together, loved one another. But fantasies and dreams were all that would ever be. Even today sitting on the deck of my new home, overlooking the ocean, and wondering if she would ever share this moment with me. Probably not without constant criticism, I truthfully reply to myself.

But instead, what I will never forget is the afternoon I was at home, cleaning and in a loud sob, after months of angry, abusive, conversations with my mother, I told myself that today was the day I would stop loving my mother. Imagine if you will, that moment for yourself, to say I no longer want to love my parents. Because loving my mother was killing me and I needed to sever that tie to her and to my heart. My poor heart aches for her loss as it ached for her love as it aches for me when all I wanted was a mom. I was 40 years old.

My mother was born in Atlanta, GA on November 11, 1948. She was born to two alcoholic parents. Dorothy Dix Davis and Laverne Lee Leverette. Two parents who should never have been parents. Two people who should have never married, at least not each other. Two very selfish humans. Two people with so many demons of their own thrust those demons on their children. My mother was verbally, physically, emotionally, financially, and sexually abused, her entire life. Even when you leave this situation it still sits with you, eating away at you, haunting you. Abuse is hard to get over, to understand, to heal from, and makes it hard to move forward with any normalcy. However, there are those people I know that grew up abused in some way, shape or form and turned out to be brilliant, stable, kind humans. I would never want to make any assumptions as to why someone or how someone came through abuse. Honestly, I do not know how some people do it. How do they get through it and move on?

I see people who never do, and who pass that abuse on and down to their families. I see people who live as victims. I also see people who seem as if abuse never hurt them at all, when I know it tore them to their very soul. Humans amaze and frustrate me all at the same time.

My mother never had a chance at anything that resembled even an average life, childhood, or experiences. I think, if I believed in destiny, she was destined to be miserable, make others miserable and die young and miserable. That she was destined to ruin the lives of those she touched. To let everyone know she was unhappy and to make us live with that, without question. Though as I was just reminded, if she had not been who she was, I would not be who I am and as egotistical as it sounds, I believe I am an ok human. A bit bent, but no longer broken, but I am ok with that too. Bent is better than not living at all in my opinion.

I do not have much information about my mother's young days. She spoke briefly about her life. But I have put together pieces and parts from others, and from some things we talked about later in life, and the years she was ill and while she was dying. Those very brief conversations left me breathless with emotional pain and anger.

I have a photo album that I have pieced together with the help of my child of old photos of my mother and her family. They celebrated holidays, they went on camping trips, road trips. Sat by the lake, fished, hiked. I saw smiles in those photos, and I can only imagine that there was a time when my mother was a child that she did have some fond memories of her life. But the only answers I got about that were from these photos. She never spoke of those things. Good or bad, not really.

The time she told me about her father beating her and taking away all her stuffed animals, putting them in a rat-infested closet and letting the rats eat them up. Or how she had to beg for new clothes. How her mother and father screamed at one another and were drunk all the time. How she watched her father beat her mother on a regular basis. How the abuse in the home was so bad that guns were pulled, more than once. How she was never loved and every day of her life she was afraid for her life. Afraid to be beaten or raped by her father. Or raped by her father's friends. Afraid to be beaten by her mother, or emotionally or verbally abused. She never talked of a single positive experience as a child. Not even in school. I never knew if she was a good student, did she have friends, did she play an instrument, was she interested in college? I knew none of that. She spoke of none of it.

And she saved nothing from her youth. No yearbooks, a few photos of herself taken in school. I have a photo album that spans her life, but there are very few photos in it. None of them tell a story, they just tell of a single day here and a single day there. If you inspect the photos, you see a few smiles, but mostly forced. It was as if she was just going through the motions. Which I believe she did until she died.

It has taken me over 40 years to put together the women I knew as my mother. And it has been heartbreaking. She never dealt with her life, and she wasted most of it on hate and bruises and demons that she chose not to heal. I say chose because I believe that everyone can be in control of their own life, everyone. You must be aware of who you are, what controls you and what you allow to move you day to day. My mother allowed her demons to control her then she used that control, to control others.

My mother instead, just put one foot in front of the other, one day at a time, whatever comes next. Which in a tragedy is an acceptable way to get through each day, but it cannot carry you through your entire life. This behavior is only if you want to exist, not live. And my mother was only existing, painfully.

My parents were married. My mother was only 19 years old, my father 24. But no one who knew them back then, not even my mother's brother, could give me any details regarding their wedding. Even a woman who claimed to be her best friend back then, said she cannot remember their wedding or why they married when they did. On my birth certificate my mother signs her name both with it maiden, Leverette and married, Robinson. I only have court papers showing her fighting for custody of me from my father's parents but have not been able to locate even their divorce papers. (yet later in my writing you see I did receive some papers)

I figured she married because she was pregnant with me. Which if we do the math could mean they married in August 1967, 10 months before my birth. Something I only guessed at. Or they could have married right before my birth, in May 1968. Not sure it matters in today's conversations, but in the 60's those things mattered. In my research, I did find a birth and death certificate for a baby girl, born in 1967, in Marietta GA, my birth city, with my exact name. And I mean spelled the exact way. Mom misspelled my middle name. And to see it on these certificates of another child made me pause, but never ask. I would later find out that my mother had Dyslexia, which she never spoke of, or received help for, again the 60's, not something people readily discussed. Hence the misspelling. Some of that was generational, some was just my mother's obstinacy. She always thought she knew better than anyone or anything. But the subject never got broached. She would never admit her weaknesses. And looking back on my mother's years I can tell you that her dyslexia was something that she struggled with daily. Either way I still had a couple of questions unanswered.

Just today while writing I did find that my mother married my father, Thomas Eugene Robinson, on May 6th, 1967, the same year she graduated from high school. I did find one state record of them getting married, in Montgomery, Alabama. So, I suppose she was not yet pregnant with me when they married.

Most of the questions I have spent my life looking for were easily answered in today's quick search technology. Though I have been looking for a long time, this information looks brand new. I do not remember seeing it before today. But it still left one question unanswered why did they marry before she graduated high school? I remember one quick conversation she had with me where she said that if anyone knew they were married they would have kicked her out of school. But why they married before her graduation, especially since I was not born until the next summer, is beyond me. And honestly, I am exhausted trying to find out. No one seems to remember, or they simply do not want to say.

Going back to her Dyslexia would explain many things about her. Some of the reasons she would get so angry at even the smallest suggestion of turning left or right while driving. She would need someone to point in the direction not just speak it. How she would struggle for years to read a book in a timely manner. She could not read a map; she never filed her own paperwork but got terribly upset if her desk was messy. It was the insignificant things that I now see were her struggle with years of dyslexia.

Having a bit of Dyslexia, myself, I can look back and now understand why she would get so frustrated with herself when she would read but not be able to comprehend quickly what she just read. But it also kept her ignorant, not just because of the church she was obsessed with but because she could not admit a weakness or get help for a weakness, therefore she just lived her life making a fool of herself over facts, because she rarely had them.

I had believed for a long time that Eugene may not be my actual father. Mostly because there were never enough conversations or facts put in front of me to believe he was. But as the years went on and my research intensified, I now believe that he was indeed my biological father.

However unfortunately as I write this it is with broken and confused sadness, I must report that my father Eugene died from COVID-19 on February 2, 2021. Just one day before his 77th birthday. And because of COVID-19 there will be no service, just a burial. I, like thousands of others around the world, had to bury my father over Zoom. What a thing. However, I did receive facts about his life and my life from last summer and from his death that I will share in this chapter. (Death certificate in later chapter)

I was born in May of 1968, in Marietta Ga. My mother did not speak of that birth, or her wedding, or my father, ever.

She never spoke of being a wife or what her marriage, though brief, was like to my father. In fact, my mother never spoke of my father at all. I was forbidden to talk about him or to ask her questions about him. My stepfather never mentioned him, except once, in a fit of anger when I wanted to meet the man, I knew to be my biological father.

I was just told in 2017 that mom and dad were happy, that they seemed happy at least. And that they were extremely excited to be having a baby. That would be me.

Some people told me recently that my mother was always quiet, a wall flower. That she never really spoke much, did not have much to say, and had few opinions. Which was certainly different than the woman that I knew all my life, opinionated, arrogant, misinformed, ill-educated, and angry. Always so angry.

But in my research, you will read that I believe my father was abusive to my mother and it could explain why as a young woman she was considered a wall flower. She had already come from abuse, into abuse.

My father had been in several musical bands, immensely popular bands. The Misfits, the Onyx Blues Band to name a couple. (Figure 25 The Misfits newspaper article, Figure 27 Onyx Blu's Band poster) They made headlines and did a lot of gigs in the area. The Onyx Blues Band was the last band he was in before the accident. I have some of their early music on 45's that one band member, John sent me, re-recorded music that my friend Steve made for me and signed photos of the band and posters announcing their performances. I have attached numerous things so that the reader, that is you, can see that I did not just make up shit along the way of my life.

One of the band members is still alive, Larry. Randy committed suicide in 1976. (Figure 6 Randall Wilkins death record) John just passed in 2020 and my father just passed in 2021.

My mother, as I was told, was supportive, coming to the shows, but did not seem extremely interested in what was going on. I was told she just stood in the corner, did not embrace any of the fans, nor any of the family members who came to see the shows. My mother always had a musical side to her, perhaps she wanted to be part of the band too. That I will never know. She never embraced her musical side. But my absolute love for music came from both of my parents. She had a beautiful voice, she rarely showed it but sometimes I would hear her singing and I could feel the sadness in those notes. It was a rare occasion that she would ask me to sing with her, which I always felt was such an honor. Until she also used those occasions to tell me what a terrible singer I was and that I should not embarrass myself trying to sing in public.

In August of 1968, three months after I was born, there was a horrific automobile accident. I was originally told it was a drunk driving accident but then I was told it was just thoughtless driving. A girl driving a car that was too powerful for her. A blue 1967 (though the newspaper article called it a 1964 coupe) Corvette with a slanted rear window, a car built for two. But many years later picture proof would show that the accident was indeed alcohol fueled. People who had been at a party shortly before the accident, with the people involved, knew for certain they were drinking and driving.

I have photos that were given to me recently, showing the party they attended just moments before the accident.

This sports car meant for only two passengers, but holding 4, slammed into a tree at tremendous speed and was destroyed beyond recognition.

I recently went to the spot of the accident in Georgia. It was a bit hard to understand or quantify it. If the newspaper was right, the car overtook another, went through a stop sign then went only a few feet, across the street and smashed into a tree in someone's yard. But and I am only speculating, that would mean the driver had to accelerate from a stop at an incredibly high speed for the car to be destroyed just a few feet in front of them. And for two people to be killed and two to be thrown from the car. My parents were lying in the window of that car in the back, if you look at photos of that car, you can say that it was almost impossible. And to me it was almost impossible that my mother survived this crash.

I stood on the very street that accident happened. I do not think the newspaper article was right about how the crash happened. Imagining how fast that car would have been going to kill its two front passengers, immediately after leaving a party, but never actually entering any large road, only a side road, then a tree.

There was no other automobile involved in the crash. The police reports do not mention witnesses or any other automobile on the road that evening. Though the newspaper would report it differently.

For years I was obsessed with how this could have happened. But my mother never spoke of it. Not a clue, not a tear.

In my years of research, I had received an email from a woman who was just a young child when this happened. Living in the house where the car struck the tree. Her father had gone out of the house to see the commotion, he was the one who called 911. That emergency number was just created a few months before this incident by Speaker of the House, Rankin Fite out of Alabama.

There were police, ambulances, and everyone waking up coming out onto the streets. She said her father was shaken his whole life after what he saw that evening. It was incredibly violent and tragic. And he tried to help the people who were left alive, but it was too much for him to bear. He left the scene and left it all to the emergency workers.

My mother and father were thrown from the car, when the back window burst out on impact, but the passenger, Sydney Boyd Burrell, the manager of my father's band and his girlfriend, Donna Ray Schulten, were both killed in the accident. I requested death certificates for the two-people killed. (Figure 2 Sidney Burrell certificate of death, Figure 3 Donna Schulten certificate of death) The certificates do not say anything about alcohol, just their injuries, much of the certificates were redacted. As to why I do not know, I have tried to ask as it is not necessary to redact a death certificate 50 years later unless there was an open criminal investigation, which I have not been able to find if it exists. Though I did speak to a couple of older police officers who remembered the crash. But now two young people, in the blink of an eye, were dead. The certificates say they were both killed by blunt force trauma, head injuries, and bodies crushed from the impact of the car with the tree. They both lived only for a few moments and or hours before they were pronounced dead.

My father had severe spinal and brain injuries; he was in a coma for 4 months.

My mother broke a few ribs and had a huge scare on her left arm, road rash. I believe she may have had a skin graft done, or it could have just been the way the scar healed. We never spoke in detail about it. But it was there to remind her, every day. It was there to remind me every day of the details and harsh topics my mother would never speak of. She might mention it on sunny days when the heat from the sun would burn that section of her arm and make it ache. But that was rare.

The accident shook the community and families. Since my mother was the only survivor, people pleaded with her to tell them what had happened that night. Families could not make sense of it. The newspaper, the police, no one made sense of it. A car, 4 young people, leaves a party, runs a stop sign, slams into a tree with such force that it kills two passengers. Is that the whole story? Now I will never know. My mother said she did not want to speak about it to anyone. As far as I know, she never did. She took many secrets with her to the grave. I believe this was the largest of her demons.

I was told that she did not even attend the funeral of either of her dead friends. And she just moved forward with life. PTSD would eventually take her over.

I only remember twice in my life that she was racked with guilt over it, when a friends two sons were in a terrible accident that almost killed one of them, and when another friend's son was drinking and driving and three of his friends were killed. She cried, called me on the phone both times and started talking about stupid kids, drinking, and driving, selfishness, etc. I tried to be as patient and empathetic as I could, but it was difficult since she never confided in me about that night in 68, so I had no reference as to how she really felt about it. Though she lived her life with the guilt and pain of it. I am not sure that PTSD is a strong enough word for what she felt every day. Nor am I sure that there is a strong enough emotion to describe how a young woman can move ahead with life after she witnessed her two best friends being crushed to death in a car.

I never outwardly called it survivor's guilt, but that is exactly how I would describe how she lived for the next 40 years of her life. Her two best friends, and her husband had been killed and or severely injured in this accident and she never spoke of it, that is neither healthy nor natural. And her lack of discussing it not only produced her PTSD, but it never answered questions that others had regarding the death of their friends, loved ones. Her blatant refusal to never speak of it also left 3 families to grieve and question their whole lives, what happened in an instant that evening in August of 1968. She thought she had just left it behind, but it ruled the rest of her life. It ruled my life as well. It ruled every decision she made from then on out. Her abusive family, this accident. How much more would she able to endure?

The man killed in the accident left behind a 4-year-old son. Stephen. More on that later.

My mother was forced to move back in with her father and step-mother, after the accident. She had a new baby, a husband in a coma and her own physical and emotional injuries. My grandfather had since remarried to a woman much younger than him, a woman who was close to my mother's age.

Her father, my grandfather was an abusive alcoholic, arrogant, asshole, know it all. This would be how he was remembered even in death. No one wanted to attend a funeral for him. He had spent most of his life drinking his days away, beating his children and wives, raping his children, and wives, and abusing them with his words and actions. He had no business being a father, or a husband for that matter. I never heard my mother say a single positive thing about her father. Never, not once. Yet I know that she tried hard to make peace with him, or at least to make peace with herself regarding this man, her past, his actions. That peace never came. And I genuinely believe that her cancer was partly instigated because of all the hate she was carrying around in her body about her family, the accident, and so much more. And her lack of caring for her health daily. She just simply did not give a shit. And she took a lot of secrets to her grave. A lot.

I want to point out briefly that my grandfather was the only male influence I had in my life. We spent most of the days together. We worked in the barn together, we made homemade ice cream together, we BBQ' d, rode horses, went hunting, listened to music, shoed horses, read books, read the newspaper. We had cantaloupe with salt and pepper almost every morning. We roasted peanuts in the shell. Our favorite song was Freddy Fenders, Wasted days and Wasted nights. I loved riding in his old truck. He called me darling, he was kind to me, and he was special to me. My memories of him were mine. I never thought I would find a man that was like my grandfather. And though he was not a kind man to others, and drank too much, and was terrible with his money, those were not my childhood memories of him. So, I will keep my memories. And though people might say that it is not fair to give him any kind of platform because of the way he abused others. I say, I never excuse an abuser, ever. But my memories of him, with him, were not those of an abuser and honestly, I did not have a lot of good memories as a young girl, so I will happily keep those that made me happy during a very rough time in my young life.

My grandfather died in December of 2000; he was 79 years old. (Figure 7 Leverne Leverette death record)

My grandmother Dorothy died in 1984, she was 66 years old. She literally drank herself to death. I have zero memories of her. My cousin Francis talks about her as if she were some amazing woman who had lots of money and looked like a superstar. My uncle also talks of her as if she was some glamorous superstar. I do not know those memories. And my mother loathed her and was haunted by her everyday of her life. Haunted in a way that can only be described like the movie Amadeus, how it described Mozart being haunted daily by his father. It creeps into your bones, and it never leaves. But again, I can count on one hand the times my mother spoke of her mother. Anything I knew about Dorothy, my grandmother, I learned years after my mother's death. (Figure 8 Dorothy Leverette death record, Figure 9 Dorothy Leverette grave site)

I do have photos of my grandmother, with the kids, and the family. Camping, wearing fur. Always looking regal. But I have no memories of her.

If mother cared about one thing, it was her looks and how she was perceived by others. She spent a lot of time making sure she was dressed properly; her hair was always done and her makeup always on. Even if we went camping or she was at home cleaning the house. She made sure that her outer appearance was perfect. But what she should have worked on, or improved, was her inner self. Her physical and mental health.

As a child I remember my mother being young, attractive, sometimes happy, and trying to move on with her life. Though that is how I describe it now, back then I had zero idea what was going on in her life. But she was going out with friends, working, buying us a place to live, trying to be normal after the accident.

I am not sure how long we lived with my grandparents; I think it was a few years. My mother had to get on her feet financially, she no longer had a second income. I have many many memories of those years at my grandfather's home. And to be honest those memories were all positive. I almost believe my mother hated me for "glamorizing" him. I was a child, I did not know any other man in my life but him, and he was my entire world for the most precious times in my life. Anything that went on with mom and her father had zero to do with me.

I have many photos of me with my grandfather and step grandmother. I seemed happy and loved. It is those memories that get me through some days, as they were some of the best I have of being a child.

My father was in a coma for approximately 4 months. That is what everyone I have spoken to has told me, mom might have mentioned it to me once, but never at length and never start a conversation. My mother decided to divorce my father. I never understood this decision until I was much older. My mother could not wait to leave her father's house again.

This man was nothing but abusive to her, to everyone he encountered. My mother had some exceptionally large decisions to make about her future, our future.

My mother worked for The Bell Telephone company, and she seemed to really love this job. She made approximately $98.00 a week. And you would never know we were poor. I had everything I needed.

She bought a small trailer, an Airstream, and put it on a piece of land. I thought it was a random piece of land, but my cousin told me that that land belonged to my biological grandmother, Dorothy. I am not sure how much of that was true, as many stories coming from my family and especially my uncle were or are rarely true. I never understand the need to lie or exaggerate when it comes to family or life or situations. But my family seems to excel at this. It is hard sometimes to know what truth is and what fiction is. I have had to rely on solid facts, certificates, awards, newspaper articles etc.

But we lived in that Airstream trailer for a few years. I do not remember it being uncomfortable, or small. I was a small girl; I was happy with what I had. But it was during this time that I remember my mother being irritable all the time. She spent a lot of time with her girlfriends, partying and leaving me with my grandparents. She also went to Idaho a lot to ski, though I do not know how that transpired. As a young girl it is hard to know if someone is unhappy, grouchy sure, hurt, ok, but unhappiness can mask itself in many ways. And her unhappiness was growing bigger than her.

It was also during this time that my mother asked an older lady, Rose, if she would babysit me during the week while she worked. It was Rose that really helped me become a young woman. She taught me how to bake, how to measure ingredients, how to iron, how to pick vegetables from the garden and wash them and cook them, how to break an egg. She taught me how to do laundry and hang it out to dry. She taught me how to mow the grass, to sew, and to make a bed. We planted Sunflower seeds, and we caught fireflies and put them in jars in the evenings to watch them light up and fly around. My smile is big when I speak of her and her husband Bill, even now years after their death.

She taught me how to be kind to others, she had an enormous laugh and heart, and she is one human I think about a lot. I miss her and her husband Bill very much. I credit them for helping me know what it was like to be good humans, to teach and to love. And to be tough. This woman was one tough individual.

She even told me a story about how in 1968 she was in a terrible car accident that collapsed one of her lungs and when the doctors said it had to be removed, she said HELL NO. You will not remove my lung; I will manage it myself and eventually it will reinflate. And guess what, it did. She kept her lung and honestly, I never remember this woman ever being sick or hurt. She was amazing. To me at the time, she was one of my heroes.

My mother was in the middle of a custody battle for me from my paternal grandparents, Dana, and Mildred Robinson. They wanted full custody of me. And listening to my mother tell it, she fought like hell to keep me. I thought it was because she really loved me. But I got the impression as I got older that it was about the money. The money she was getting each month from social security, because my father was now disabled and unable to work. My father was also a Veteran, a Marine, Private First Class. He served for only 10 months in the military, but he was honorably discharged in March of 1967. (Figure 13 Thomas Robinson Marine Discharge)

Those social security checks were $250.00 a month along with her $98.00 a week in income, was a lot of money in the late 60's early 70's. Single mother, I can see why it mattered.

My step grandmother Jan years ago told me that when mom and I moved out of their home and into our own, that she loved me so much, she wanted to take custody of me herself. But then when I was much older, she began to blame me for ruining her life because she had to put her life on hold to take care of me after the accident. That really hurt at first, but then I realized, slowly but surely, that Jan is sick, dementia perhaps or mental illness. Borderline personality disorder as one person described it. She does not even speak to her only son. She now refuses to speak to me and honestly blames everyone and everything for the choices she made. She is selfish, rude, and ignorant and her anger spews from her like vomit. One person described her as a parasite. She is also an alcoholic. That was a theme in my family. I keep my positive memories of her, the way she taught me to do my hair, to sit up straight to dress as a lady should dress. But I have chosen not to speak to her anymore because I would rather have those positive memories and keep her toxicity out of my life.

Since my father was now disabled and though mom and dad were no longer married, I qualified until I was 18 to receive social security payments. I, however, never saw them; my mother used the checks for the family, which looking back, was fine. But I do remember a HUGE fight with her when I was older and asked her to let me have the checks she refused and of course called me a selfish whore who never thought of anyone but myself. When I threatened to leave home before my 18th birthday, she threw a fit because then I would have to be getting those checks directly and she could not have or use the money. And when I asked why my stepfather never adopted me and why I had to use his last name at church but not at school. She said if he adopted me, yep you guessed it, I would not be eligible for those checks any longer.

I understand that my father Gene had huge anger issues. I surmise that those anger issues leaked into my parent's marriage. My mother even told me that my father slapped me once in the hospital, he was there still recovering from the accident and that was when she said she decided that it was no longer good for her or me to be part of his life. More in another chapter in better detail.

This however carried into her life when it came to her choice of men. She always made and assumption and a strong one, that if a man had a powerful personality, if he was an A type as we call it today, that he was automatically an abuser. I assume that is why her second husband was a man she could walk all over. And though I have no ill feelings about my two brothers in law, they are both men that are soft and can be walked on by their mates. We do tend to marry spouses who are much like our parents. I married the second time to a man who has more of a strong personality like my grandfather. My sisters are married to men like their father, my stepfather. He was a weak, easily led, man who never stood up to his wife. And though I do not think my brother in Laws are like this, my stepfather was also a habitual liar. To the point of it being an illness.

After my father came out of the coma he was now in the care of his mother and father. He was now 24 years old. His mother refused both physical therapy and speech therapy for him. I was in the dark as to this until about ten years ago. In my conversations I was told several things, one was that she, Mildred, thought it was too painful for him to handle. But as the stories came to the surface, that was part of it, but also my father's mother was an evil human being. No one liked her, zero of my parents' friends, especially not my mother. She always shouted and was abusive to everyone she encountered. In my research for this book, I was told by a lot of my parents' old friends what a horrible human my grandmother was. My father could have walked again, he could have worked, played music, lived a normal life. But my father's mother was so evil that she used this as an opportunity to sexually abuse and rape my father. Until her death in 1977. And just recently I was told that my grandmother had always sexually abused my father even before the accident. I will give details on this in a later chapter. With him in a wheelchair it just made him an easy target, easy prey. He could not escape, and he was not about to tell anyone about it. As far as I know he did not speak of these things until the late 70's when his mother had died. I know I sprung that on you, so let me say that though this does not make it better, come to find out my grandmother, my father's mother, was his adoptive mother. He had been a twin, separated from his brother at birth, and adopted by this monster of a woman and her husband. It is no wonder my mother did not speak of these things.

As of this writing, I found out that this is indeed a lie. Not the sexual abuse part but the adoption part. I left it in the book because I wanted you to know what I thought I knew as truth and what I was told by my mother during those times she decided to speak of her life, my life. My father was not adopted, and he was not a twin. My father Eugene is my father, he was born in 1944 to Dana and Mildred Robinson, and I am his biological daughter. He was indeed being raped by his own mother for 11 years until her death and until he began being cared for by a private nurse in his own home. He later had to move into an assisted living home when his nurse could no longer care for him, and both of his parents were now dead. My grandfather Dana dying in 1981.

And as of this writing as I spoke of above, come to find out he had most likely been sexually abused most of his life by his mother.

As a side note in my research, I did find out that my grandfather Dana was in the military also, the Army. He also served as a police officer in Georgia up to the time of his death. He was 70 years old when he died. My grandmother Mildred F. Robinson died in 1977 at the age of 59. (Figure 18 Mildred Robinson certificate of death)

My friend John, now deceased, told me that Gene was told in his 20's about his adoption and was not aware until then. As I have said, lies upon lies, why, I have yet to figure out. But I was told just recently that there is no way he could have been adopted. And when he passed, the truth came to light. Though in doing DNA on Ancestry, there is a man who claims to be the twin brother of my father Gene. I have since learned that this person was just a scammer trying to get money from people. His granddaughter was helping him to defraud people, how that works on a DNA site I am not familiar with, but I put all that to rest when I saw my father Genes actual birth certificate. It clearly states he was born, one boy to Mildred and Dana Robinson.

I just wish someone would have told me the god damned truth after all these years. I wish someone had told me the truth about a lot of things.

I digress, my mother knew about my father's abuse, but not only did she refuse to discuss it, when it was finally time for me to meet my father at the age of 27, she never told me about it. You would think that this was something you would want to tell your daughter, that her father might be a sexual predator because of the abuse he had sustained at the hands of his mother. Instead, she just said that I might not want to meet him for fear of opening "a can of worms". That was, as I would find out, code for, your father might try and grope you or worse.

When I finally met my father, he was in a VA assisted living home. Those homes are awful. They are sad, dreary, and lonely. They smell terrible and the people in them are sad and lonely. The staff seems nice but that must be such a hard and thankless job. I had only known one other person in my life living in such a home, and that was my first husband's grandfather. And though we visited a couple times, I was always uneasy in these homes. Death all around you, I have always thought it sad how our American society tosses aside our elderly like this. Though my father was in a home due to his injuries, it was still constant death and darkness there.

I waited outside his room for what seemed like an eternity before I decided to knock and meet him for the first time as an adult.

To see my father older than he should have been, with hardly any speech capabilities, wetting himself and bent over to the side because of his spinal injuries from the accident now almost 30 years down, was extremely hard. He knew the second I opened the door to his small room who I was, though he had not seen me since I was 6 months old. I took photos of him as a girl, we talked a bit, very slowly and painfully about the past. I was extremely uncomfortable but felt it necessary to ease my mind a bit. He was the one who gave me a copy of the newspaper article regarding the accident. Something I had never seen up to that point.

My second visit to see him went as follows, I was not there exceedingly long when I bent down to hug him, and he pulled me tight to his body and put his hand down my blouse and started groping me. In shock I stood up and walked out. The last memory I have of him is looking at his broken body in his wheelchair, he turned away from me either because of guilt or perhaps he simply did not understand what he had done. And my anger for my mother boiled inside me. She knew this might happen and instead of protecting me, she just let me do it. What kind of a mother allows her child to put him or herself in a position where they could be abused?

I spent 27 years of my life wanting to meet this man. I traveled from Seattle to Georgia, I drove to the assisted living home myself, I had put all the information together to find out where he was living and I did what I needed to do just to meet this man, and everything was shattered in a moment. A moment that did not have to happen. I could have protected myself, but I did not have the tools I needed to make that choice.

It was as if my mother was punishing me for wanting to meet him. And when I told her about it, all she said was, I told you there was a can of worms.

I will never forgive my mother for this. Ever.

I hated my mother for never telling me these things, and never being honest with me about a fucking thing regarding my childhood, her childhood, her marriage, nothing. Her lack of honesty and arrogance pissed me off more than any other trait she had. And her lack of honesty with me put me in danger all the time. Danger because I would put myself in positions to be with sexual monsters, or abusive men and not even know I was because she just shrugged it off.

The fact that she never spoke of my father, or even the things that went on with her father as a child, confused me. I wanted so badly to understand my mother, but she never let me in. Just more things for me to hate her over.

When we moved from Georgia to Phoenix Arizona in 1975, my mother was now newly married to a man she had only known for 3 months. It was not love. It was not sex. Her marriage was so that she could keep custody of me. After 4 years of fighting for me, marriage was her final option. No judge in the 60's or 70's was going to give a single woman full custody of a child. Marriage, according to the added information I have recently received, was the only way she was going to keep me. I thought it was because she genuinely loved me, and perhaps she did, for a while, in her way. But that custody was also so that she could get the money from the government. And I know she knew about my father's sexual abuse at the hands of his mother. So, I want to believe she was also protecting me. I wanted to believe a lot of things about my mother.

We moved from Tucson Az, in 1979, to WA state. Bellevue Washington, where I still live today. I did not realize it then, but today I recognize that that move literally saved my life.

At the age of 12 I was devastated that we were moving again. I was happy in GA, I was happy in AZ. As luck would have it, I would be miserable in WA State. At least as a young girl.

It was at this point in my mother's life that she became impossible to live with. From the day we settled in WA state, she was an angry hot mess. I do not remember many days with her, living with her or living on my own, that she did not scream, berate, criticize, or cry.

My mother was hateful, abusive, and manipulative to me. She would gaslight me, lie to me, hit me, ground me, keep me from my friends. Embarrass me, make me go without something, tease me, torture me with her words, and do everything in her power to make sure I was as miserable as she was.

Everything that she was feeling from her youth, from the accident, the abuse, the death of her friends, her divorce, her health, her ridiculous new marriage, was now catching up with her. Though this is something I pieced together while authoring this book. Back then, I just hated everything about her.

And then as if life as I knew it was not hard enough, the year was 1972 when my mother would dive headfirst into the cult, Jehovah's Witnesses.

Though my mother diligently practiced her faith, in the end it was her undoing. *I cannot put a finer point on this part. That religion, that cult, was my mother's undoing. It did not save her, it ruined her. It killed her, literally.*

The cult was vastly different in WA state than it was in AZ or even GA. It was stricter, more judgmental and made people more miserable than I had ever seen. I do not remember being unhappy in the cult before our move to WA, but nothing made me unhappier than being in this cult, here in WA state.

My mother immediately tried to make friends. Fortunately for her and us, a few of the friends we had made in AZ had also moved to WA state during that time. I always thought it was because there was more work there, and that the weather was milder, nicer. And that was partially true for others. For us it was a faraway place to run from the drug lords, and from my stepfather's Ex-wife. My stepfather was not an honest man and he put our family in danger more than once.

I remember the afternoon in Arizona, quite clearly, my mother putting all her personal things on the porch, clothes, furniture, everything. She was crying, a lot. I asked what was wrong and she just said that we had to move. And that she could not really explain it.

We sold everything we had, except some dishes, and a few clothes. We gave away my dog and packed my sister and our boxes in our van and began our journey to WA state. It was in the middle of the night, it was abrupt, and I was told to forget about that place, to forget my friends, to never talk about or contact any of them ever again in my life. My twelve-year-old heart was so sad. And my dog, well come to find out my stepfather just dumped it out on the road somewhere, left her dying in the desert. I cried for days. I grieve that dog today. I never had another dog until I was in my 40's. I was not sure my heart could handle it.

I remember the entire drive my mother pressing me on being a better bible student, that I needed to study harder because she expected me to be baptized in the church very soon. A decision I deeply regret.

Things changed very quickly in WA state. My mother was no longer a young mom with demons, she was now a 31-year-old, angry woman who hated her life, her husband, me, and everything about the next years to come. She was a mother of two daughters now, and more uncertainty.

One thing to note is that my mother was a proud woman. She was overly sensitive about her physical appearance and how she appeared in all ways, to others. Moving to WA made her feel insecure around others. Because of her financial status and because of her lack of knowledge regarding many things. She was miserable, but she pretended to fit it, to understand and to be part of the crowd. She never really was, and it was killing her slowly.

By this move my mother was only 31 years old with zero real-life experience. Born and raised in the south, her 2nd husband, in a cult and knowing nothing of the world around her. She had a lot to learn but chose to stay ignorant. Her ignorance was hurting her, and it was hurting me.

We had no money and had to live in the basement apartment of a friend's house. My parents, trapped in the cult, had no education, no savings, no job. My stepfather started cleaning windows and my mother started working for AAA and some receptionist's jobs. I believe, if memory serves, she was also working at night. She then began to clean houses, it paid better, but she was not happy. She was never happy again.

We lived in this basement in the dark. No lights could be on, no phones, no one was to know where we lived. We were still hiding from drug lords and from my stepfather's other family. We literally lived in the dark for months.

My mother had this bizarre idea about work about life because of the cult. It was that it would be better to own your own business and only work with people who believe the same as you than to work for what they called "worldly" people. Or people who were not in the church with them, who did not have the same beliefs. So, she and her husband started their own cleaning business. Not hiring anyone inside or outside the church, just cleaning buildings at night, the two of them. It was easy to do since many people in the church, most of them without education, were janitors, window washers, mechanics. They had no life experience, and they had no training of any kind, none of them. Cleaning houses and buildings was their purpose. It was as if that was what defined them. Working hard and having nothing to show for it.

Eventually, I would say about 6 months into our life in WA, we rented a home of our own. I remember it because it was the first blizzard I had ever seen, and we were stuck at home for days. Our new home was a small house, but it was what we needed. Mom and Lloyd worked all the time, day, and night, and still, it did not seem to be enough. But I do not ever remember going hungry, or not having things I needed. But as a girl I remember that all my friends seemed to have way more than I did. They did have more than I did. They always had new clothes, shoes, fancy coats, anything they asked for. I had just what I needed, nothing more, nothing less. And I had better damn well be happy that I had anything at all.

My mother made it seem as if I was burdening her because she was a mother. Instead of understanding that she was a mother by choice and my existence was something she needed to manage, to take care of, to feed, to educate, to love. But instead, every day with me she made it seem as if I ruined her life, though I had no choice in coming into this world, into her world.

But that was also part of my mother's thinking. That I was not the most important person in the house, so I should be perfectly happy with hand-me-downs, or nothing at all. And she made me feel guilty for wanting or needing things. I will remember that it was COLD here in WA, and I did not have a proper coat. Remember we just came here from Arizona. But she was not about to buy me one. Especially if I found one that I really wanted. I had to pay for it myself out of money I had made babysitting. But when it came time to buy one, she made me buy one that she knew the other kids would make fun of me for wearing. She loved it when I was humiliated. This would not be the last time she treated me with this toxic behavior.

We always had food, but there were times when the food was sparse, but we never went hungry. There were so many conversations about food in my house. You can use milk for cereal but not for drinking. You can have Kool-Aid but not coke, you can have generic cereal and wheat bread because white bread is for the wealthy, you can have cookies if you bake them yourself. No cheese, no chips, no miracle whip, no fancy ice cream, no fancy cereal, nothing that appeared extravagant. We were too poor, my mother would say. But please know that no matter what we went without, or how challenging times were, we always had beer in the refrigerator, always. In Georgia, in Arizona, in Washington state, we always had beer.

Beer represents something larger to me. Not just the hypocrisy of my mother and her husband but the times we were living in. In Arizona, my mother was still young, in her 20s when we moved to Phoenix, and she still liked to party. I have been in contact with some old friends from Arizona who still live there, and they told me the one thing that they remember about my family is that my parents loved to party, and they did party. There was always music, always food, even in the hottest Arizona summers. There was tons of alcohol, beer, and bodies.

That beer represents a time when my mother was still enjoying her youth. Still smiling, still enjoying friends and life. Beer is not solely about the drink, it is about the time when our family seemed normal, when we watched sunsets, and listened to music late into the evening. When friends came over and we laughed, played, and danced, we had no cares, and my mother had no cares - until she did.

Today I have a strange habit of not eating the last piece of food on my plate. I believe it comes from the years of being a child and being told that I was not important enough to eat or drink the last of something in the house. The last scoop of peanut butter, it had better be there for someone else, everyone else in the house was more important than me. The last of something always went to someone else and we could not afford to replace it. Yet, you better believe, we always had beer.

I would never be important in my family; I would go without and not question it. It was as if until I got kicked out at 19, I became the stepchild while the rest of my family moved along in their pretty little bubble of what my mother wanted for a family, me on the outside, useless and forgotten.

If I have one and only one good thing to say about my mother, it is that she was never lazy. She always worked, always. She always paid the bills and we always had food, a roof, heat, clothing. Whether she was single or married. One negative thing I can say about my mother is that she always worked. She never took time for herself. She did not actually believe in time off, or free time. She was the, if you have time to lean you have time to clean, kind of woman. It pained me to see her not enjoying any free time. And not to allow me to have any myself. Something I had to learn years after her death and the years I have lived outside the cult.

She loved to read and paint, but she never took the time to relax or enjoy her life. For her it was that you work and then you die. And that is what she did, worked then died.

As my mother got older, and her health was worsening, she spent time reading mystery novels. She had many of them on shelves when she passed. But I wondered did she really took the time to enjoy those novels, was she ever at peace in her life.

Because my mother worked so much, I oversaw raising my sister, who was two at the time that we moved from AZ to WA state.

My mother was at a point where she could not stand the sight of me, I had no idea why. I loved my mother more than anything in the world. But I was also beginning to hate my mother more than I ever would hate anyone else in my life, even to this very day.

As the years passed, we would move several times into different rental homes. My parents did not believe in buying a home. Because of the cult they thought that Armageddon was going to come any day and they would have no need for a home. The cult rationalization regarding this teaching was that if you owned things, or nice things, you would have a tough time giving them up when Armageddon came. So, it is better to just live paycheck to paycheck and only have what you need so that when it was time for Armageddon, you could easily give those things up. This is a teaching my mother fully embraced, fully believed in. Though it clearly made her miserable. Especially now that we lived in a more affluent area, where people drove nice cars and had beautiful homes. She would say "it must be nice," a lot. But what she meant was that she wished she could or would allow herself to live the kind of life others were living.

But also, my mother was a terrible money manager. They made over 6 figures a year at their business and never had more than a few hundred dollars in the bank. Even if you believe the world is going to end in a few months, having a small amount of savings is never a bad idea. My mother taught me to balance a check book but never how to save money. Never the importance of what the future might hold, savings, retirement, 401K, never conversations in my home.

Mom never tried to better herself or better our lives. And not just with things, but with education, with facts, with life. They bought used cars, rented homes, bought us the basic things we needed, and made sure we knew that we had better be damn happy with those things. And they kept us ignorant. Basic education and no plans to move us forward to college or a career.

Not that there is anything wrong with the belongings we did have, but her thinking was flawed. We lived like that because she was literally waiting for the world to end. Not because we had to. She was hard-working and bright. She could have given us any kind of life she wanted, but she chose to allow the cult to dictate to her what kind of life was acceptable.

She made choices that affected all of us. Which might seem like the thing that parents do, but her own demons put us all in jeopardy. Her unhappy marriage, her cult thinking and her view of life, education, and money. It stunted all of us in many ways.

I could see it pained her because even some of her "friends" had nicer things, took trips, drove nice cars. And even though she was pained by it, she would turn her pain the other way and make remarks like, those people will be sorry when they must give those things up so that god will allow them into the Paradise. It is a very twisted way to live your life. Every day having to fight the urge to be a real human who naturally wants real things, vacations, material things, education etc. You only get one life; this is not the way to waste it.

When I was 13 years old my mother got pregnant with my 2nd sister. She was so upset about this, I remember her clearly, crying and saying how much she hated being pregnant, how would she have time or money to raise another child, how could this have happened.

And even at 13 I wondered why in the hell if we could barely afford the things we now have, could we afford another mouth to feed? But I also knew that my life was about to get worse. I was already cleaning the house, going to school, and raising my sister, now I would have double the work and my childhood would be gone in a flash. And as luck would have it that is exactly what happened.

For some reason I remember mom going to all her friends telling them that she was pregnant. My stepfather was super happy about this for some reason, but mom was broken. The last thing she wanted was another child. And her husband was of the old thinking that you have sex to procreate, so why use any kind of birth control? Seriously? And it was not as if he was going to be some fantastic father who came to the rescue and helped with the kids around the house, etc.

I would find out years later that one of the reasons my mother was so unhappy by this time was because her husband had been cheating on her. Not just once but often. It was a long time before I understood some of her misery, and why she cried a lot about things that seemed trivial. But her husband could not seem to keep his pants zipped around other women and as I found out, other men.

I was told by a "very reliable" source that these things are true. I was told by him, her husband, my stepfather. Now do not get me wrong, I do not always consider, nor have considered my stepfather to be a truly honest man, but why admit you were cheating, if you were not. I would think that is not a subject you would brag about. Nor would I think you would brag about being a gay man who continues to hide his sexuality and hurt those along your path of life with your lies.

Why mom did not leave this man, is beyond me. I know she had a very dedicated view of her faith. And that women and men should stay together, they should never divorce under most circumstances. I know she even believed that if a woman was being beaten by her man, that she should stay faithful to him because eventually god would make things right. But the cult also teaches that if your spouse cheats on you, you have every right to divorce him or her and you have every right to remarry. But she did not, why, I cannot say. I was even a grown woman with a child of my own when my stepfather was caught cheating on her with a man, and still she stayed.

But she was miserable, and in turn making us all miserable with her. I only remember a few short years when mom seemed happy with my stepfather. She smiled a lot and laughed. But that ended quickly. It all stemmed from us moving from GA to Arizona but that also seemed odd to me, especially since mom wanted nothing but to get away from her own father.

I think it was that mom was not in control of her life. Life was controlling her, and she did not know how to handle that. Life was pulling mom forward and she pushed back a lot.

Mother was only happy when she was unhappy.

She had such a distaste for sex, and she thought that every decision a person made, from their make-up to their clothing choices meant they were having sex or thinking about having sex. She used to call me a whore if I wanted to wear a dress to school because she had a belief that girls only wear dresses to school so that the boys can look at their vaginas. She thought a girl wore stretch pants or leggings only because she wanted to show off her body for a boy, so they could have sex. She believed that anything you did, was because of sex. The need for, the want for. And she treated sex like the evilest thing on the planet. And the teachings of the cult did not help. They taught that sex was only missionary, and only with a man and a woman. No anal, no oral, no masturbation. Sex was never to be enjoyed! The teachings of the church about sex were and are some of the most disgusting and disturbing of teachings. Yet my mother spewed them at me all the time. It was toxic to its core.

Mom had the most unusual views about life. I used to think that her words were law. But as I grew, as I approached 50 especially, I realized that her opinions were based on nothing. Perhaps her own firsthand experiences but she was usually just talking out of her ass.

Oh yes, mother had an opinion about everything and everyone, and most of the time her opinions were just flat out wrong. She rarely had facts to back up her views, but she did not care. I remember once she told me that people just do things or obey her because she is who she is. In many ways she had an extremely high opinion of herself, in other ways she was broken.

It took me years to even fix my views about other humans, mostly because of the influence she had on me. I used to think that no one can change, you will always be who you are. Mom always thought that if a human were bad, they would always be bad. She rarely gave people chances, especially not second chances.

Mom's views about people, things, were always negative. It was exceedingly rare that you heard her say that a person was kind, or lovely or smart. Everyone she encountered had something wrong with them. Everyone.

Everyone was either too rich or too poor, too fat, too thin, too opinionated, too something.

She believed that she was right about everything, and she made sure that everyone knew it.

The fact is, she was not. She was wrong about a lot of things. And when she became ill, she was even wrong about how she handled that.

I hated my mother so much, which pained me because there was a time when I loved her more deeply than anyone.

I wanted her to accept me, love me without conditions. But she could never do that. Even on her death bed she treated me with utter disrespect.

It was shocking but honestly, not shocking. Why should I be shocked that she behaved the same way toward me all the time?

At 19 I left home; it was a pretty brutal time. To me it seemed like the normal thing to do, leave home, get married. To my mother it was an affront to who she was. But the reality was that she did not want me to leave home, not because she loved me but because she needed me.

She needed me to keep cleaning her house, raising her children, doing her job as a mom and wife.

That was a challenging time for me because I needed to leave home for my own sanity. But in doing so I left behind my sisters. The two young girls that I had been raising for almost 10 years.

As luck would have it my mom now used this time to tell them what a horrible human I was. She lied to them about me constantly. They used to say things to me that made no sense. And I could not understand why my mother could be so evil regarding me all the time.

Mother used me, abused me, and turned others against me. Whenever she had a chance, she threw me under the bus. I do not remember a day she ever stood by my side or protected me. Leaving home just gave her more fodder.

She was so bitter that she now had to raise her own children that she used that time to undermine my years of being with them, of raising them, reading to them, holding their hands when they were sick. She made me out to be this evil horrible human when all I did was leave home. And leave mom to be a mom.

One of my sisters was so traumatized by my leaving home that she spent years in therapy. Thinking that she had done something wrong, something to make me leave home.

Of course, my mother did nothing to change her mind about this. It would be many many years later that my sister would reach out to me to get this subject settled. My heart still hurts today even thinking that my sister or sisters thought I left home because of them.

What mom should have done was tell my sister that she, mom, was such a horrible human all the time that she drove her oldest daughter out of the house. She should have been open and honest about her own demons, with all her children. But she always found a way to blame me for her problems and the problems she put onto others.

My mother was so livid all the time. I honestly do not know how someone can live their life, day in and day out, yelling as much as my mother did.

Though the word yelling is sometimes used to simply express the way a person reacted or acted. My mother LITERALLY yelled all the time. Sometimes so often and for so long that even the radio in my room could not drown her out.

Looking back, I do not know why she yelled so much. Everything triggered her. A plate on the counter, a chilly day, a bad night's sleep, a song that made her think of something she hated. It did not matter, she lived her life screaming and yelling, and not just at me, with anyone and everyone.

She never had a kind thing to say to me. And it was not just mom being belligerent. My mother would say things like, you are dress like whore, you are dumb, you are worthless, and you are only good for being pregnant and dumb. She made fun of me so much, the way I looked, the way I laughed, walked, hugged, sang, ate, smiled, that to this day I still have visions of her angry rants at me, and I still have huge self-esteem problems. Sometimes I even get scared to do a task for fear that she is waiting to yell at me at any moment. Like cooking eggs, spreading butter onto toast, folding sheets, putting on make-up. Everything is a haunt.

Yes, therapy helped but when the one person who is supposed to love you abuses you instead. That is not something people easily move forward from.

I have tried hard to not let my mother's past abuse affect or define me as an adult. But it has been hard. I am fortunate to have a supportive partner who loves me unconditionally.

I got married the summer I left home. My mother not only did not support that marriage, but she also did not help with the wedding or come to the wedding. She stopped speaking to me all together. Her abuse, her hold on me, was ruining my life, paining my heart.

And nothing I did was going to bring her to me. Nothing I did was good enough, ever.

At 22 I had a baby, thinking that this would bring us closer. When I told her I was pregnant she screamed at me on the phone, called me an idiot and then hung up on me. Said that I was stupid, and I would never survive motherhood. And in those early years of being a mother, my mother used that time to tell me what a horrible parent I was. Every day practically telling me how I was raising my child wrong, dressing them wrong. Mom spent a lot of time with my child, picking them up from school, taking them to church, shopping, baking. But those years did not last. As soon as my child was old enough to start having an opinion of their own, mom would have none of it. Mom would yell at me about why I was raising my child a certain way, that I needed to do things differently, that she did not approve of their personality, their independence, their views, their outgoing spirit. Blah blah.

It was just more years of my mother being abusive and self-righteous. Nothing changed, as I would painfully find out, it was never going to.

Have you ever wanted something so much you would almost give anything to get it? That is how I felt about my mother's love. Her acceptance. Her time. I would have given anything to get it. I practically did. I still cry sometimes when I look at myself and know that I am a good person. I have always strived to be a good person, a kind person, a loving person. And yet my mother still tossed me aside with no regard to anything but herself.

At 51 years old mom told us all, in a family meeting, that she had breast cancer. What a gut punch that was. I think the thing I remember most was that her father had recently passed away, and now, her words to me were that she now thought she could really live her life with this monster dead, but instead she had cancer.

She made choices regarding her health and let me be clear not just about her cancer, but with her health her whole life, that were disastrous. She never took care of herself. She was of the, just take a Tylenol and it will be fine, mentality. But it was never fine. At a youthful age, she started having major health issues. Gallbladder removal, kidney stones, bladder problems, Colon issues, stomach issues, I believe once she even had a heart attack but never ever sought out a doctor for that or for much of anything. She also had the thought that if you are sick and you go to the doctor and he confirms it, then you could die. If he does not confirm it, you may live. Ridiculous ass shit like that made me want to scream.

So, when she got cancer, she went down this unusual path. First, she told us that she had had a lump for over a YEAR and that either she did nothing about it, or her doctor told her it was nothing. I do not know about you, but if I had a lump for a day, I would seek one, two, three different opinions and get on the path to getting healthy as fast as I could. But she did not, she waited and then she decided NOT to do chemotherapy. Only to have the lump removed and do radiation and medication. But she had let the lump go on for too long, and her decision to not do chemo, in my opinion, was her death sentence. And her decision to not have her breast removed was also, knowing what I know now, a huge mistake.

But to be clear let us wrap this in with her mental status. She was miserable, she hated herself and her life, so now that she had cancer, it was her way out. I believe that she only lived long enough to make some amends, to have a few years where she forced herself to be happy, and then she could see her final days.

She lasted 10 more years and at the age of 61, died from complications due to her breast cancer. The cancer had spread to her bones, and she died an agonizing death. She was in hospice 23 days. The last few days she was in a coma.

Her days in hospice were not only miserable for her but for me. Her fake friends, the Jehovah's witnesses with their fake tears, their zombie emotions. Rude people telling me that her cancer was my fault. People pretending, they knew me and what I had been through with her. People are trying to tell me about my mother. When I knew damn well that these people, these fake friends, knew nothing about me or my mother or the misery she had been through or put me through my entire life. I really wanted to tell them to fuck off and leave me alone. And leave her alone, let her die the way she wants, a martyr.

I had this silly dream that her and I would be at peace when she died, that we would talk about a few things, and we would finally put our demons to rest. But not only did that not happen, she was rude and condescending to me on her death bed. She lied to me, and she even said that my dear husband was not allowed in the room with the family as she was dying. The only words that crossed my mind, were cold hearted bitch.

Everything I wanted to say. Everything I wanted to ask. I never did. I regret it sometimes but then I must think that she would not have told me the truth anyway. Because that was her way. She asked me the first day I saw her in hospice, If I had any questions. Of course, I did. Did I ask them? I did not.

My mother died a 61-years-old a lost and broken woman. She was uneducated, depressed, angry, and despondent. She had nothing to show for her life, and her three children were at odds over everything. Her husband lacked integrity, was a compulsive liar, a cheater and seemed almost happy that she was dying. He even lied to her on her death bed. Told her he would never remarry, yet only a few months later, he was married, to his ex-gay lovers, widow… yes that. I could feel how broken she was, and yet she held her ground. She still spoke of nothing uncomfortable, nothing with conflict, nothing of things that I needed her to talk about. She was closed and cold, just like she had always been.

She told me in those last days, that if I was not going to come back to the church or to Jehovah her god, that I and my husband should just commit suicide, because god was going to kill us anyway. Those were all her last words to me.

I hear that people who are dying want to make amends, want to confess, want to forgive or be forgiven. But my mother seemed too just be. She cried a few times, she died the way she lived, without release, without real emotion.

I see my mother sometimes in my dreams, in my thoughts. I see a beautiful bright smiling woman enjoying her life. Sitting on the deck enjoying her wine, her coffee, watching a sunset, sunrise, laughing and crying with her children, her grandchildren. I see a woman she could have been but was not.

She was a miserable human being who allowed her past to define her future. She allowed a cult of people with false dreams and false hopes to manage her day-to-day life. She allowed all these things to come between her, her children, and her spouse. And she allowed it to control her happiness. She only felt comfortable being miserable and making others, especially her children, miserable.

She was only happy when she was unhappy.

Even today 13 years after her death I find myself keeping a clean home or questioning the way I dress, for fear she may walk in the door any moment and scold me for not being perfect or not doing things her way. Or god forbid, drinking the last beer.

I admit that I miss her. But I missed her when she was alive. But what I miss is the woman she had been for a moment when I was a child, and the mother that I wanted her to be. I miss what I did not have and sometimes I miss her touch.

Though I am grateful for the life I now have, my years with my mother were nothing but torture day in and day out. I would not be who I am today, had she not been who she was. But it still does not stop the pain in my heart most days.

If you have a mother that you love, that loves you, that gave you a good life, with kindness, empathy, and support, cherish her and or cherish those memories.

If you have not spoken to your mother in a while, pick up the phone, she might need to hear your voice.

If you have an extra beer, invite her over to make memories with you. I assure you; you will not regret it.

TINY STONES

"No one gets more upset than a narcissist being accused of something they definitely did"

~Anonymous

In March of 1974, my mother remarried. She was 26 years old and 2 years off a divorce and a custody battle for me from my paternal grandparents.

She married a man that she had known for barely 3 months. I called him dad right away, before they even officially married. It did not occur to me, not to. I did not even know what it felt like to have a father, a man in the home, someone for mom to love. I did not know that people had fathers, or it did not occur to me that I did not.

At the tender age of 6, I had no idea why I did not have a father. The father figure I had known to that point was my grandfather, Lee. I never thought about why mom did not have a man in her life. Though I knew she had a few men she had been interested in. Rick Welch, a nice-looking man who I think she was having sex with, but that relationship never went anywhere. Rick would die years later in a freak accident where he was electrocuted to death.

Henry, he was married to her best friend Myrna, he died in a swimming accident. He went swimming alone and drowned. I always wondered if that was the whole story, but the newspaper told the same story. My mother spoke about him for as long as I remember. I believe she loved him even though he was someone else's husband. She was deeply hurt by his death. For years she spoke of him, showed photos of fun times they had had like going on ski trips. It was touching to see her care so deeply for someone. As I did not get to experience that much more in her life. All her caring was on the surface, even for her children.

Ron Porter, who was also married to a friend of moms. I think she had real affection for this man, but what I really think is that she had a desire to be with a man, a good, hard working, strong man and all these men fit that bill. But what she chose instead was none of these things. Because as she aged, she made it clear that any man who was bold, strong willed, or drank, was automatically an abuser. So, she chose someone who I think was the very opposite of her father.

It never occurred to me to ask why mom was single. I had everything I needed, food, shelter, love, though mostly conditional. Mom for the most part gave me those things, having a father was never a necessity.

Mom and Jack got married in March of 1974. He seemed like a nice man. He was, for the most part, nice to me. I do not remember any time, at least for many years, that he was not nice to me. He seemed to jump right in and take over the father's role. But looking back I think he was just going through the motions of being a father and I cannot really say why. As you will soon find out.

He worked hard, he seemed to spend most days in a good mood and mom seemed happy. But as time would show, mom wasn't happy with Jack. Actually, mom just wasn't happy.

In 1975 or 76 we moved to Phoenix Arizona. I remember parts of that trip - us packing all our things into a U-Haul and mom driving the U-Haul one afternoon into a Burger King drive-thru and smashing up the roof because the U-Haul was too tall. We knew it wasn't going to fit, but she insisted that she could make it work - but as luck would have it, it did not fit. That was a story we told for many years at parties, camping, until mom got tired of being laughed at and told us to stop telling it anymore. It is one fond memory I have of mom because it was unlike her later in life to just take chances and then laugh about an outcome, good or bad.

I have a faint memory of us running in the middle of the night, to our truck, running as if our lives depended on it. We were running for a new life as it would turn out. And our lives did depend on it. And this would not be the first or last time we would run.

We lived in several homes while in Phoenix and Tucson, a couple of apartment buildings, a couple of town homes, finally settled in a single wide trailer. This had been the third trailer I had lived in in my short life, it never occurred to me to be bothered by it, until I was. But being poor is hell. And though I was never so poor as to be in need of something, I was poor enough to be embarrassed about it, especially when I got older. But truth be told, I never felt unhappy, until I was.

I was not sure why we moved from Georgia to Arizona. But there were numerous factors that played into it. One was that my stepfather was running away from his first family, from his obligations. He had been married before, his wife being only 13 when he got her pregnant the first time. As shocked as you might be by that I can tell you now that that story is not true, though it is the one he told me my entire life and loved to tell at parties. His wife was actually 20 when he married her, and she was not pregnant with their first child. My stepfather liked to tell false-hoods, stories, lies, and embellish everything. It was incredibly and deeply psychotic. Why would you tell a story of being what we now today call a pedophile? He said that he was 19 and she was 13 when he knocked her up. And he used to tell this story as if he was proud of it. As if he was a big man who committed child rape and then married his victim.

But he did marry her, Sammie, and proceeded to have 4 children, daughters, with this woman. But one day in a fit of anger, he just walked out on his family. He said he fired a gun inside the house, yelling and screaming at them. Telling them he did not love them anymore. But I found that hard to believe since my stepfather was a bit of a weak human being. And as it turns out, that story was also not true. He left his family because he was in love with a man, Butch. Yes, the man's name was actually Butch. He had been having an affair with that man. And though he could not stop making his wife pregnant, he had ZERO intentions of staying with his family. And he had zero intentions of being part of their life ever again. When he left his family, his youngest daughter was only 3 weeks or 3 months old. My facts are a tad incomplete on that one.

When he left them, he also had zero intentions of paying child support. Because as you will see at the end of this chapter, this man has zero integrity. He is a liar, a thief, and a cheat. The fact that he had had a family, left them, did not pay child support and was a gay man living a lie, were things he probably should have let me mother in on. To this day, over 50 years later, he has barely been in contact with those children. They are mere strangers to him. They all have families of their own and those families have families. And the part that gets me the most is that he does not even care. I never saw him shed a tear over that lost time, or grieve for them, or speak of them, or want to be with them. Never. I never heard him say he was sorry or feel any remorse for his disgusting behavior. Mind you I do not care that he is a gay man living a lie, but I do care that he left his children with zero intentions of ever thinking twice about them again. What kind of human are you that you do not have any kind of emotions for leaving your family?

I can tell you that just these past couple of years I have been in contact with his oldest daughter from that situation. We are also friends on social media. And we talked and chatted about her bio father. She said that she was 7 when he walked out on them and that she had spent most of her life wondering what she did wrong that made her father leave the family. And though her mother remarried, her stepfather molested them and was not a very respectable man. But she said she just moved forward and accepted things as they were. That is a pretty heavy weight for a 7-year-old to carry her entire life.

This made me loathe my stepfather more than I did before I knew more stories of his past. I must admit I did not take many of his stories to heart until authoring this book because I never knew what was true and what was a lie. His stories changed from day to day and year to year. He even told us stories about things that were happening with his children, illnesses, events, vacations, etc. Things that LITERALLY never happened. But now that I have most of the facts and understand that real humans were involved, I have made a solid and easy choice to erase him from my life.

My mother, as I remember her up to a certain point in life, always worked hard, she saved her money and paid her debts. That was not always the case as life moved forward and she got older. But as a single mom she was not one to just skip out on her obligations as a mother or in any other way, yet here was her new husband thinking that it was acceptable not to pay for his children or even be there for them. And it did not seem to occur to him to be bothered by it.

Our time in Arizona was the best time I had with my stepfather. We got along well, had a few laughs, I considered him my friend, someone I could trust. We rode bikes together, went to parks, told stories, lay in the sunshine looking for 4 leaf clovers. In the summertime he had this job delivering Co2 tanks to restaurants, and he would take me along to ride with him. It was fun! I used to meet nice people, get free sodas, and spend some quality time with him. Those summers were hot, but they were my own memories of my stepfather and what we shared alone. I always assumed he enjoyed our time together. But looking back perhaps he just thought he was "doing his job" as a father. Not that being a father was something he had proved to be good at, at any other time in his life.

I would later find out that this job allowed him to sell his drugs, easily, heroin, cash under the table, no questions asked. While I was getting free soda and soaking up the sun, he was selling drugs. I know this seems like an odd way to spring it on you that my stepfather was a heroin dealer, but trust me when I tell you, that the way I found out about it, in my 20's, was as if he was just talking about walking a dog. And all his friends, our friends over the years kept this dark secret from me. And Jack did not care about the pain that he caused our family, especially my mother. Nor the damage that he did to our family. Because damage to families seemed to be what he was good at.

And remember I told you that not all his stories were true. In fact, I can barely count on one hand any story that he told us that was true. So, to verify this I had to dig deep into his past, and talk to people that knew him and knew us when we were in Arizona and people far back in his past, as a teenager, young man, etc. As well as speak to his oldest first daughter and his Ex-wife.

One thing to add was that I will never forget once while still living in Georgia, he told me a story about why his teeth were all fake. Why did he have so much dental work done? That he ate so much candy as a kid that his teeth all rotted out. As an adult researching this book, I can tell you that his teeth rotted out all right, but not because of the kind of candy you buy at a drug store.

My first sister was born in 1977 in Tucson, Arizona, I was 9 years old. And my life and relationships with my parents were about to change drastically.

My mother had a rough pregnancy, and she cried a lot. I remember my stepfather asking me one day to be a good girl, not to make mom mad, and to just take over all the chores around the house because mom couldn't handle it for a while. And not to make mom cry because it could make her lose the baby. Do not make mom upset, she could lose the baby.

Holy fuck! No pressure there. Blame me for mom potentially losing the baby. What kind of thing is that to say to a child? I was happy to be a big sister, and though this is not my sister's fault, I was happy until my parents made it my responsibility to raise my sister, keep house, and set aside my childhood because they did not have the time or means to raise their own kids.

After a few years in Arizona, we just got up and left one day. I remember my mother crying one afternoon while putting out yard sale signs. She was hanging up all her clothes outside, putting furniture outside, putting price tags on everything. When I asked her what was wrong, she just tearfully said that we had to leave this place and start somewhere fresh. She told me not to ask any more questions and to just do as I was told.

I did not understand any of it at the time. But we ended up selling most of everything we had. All my grandmother's antique furniture, my mother's clothing, it was all gone. And my mother cried more than I had ever seen her cry before. I was 12 years old.

We skipped out on the payments of the trailer. It was owned by someone else, and mom and Jack just did not pay their obligations, we just moved on. I guess mom and Jack needed every penny they could get and could keep, to once again move us. My stepfather not paying his obligations once again was part of his sad life story.

We packed up all that we could fit into our big van. It even had a CB radio which was all the rage at the time. But that CB radio purchase was the biggest fight I had ever heard my mom and stepfather have. You see, not only did my stepfather not like to pay his debts, but he also liked to spend money that we never had on things we did not need. And he was going to do it for as long as they were married. It was a huge burden on my mother. And as usual my stepfather did not care.

I had a dog named Jet; I loved that dog more than anything in the world. My stepfather got her for me. I deeply wanted a pet. I was lonely. But I was told we couldn't take it with us. I absolutely could not understand why we couldn't take that small dog with us to our new home. I cried and cried and begged my parents. My stepfather came back from an errand the day we left for Washington state and said he gave my dog to a trucker who needed a companion. But I know years later that he just took that dog out and dumped it somewhere in the desert to die alone. My stepfather has zero emotions about what he did. My heart ached for that dog for most of my life. I never really got over that loss. That dog was really my only devoted friend. I even found that getting another dog in life was a painful decision because I did not know if I could love it or let it go when I needed to.

We then drove for days until we ended up in Washington state. That is where we would eventually settle down. This is where I still live today.

I never understood any of this. Why did we have to keep moving, why did we have to keep moving so far from friends and family? Why was I told, each time we moved, that I was never to have contact with my friends or family that I was leaving behind? Nothing made sense, and once it all came together, it still did not make sense.

This is a story that I will tell but downplay today. Though the trauma for me was very real. This event changed my life for the worse but also years later for the better. But even recently when I was back visiting this place, the very place I fled with my family on that dark and chilly night, I wept remembering how broken my heart was for leaving a place where I thought I was happy. A place that we left with zero explanation. A place once again where my parents did not take my feelings into consideration.

I used to ask people why we had to move, why are there so many secrets? Adults always told me it was for my own good that I did not know. But the truth was, not knowing, was worse than knowing. Because as we have all done in our lives, we make things up in our heads, we can become haunted by stories that we do not even understand or have facts over.

Come to find out my stepfather not only left his first family, but he was into drugs then too. Using and dealing. He had refused to pay child support for his first family and had hoped and wanted not to be heard from or seen again. Of course, this was way before social media, but his Ex-wife found out where we had run, and she filed a lawsuit for back child support for his 4 daughters.

Speaking to one of his children we deduced that he may have gotten into the drug situation, using, dealing, during the 5 years or so that he was single after he abandoned his first family but before he married my mother. The daughter says she does not remember drugs or talk of drugs. But she was also incredibly young when he left, how he got into drugs and when is something we just put together with the facts as we know them.

Also, his first wife had called the police and had him put in jail shortly after he left his family, because he refused to pay child support.

There was no way our family could afford the back child support for his 4 children. It actually would have been 3 children by the time the court found us, because his oldest was now 18. Money was always tight, and mom cried about this too. I think she cried mostly because she had zero idea what a shady ass piece of shit she had married. But she was slowing finding out. By now they had been married 5 years. To me seems like enough time to tell the truth to your spouse about your life before her and the shit you continued to pull.

But the biggest and only reason we left Tucson Arizona was because we were being chased by drug lords. My stepfather apparently had been in deep with them for Heroin/drug debt. He had been dealing, and using, and Tucson, come to find out, was a huge hub for these dealers, especially in the 70's. That is why we ended up there. Not so he could get away from his past, but so he could end up smack dab in the middle of that mess. Another mess he created. He dragged my mother and I right into his demons and then made my mother miserable while trying to dig out of it. And put us in danger at the same time.

I do not know if my mother knew this, or if she just went along with her new husband because it seemed like he knew what he wanted, or what he was talking about. Maybe he told her he would change, or that he would be a better human than he had been in his past. Or maybe she was just tired, to this point in her young life, she had been through plenty of tragedies. Maybe she was tired of fighting for everything all the time. Or maybe her new husband just seemed like a better choice than her first.

My stepfather told so many lies in his life that I do not think he knows what the truth is anymore. And sometimes even when I find out the truth about a story he told, I question its validity because there was never a time in my life with him that he did not lie to me.

And this plays in well with most of the men in my life on my mothers' side of the family also, who as I found out sometimes painfully, were also nothing but liars.

Please do not get me wrong, my stepfather did some pleasant things for me. I have a few fond memories.

Once while living in Phoenix, I fell out of bed and cracked the top of my nose, cracked the bone. It was very painful, and I had to have a butterfly bandage put on it and I had to have it cleaned out with this product that I remember stung like a mother fucker. But my stepfather felt bad for me and literally went to the toy store and came home with this huge bag of toys to make me feel better. It was filled with everything from figurines to stuffed animals to candy. It was an extremely sweet gesture and I remember feeling really loved at that moment in time.

One year I wanted a ten-speed bike, we were living in Washington state at this time. All my friends had one, and there was one in particular that I wanted, a Red one that I had seen at a local store. My mother insisted that we did not have enough money for this bike. And said I did not need a bike just because my friends had one.

But my stepdad went out and bought it for me. And gave it to me as a gift. It was the coolest bike I had ever owned. I was in love with this damn thing. But all it did was make my mother angry at me and at him. Things at home, well they were beginning to boil over.

And my heart was broken a few weeks later, when someone broke into our garage and stole that bike. Over the years I have spoken to people who lived in my neighborhood at the time and asked if they knew who stole it. I had assumed it was the neighbor boy who lived across from me. But he claims he did not steal it. I had my ideas about who else it could be as I was bullied so much in school that any one of the kids who lived around me could have stolen it. But the bike was returned about 3 days later. I think that my crying at school may have made someone feel bad and just returned it without question.

My mother, in her way, blamed me for it being stolen, said I must have taken cash for it. Nutty.

But that bike represented not only kindness from my stepfather, but it seemed that at that moment he was beginning to stand up to my mother and my mother's bullying. But as luck would have it, that did not last.

It was the 80's and all my friends had boom boxes, I wanted one so badly and my mother said no. My stepfather went out without mom's permission and bought me one. I played that thing until it literally just stopped working, many years later.

Jack did a few positive things for me; he prevented me from marrying a few losers. Because I was in the church and because my home life was such a fucking mess, I wanted to get married to leave home. Not the best way to do it, but it was complicated. I had several boyfriends, a few that wanted to marry me and almost every time, Jack would say, "Do not do it" or "Are you sure this is right for you." One of the last times we had that conversation I was about to marry an abusive man who was into bestiality, yes you heard me right, bestiality. Oh yes there is a chapter for this too.

Jack was incredibly supportive of my decision when I said this does not feel right. So, I dumped that man, thank goodness for that. I mean you would think that bestiality was a deal breaker, but living in the abusive toxic household I was living in, bestiality was not a deal breaker. I was a vastly different person back then.

My stepfather always worked hard. I do not remember him ever being lazy. But when he did not want to work or he did not feel he was getting the kind of attention he felt he deserved, watch out. He frequently had fictitious pains in his chest, pretend panic attacks, apparently, he went blind for a few weeks, he would pass out in crowds for no reason, he was simply a drama queen. And I am not using the word Queen lightly, I assume you will get the picture.

He really proved it as the youngest of the three children. I never really saw him show much emotion about anything. Or have any kind of attachment to anything except himself of course. The only time I remember him really being broken up about something, was when his sister died suddenly in her sleep of a heart attack. But boy did he milk that situation to get as much sympathy and attention as he could. Mind you when she died, he had barely seen her in 20 years.

After my mother died, I had several long conversations with him about some of the years of our lives I could not piece together. My mother seemed very unhappy with him most days. Come to find out he had been cheating on her a lot. At least with three women in the congregation, according to him. And with one man. But was this true? I can never tell.

The man however, eventually died of AIDS and asked to see Jack while on his death bed. He was in love with my stepfather, and they apparently had had a secret relationship. The rumors during that time were flying. The congregation was in an uproar over this new-found gossip. Was he or wasn't he gay, could it rock the congregation to its very foundation? Well of course my stepfather denied all of it. Said the man on his death bed was a liar, hallucinations, drugs. But I knew it was true, I remember him sneaking around, the phone calls. And this dead man's son, he confirmed everything I knew and had suspected for years, my stepfather was gay, or at least Bi. No shame in it unless you allow it to ruin your family and you lie about it until it hurts others.

My stepfather is now married to the wife of this man, his gay lovers' widow. As if things were not weird enough already.

I had a suspicion that my stepfather was gay and most people who met him would tell you they suspected the same thing. But being in the church, and him being an elder in the church, homosexuality is forbidden. So, he just hid it, cheating on my mom with several woman and just lived his life as if nothing were wrong. All the while still breaking my mother's heart.

There was a woman in Arizona who was young and pretty and became pregnant out of wedlock. She was a member of the church; her father was an elder in the church. She was very secretive about who the father of her baby was. It would not be until 2016 that I was told that the probability of Jack being that baby's father, was extremely high.

He had a tendency of putting his penis where it did not belong. And since he did not really believe in birth control, for whatever reason you've got me, then the fact that she became pregnant after only one night of intercourse, would make sense. That's the story she told. She never revealed that baby's father to anyone, as far as I know. And she left that kid to be raised by her elderly parents. That baby girl, Brandi, looked exactly like my stepfather and like my middle sister. If he is the father, like so many other things, I will never forgive him for being the fucking coward who once again left his children behind.

I do not know what my mother saw in him. She was a lovely woman with many talents, and I could not figure it out. I used to see them together and wonder what she was doing with him. He was not a terrible man, but he was certainly not moms forever husband. That is if she made different choices that were not controlled by the cult.

But in my late 40's I understood quite clearly why she married him. She married him so the judge would give her custody of me. And though our relationship would turn out to be difficult at best, I now understood. It was the 60s and judges were not prone to give custody of a child to a single parent. Especially one who had been through my mother's trage-dies. I believe that lawsuit was settled in 1973, and a few months later my mother was married to this perfect stranger.

Jack did not make my mother happy. There were plenty of times I saw her cry over the years regarding their relationship. I did not hear them fight much. Money arguments, sometimes Jacks childish behaviors, but not many outward fights. I think my mother was just resigned to the deci-sions she had made. I knew she was never going to divorce him; she would never give herself satisfaction over that. And of course, since she was so loyal to the church, divorce was simply out of the question.

I think Jack wanted to be my ally. I think he wanted to fight for me, even when mom disapproved. I know that when they married, they had an agreement. This agreement was one that really put a strain on my family dynamic. Jack agreed that he would never interfere with her discipline of me. So, she spent my entire life, almost up to her death, chastising me, berating me, abusing me with her words and hands and deeds, making fun of me, yelling, laughing at me. And he never interfered. He just let it all happen.

He pretended to be sorry for that. He pretended, when she was dying, to be sorry that I had been through what I had been through with her. He bought me roses and said that if anyone deserved them, after all I had been through with her, I did.

Yet here we are 13 years after mother's death. And he has once again moved on with his life. He married very quickly after mom died. He stopped speaking to me or my daughter, and now he barely speaks to his other two daughters, my sisters, from my mother. And his two other grandchildren, he just up and left us all behind, typical of him. Moved on with his life with a new wife. A woman who is deeply abusive and hateful to his children, my two sisters. Does he care? He does not seem too concerned about it. Moved back to Arizona and left us all behind, again.

I hope there comes a day when I get a chance to tell him how much I dislike him. How much I hated him for turning our lives upside down. For breaking my mother's heart. I dreamed of that day.

I actually took that chance a couple summers ago on the 10-year anniversary of mom's death. I sent him a letter that I had written about how much I despised him, his lies, his lack of integrity and how I would never again think of him or refer to him as my stepfather. The letter was not kind, and it was filled with many emotions not only about me but about all the people he had hurt and left behind in his life.

I am not sure that he ever read the letter. His new wife has such control over him that she probably saw it in the mail and threw it out. But I hope that he did read it. Not sure that he will care as he cares for nothing and no one but himself. But I said what I needed to say to the person I needed to say it to.

I suppose looking at my life now, I can thank him for one thing. If he had not royally fucked up his life, then my life wouldn't be this good. Our move from Georgia, to Arizona, then to Washington state, was the move that would save my life. If not for him, we would probably still be in rural Georgia.

I dislike that man for so many things, but I mostly dislike him for taking on the role of a father but never actually taking it seriously. Not only for me but for the 4 girls he robbed of their father because of his selfishness.

I dislike him for allowing me to love him, and never returning that love, not really.

And I hate him for his lack of integrity and his lies. At first, I found it hard to say that, but it is the truth. I needed a good male role model, and I had none. My grandfather was an abusive alcoholic who alienated everyone in his life, my biological father would spend the rest of his life in an assisted living home because of his injuries and my stepfather turned out to be a lecherous lying disingenuous weasel.

I wonder why I surround myself with strong men as friends but honestly there is no question. The woman in my life that was supposed to be my role model, she was a hot mess up to her death. And the man that raised me, well, he lacked everything that a father should have. Raised me? Not really, he was only in my life for 12 years, then off he went to fulfill his own desires, again.

I wonder sometimes how it is I got here instead of sitting alone somewhere miserable, drugs, watching my life go by.

I will tell you that I do not think I can ever forgive this man. I am not sure that he can ever do or say anything that will allow me to forgive him for the hurt and mess he caused us. Ever. When he passes it will be better for everyone he has hurt along the way.

Did he love my mother? Who knows. He used to be attentive to her sometimes. But I think his marriage to her was just a convenient cover up along the road of his lies.

Did he love ANY of his children? I honestly do not think he understands what love is. He is like a man possessed by his own arrogance and sloppy handling of his life.

He could have excelled as a stepfather even though his past was notwithstanding. Yet he chooses to be neither a good father, stepfather, husband or grandfather.

I wonder if he ever thinks about me or his first family or his other children and their children, and if he ever feels ashamed of how he left things.

I wonder if he ever thinks about my mother. A poor young soul that he trapped in his lies and tangled life. A woman who would have stayed faithful to this man no matter how long they lived. Things he did not do for her.

I do know for sure that without him, his lies, his past, his fake love, his crimes, his deception, that my life would be quite different to what it is today. And I must admit that my life is pretty great.

DROWNING IN THE DESERT

"Things come apart so easily when they have been held together with lies."
~ Dorothy Allison

My memory of "the moving event" is slightly fuzzy. But this event was as life changing as they come, for me at least. I call it an event because it was done in haste, not because it was something my mother wanted. And of course, like with all our moves no one consulted me on what I wanted. I know I was young, but a family is a family, I assumed. Because I was unaware of the facts, I assumed this was chosen, discussed. Looking back, it was very traumatizing. I was being ripped from the only person I really loved, or had a connection with, or who really loved me just because I was me, my grandfather. This move would be the beginning of being pulled away from the only people I loved and who loved me. My life seemed to be a series of these things. We moved from Marietta, Georgia, to Phoenix Arizona, in 1975, and shortly after to Tucson, Arizona and then to Bellevue Washington, in 1979.

This move was less about my mother's hot mess of a family, which, to be clear also played a role, and more about the lies my stepfather was telling my mother, that he himself was fleeing his past so that he would not have to pay the debts he had left his ex-wife or pay to child support his 4 children. This was also about his drug use and distribution. And he never spoke of his previous family, at least not with me around, not up to this point, not until years later, when I ran across a photo while snooping in my mother's home office, of 4 blonde girls, and wondered who they were. I simply asked a question about the photo, and it was as if this buried secret became a pandoras box. I had no idea the outrage this would spark in my home, nor did it occur to me we had so many secrets in this household. So many book writing secrets in one inconsequential family. I was 15, I believe when this incident occurred.

I was living in a rental home, not too far from where I live now. A small back-room office, with wood paneled walls, the smell of mildew, as seems to be prevalent living in the Pacific Northwest, and one lonely photo lay almost in the open. I always snuck around my mother's home office hoping to find things about my childhood, my father, anything that she was not telling me. Which turned out to be a lot.

I do remember the moving event of being in a U-Haul truck driving cross country, for what seemed like forever. As a child, time seems to stand still sometimes. My mother drove most of the time, mostly because, as it usually was with her, she was the only one who could drive properly and apparently was the only one who knew how to read a map, so I sat in the middle with my stepfather to my right. I do not remember the contents of that U-Haul, it never occurred to me to ask, to care, but it would turn out that some of it was unbelievably valuable to my mother and soon she would have to depart with it, and it would be the beginning of the end for her.

I also do not remember who was driving our car. I know we had a car and with both parents driving the U-Haul I do think there was also someone else traveling with us, but my memory is fuzzy on that too. After doing some thinking I believe it may have been Rick Welch, the man I speak about in another chapter.

During that trip a young man who was a family friend, decided to ride his motorcycle with us to Arizona. I think his name was Charlie, though I am bit fuzzy on those details as well. Looking back, I believe my mother had an affection for him, as well as several other men in her life. But she stayed faithful to her new husband. Her husband, however, rarely stayed faithful to her.

My mother had been in love with plenty of men. Ron Porter, who was married to a woman who remained my mother's closest friend up until the day my mother died. Rick Welsch, who ended up passing away from a freak electrical accident. Also, Henry who died in an unfortunate but all too common swimming accident. He went out swimming alone and drowned. My mother spoke about him for as long as I can remember. She used to show me photos of the trips they would take skiing and talk about the fun times she had with him. I know she loved him. And I do have at least one memory of her being with him, laughing, hugging, kissing. I do not think she knew I was in the room. Henry was married to my mother's best friend at the time, Myrna, and I think if he had lived, she may have stayed with him, married or not. But her heart was broken when he died. She wept for him often.

His official name was Henry Otto Hull, born June 15, 1937, Minneapolis, Minnesota died on May 16, 1971, at the age of 33. Son of Donald Emerson Hull, Research Physicist, and entered in "Who's Who in American Scientists."

Figure 10 Henry Hull obituary

I thought it might be fun, moving. I was young, so I was not sure of the total impact that was about to have. I trusted my mother to make the right decision. As children do, trust their parents. Little did I know that marrying her second husband was one of many bad decisions she was making in trying to put her life back together after the accident.

This move was less about making a positive new life and more about covering over my stepfather's past life. His drug use, his divorce, 4 children he literally abandoned, the affairs he was having and the fact that, and I honestly believe this to this day, that he was and is gay.

But this move just proved worse for us as a family and worse for my mother. And this move would bring us to one more move, one that I knew at the time broke my heart, but literally saved my life. Something I would not appreciate or understand until much later in life.

As it would turn out my stepfather was in very deep to Drug Traffickers, Heroin, other drugs too. And in the '70s especially, Tucson, Arizona was a great breeding ground for these dealers, thugs, and bagmen. And how my stepfather got involved in any of it is beyond me. I remember him telling stories about his youth, getting in with the wrong crowd, leaving the church for a while and getting into drugs with his friends. But I am not sure how much of that is true. Jack neither did nor does have a habit of telling the truth so to ask him anything about this time in our life, you will get 100 different stories. But in my fact-finding mission to author this book, I know that he almost got us killed. I remember it as a lonely time, but it was actually a very scary time in my family's history.

Jack worked for a company that supplied CO_2 tanks to restaurants. He would load the truck and go hook them up. In the summertime I would ride with him and go to restaurants with him. It was fun, we laughed, told jokes, listened to music, I remember getting time with my stepfather and meeting some fun people. And getting lots of free soda and food. Everyone seemed to love the adorable blonde girl with a wit and false confidence.

As facts would come forward, this job was my stepfather's way of making his deals, selling his dope, making cash deals, and getting new customers. These were not just customers, but customers of his drug business and he was putting me, putting us as a family, in danger every day by not being honest with my mother about anything. By literally breaking the law.

After years without him in my life I realized that everything was about him, his comfort, his secrets, his life, him.

Apparently, he was not paying back his debts to the Cartel that he was involved with, so they threatened his life, our life. As Cartels do. He, one day, in a fit of indecision, stole money from his company to pay back the Drug Lords. Though I do not remember him getting arrested, I do remember him getting fired. And this changed our life for the next 40 years.

My mother had to call her father in Georgia, a night my uncle Lance remembers very well. And we had to ask him to borrow money to pay back the company that Jack stole from. From my conversations, I believe that if he paid the money, the company would not file charges against him and would just simply fire him instead. So, we got the money from my grandfather Lee and paid back the company, but we were now being threatened by the Mob. They threatened to kill us because Jack had made some unbelievably bad decisions, was not paying his debts, and had now blabbed his big mouth about who they were and what had happened. My stepfather treated this like a childhood game, a childhood blunder. This was as serious as it comes folks. The drug cartel is threatening your family, death. Death is forever in case that is something that has escaped anyone.

During my time in Tucson, I can tell you that I was happy. We did not have a lot of money, but we had what we needed, a roof, food to eat, music. I was a kid and I loved being outside with my friends and neighbors. This was before my mom lost her mind about who I associated with. Or simply lost her mind. My parents seemed to make friends easily, many of their friends being much younger than they were. None of their friends yet had children. And how it happened I do not remember but many of their friends lived in Phoenix, so we would regularly take a road trip from our place to see them. We had lived in Phoenix for a while, I am unsure why we moved from Phoenix to Tucson. It was about a 2-hour drive each way and the roads were long, hot and bare. But the music was loud, and my parents were enjoying life. My mother was still in her 20's and trying desperately to put her past behind her.

These road trips were crazy! We had what I call a "Shaggin Waggon", really it was a tan van with wall-to-wall carpeting, a refrigerator, I think there was a bed inside, but it may have just been a large bench. The carpet was orange and yellow and brown shag. Literally wall to wall carpeting. Two, what they used to call, Captain's chairs up front. They were big, leather and swiveled. I remember there were no seats in the back but there must have been because we used this vehicle to take us on a lot of road trips and the long journey from Tucson to Seattle. And when that happened, we were now a family of 4 not 3. Airbrushing designs on your car or van was the coolest thing you could do in the '70s so we had eagles and landscapes on our van, and we also had a CB in our car and our van. The van had a black bubble window, a CB, wall to wall carpeting and yes you guessed it, beer in the fridge, and I thought we were the coolest family in the world.

My mother's CB handle was The Phantom Pup, our friend Robin Wartman, was Rockin Robin, I cannot recall what everyone else's was, but what fun we had with that. Speeding and calling each other over the CB to let others know if there was a cop around, etc. It was in some ways like a movie I did not want to end. Or a great dream that you wish you had never woken up from. These were fun times, short years but fun times in my memory.

During the road trips, sometimes we would go to Phoenix, sometimes our friends came to see us in Tucson, my parents would drink and drive and pass beer and sunflower seeds back and forth from one car to another while we were driving. Literally out the window of the van to the window of our friend's car while they rode side by side with us on the road. Not many people lived out there in the 70's so the roads were lonely, and we owned them with our weird family trips.

Considering my mother lost her first husband and her two friends to a Drunk driving accident, looking back it surprises me that she thought that drinking and driving was acceptable. But it was legal back then and she was still young. And I almost believe that she must have put so much out of her memory that decisions like this did not seem consequential. When we moved to Arizona, she was only 26 and still wanted to party and live her life and she seemed to be doing it very well. An old friend said to me recently that my parents were THE party people and the whole town and congregation knew it. Everyone knew that our trailer was where the parties would happen.

There were lots of parties, lots of alcohol, lots of sex. I remember plenty of friends that we met while there. Steve and Robin Wartman, Jay and

Mary Bracken, Rod and Janice Kirby, Doreen and Rhodom Conrow, The Schultz's who had 7 children, the Howards who had 5 children. Most of these couples and families moved with us to Seattle in 1978 and 1979. Or moved to Washington state first and we followed behind.

We kept many of them as friends up until now. Unfortunately, Robin died of neglect and alcoholism in 2004. Her family, husband, friends and congregations literally neglected her to death. Her disease, alcoholism was ignored, and she was tossed out in the world to die, basically alone and broken. It broke my heart but looking back I was too wrapped up in my own hot mess of a life to think much about the sadness and regrets Robins death would bring me years later.

I was alone a lot, my parents both worked, and I was, as we used to call it, a latchkey kid. I walked to school every day and home. There was a corner store that I would pass every day on my way to and from school. And once a week I would go inside and buy comic books for a dime. They were my secret, my escape. Usually, I came home to an empty trailer. But I would entertain myself by listening to my mother's records, dancing and singing in the living room, which looking back was one of my favorite things to do of all time. The feeling of pulling that large round vinyl out of its sleeve and placing it on a platter still gives me chills. Music, singing, lyrics, the feeling music gave me, gives me is something that has kept me alive. Without music I would not have my memories, good and bad. Music is my life. If you know me you will recall now that most times you are with me, in my home, that I have music playing, I know the lyrics to most songs on the radio, from many eras, and I collect music from most genres. Music keeps me sane, keeps me grounded. Music keeps my head together.

I wanted to describe the trailer not because it was anything fancy, obviously, but because it is the last place I lived before my life was once again turned upside down. We did not live in a trailer park, just a single wide, on a piece of land, on a sad corner of Tucson. Not many people lived there then, so a trailer in a corner seemed odd. But this was my place, I was alone all the time, so it seemed like my very own home. I had a large bedroom and bathroom all to myself. Well, large for a young girl. I am sure if I was inside, it now, it would all seem incredibly sad.

My mother fancied herself to be a decorator. We had a white, yes white, velvet couch, two large green and blue floral chairs, spools that mom burned and shellacked that we used for end tables. Wood paneling, and on one main wall in the living room, as people did in the 70s, we had mirrors on the entire wall. The square tile mirrors, with the awkward gold splashes of lines in them. My parents had a collection of records, Dr. Hook, The Eagles, Elton John, Exile. A few I remember well. I played those records every day, danced and sang in the living room and thought my life was pretty cool. It wasn't really.

There was a young man in the trailer across from ours. As it turned out his parents owned our trailer and we were just renting from them or perhaps leasing from them, as it turns out we stiffed them when we fled in the middle of the night.

As I said, I was alone a lot. Johnny was a nice kid, I remember him being handsome, tall, funny, and guess what, he loved music. He had all the cool albums that teenagers had, the band Heart being one of them. He used to invite me to his place every afternoon after school. Of course, I would go there, he was my friend. We would swim in their above ground pool and play games and listen to records. I was 9, he was 18 as I remember.

But that friendship turned into something tragic. Yet at the time I was simply getting the attention I craved from a young man. Or the attention I craved, period. Things started innocent he would touch me over my bathing suit. He would touch my small budding breasts, my vaginal area. Just small rubs, touches, maybe a mouth to my shoulder.

Then as it escalated as these things tend to, he would invite me into his bedroom after a swim. To listen to his records. But that turned into something that I assume you have already anticipated, but hoped it was not true, it turned into full on sexual abuse.

He began laying me on his bed, asking me to touch his penis, he would finger me, kiss me, he would put his hands over my eyes and bring me to orgasm. Remember I was only 9. He would play the same song on his record player, every time. Hearts Dreamboat Annie, every single damn time. It was not until the past few years that I could actually hear that song without it turning my stomach.

This went on for about 1.5 years if not more. My memory has erased some of this. I do remember the last time it happened, but I have blocked out the actual act. I was with Johnny, we were together as we were almost every day after school, he was overly aggressive this day, same song, same stench of his bedroom, same sweltering day, but the next thing I remember was waking up in my own bed, covered in some substance on my private area and stomach. I simply got up, took a shower and did not talk about any of this with anyone until I was in my 30's. No one, not a soul. I do not remember ever seeing Johnny after that.

When I finally confronted my mother about it, in my 30's, only in a handwritten letter, she blamed me for the entire situation. Saying things that you only read about, things that victim shaming stories don't prepare you for. She said that it was my fault, I lured him to me, I was a slut, I was gross and useless, I was horny, I must have begged for it, why did I keep going back. I was nine.

She even returned my letter to me in the original envelope and wrote on the outside that I had written her a hate letter. She never spoke of it to me and almost seemed ashamed to know about it. I wondered as she was dying if she was really ashamed of me or herself for not actually protecting me, knowing, or for not being a god damned mother.

I think the thing at first that bothered me the most about the abuse is that I was not bothered by it, none of it. I was alone, I was lonely, I was begging for attention from anyone. Johnny gave it to me in an unhealthy way, but he gave it to me.

To this day that very last memory of Johnny is still blocked from my brain. Still, no matter how much I tell myself its fine if I remember it, I do not. I suppose that protection is there for a reason, so that people are not too broken to move on.

It was not too long after this that we moved, abruptly. Not because of this, since no one knew, but because of my stepfathers, illegal activities. And as I have just found out, because my stepfather was trying to keep running from his first family so that his Ex-wife wouldn't find him and make him pay for his kids.

I remember my mother weeping for days, putting all her things up for sale on our front lawn and telling me that it was fine, she would take care of it, but that we had to move.

Remember I told you about the U-Haul and how it contained valuable things? It did to my mother, furniture and personal belongings that were given to her by her mother. Antiques that today would be worth thousands. She sold every single one of them for pennies on the dollar. Almost every piece of furniture, art, clothing, everything that would bring a buck.

Some things we left behind because we had to leave quickly.

By this time my sister had arrived, it was 1979 and she would be two. We were fleeing the above-mentioned cartel. We had to, our lives were in danger, there were no longer any choices for us. Thanks to my stepfather we now had to flee our life and for our lives, a second time.

To Seattle we went. In the middle of the night, we packed our van, a few things in boxes, my sister and I and away we went. We said goodbye to no one, we took the bare minimum, and we were on our way to start fresh, again.

I had to leave my dog behind. I loved that dog more than anything in the world. That dog was my only real friend. My stepfather went away one afternoon and said he gave the dog to a truck driver who needed a companion. But I know that he either killed the dog or left it out in the desert somewhere to die. That is just one more thing I will never forgive him for. His sociopathic mindset and his lies, always lies.

And up to this point I had lived in trailers, except for the few years I lived at my grandfather's ranch house in Georgia. It was trailer after trailer, then apartments. I never even lived in an actual house, until we moved to Washington state.

In the fall of 1979, we ended up in Bellevue, Washington. I will not forget it, it was late in the evening, and we ended up right up the street from where I live now, meeting an old friend who was waiting for us when we finally drove in.

We had to stay with him and his family in the basement of their home. We had no money, nowhere to go and remember we were literally fleeing the Cartel.

We had to keep the lights off in our basement apartment for what seemed like a whole summer. And we had to park our van in the back of the house so it would not be seen. It seemed like whenever we talked, we whispered, and we never answered the phone. Ever.

I was allowed to go to school, but of course my last name was different than my stepfather's, so I am sure that was less of a worry for my safety. I was not allowed to talk about where I had come from. I was not allowed to ask questions and I was not allowed to remember these details. I was to forget anything that happened, and I was to move on.

Any and all friends who now lived in Washington state who knew us in Arizona, were to keep their mouths shut about anything private or personal they knew about us.

My stepfather was what the church called Disfellowshipped for stealing. Only for 6 months. I still cannot believe he was never arrested or killed. Or that we were not killed along with him. I assume he must have had some incredibly good connections or maybe the Cartel just felt sorry for him. I do not know, we do not speak these days, 13 years after my mother's death. But I have put together enough pieces from enough people who were there and who understood what happened, to get me this far into the story.

We eventually rented a home of our own, and from that time on all we did was rent homes. We never bought anything either because we did not have the money or because my mother had the church's view that the world was going to end any day now, so why buy a house? It might make you miss your opportunity to live forever because you might choose your lovely home over your loyalty to god.

I know that part is hard to understand but it is why for most of our lives we had secondhand clothing, secondhand furniture, not all but most used cars. We frequented garage sales to furnish our homes for years.

Nothing in life was normal or fun again. My mother became someone I did not recognize. I was angry, sad and confused.

No one seemed to care, once again, about me. It was all now about this new place, putting our demons behind us, or rather sweeping them under the rug, and making sure that my life was as miserable as possible.

I missed the desert because in some ways, though I was being abused, I was allowed to be independent. I did pretty much anything I wanted, went where I wanted, though my parents neglected me, it kind of felt a bit like being a grown-up. I had the house to myself most days, and most of my friends were adults.

When I go back to Arizona to visit friends I tear up because honestly, it was tragic. For a young girl to keep going through what I was going through. Drugs, poverty, lies, deceit, neglect, it would shape my life. It shapes lives.

My memories of Arizona are so vivid that some days it feels like we just left. When the reality is, we left over 40 years ago.

The friends we made there, we kept most of them in our lives out here. But there were a few that stayed behind and that I was not allowed to ever speak of or contact.

My time in Arizona was so filled with lies and secrets, not just mine but my family. When my mother died and this would have been 31 years after we left Arizona, she refused to talk to me about what happened and why. When my mother decided not to remember things, she just went ahead and forgot them. Even if those conversations would have been healthy for her or for those she loved.

I do remember a time when she told me that thinking about Arizona made her physically ill. But as I authored this book, I imagined a woman with so many tragedies in her life that most things she fought not to remember, made her physically ill.

The desert both haunts me and heals me. I learned so much about myself in those few years we lived there yet my life had three big life-changing moments while there. The birth of my first sister, my stepfather's lies, and my sexual abuse.

Each taught me something different, and each guided me to what decision I was about to make next. In some ways each of those things shifted my life in a direction where it would eventually land.

Though it felt like I was drowning in the desert, I literally and emotionally learned to swim and eventually rescued myself.

THE LADY WAS A TRAMP

"No matter how much suffering you went through, you never wanted
to let go of those memories."
~ Haruki Murakami

In the fall of 1979, my family had now moved from Arizona to Washington state. We had actually fled from one state to another, as I have told you, this is the second time in my life we had done this.

But it was not until this critical and final move that I began to see the stark financial differences between my family and my friends. I never knew we were poor. It never occurred to me what poor meant or was. I never thought I was unhappy. I just thought I was a girl, in a family, going to school, going to church, and wanting to grow up. This move was torture on my 12-year-old self.

Friendship is a term that many of us take for granted. We meet someone, we become friends, we trust them, perhaps we grow old with them by our side, as friends. We do not think much about that definition until that definition is destroyed by a force that seems bigger than you. In the cult, a friend is vastly different. They are cold, distracted, and I will deeply emphasize they are someone that you cannot trust with any information, with your heart, with your mind, with anything. They will turn on you and take the church's stance on anything over their friendship with you. It is friendship with conditions, and it is not friendship, it is abuse and control. These friends will not help you; they will not stand with you; they will not reach out to you. It is as if they are in a catatonic state of relationship. They know nothing about being a friend or how true friendship works. It makes thousands of very unhappy deeply depressed people.

In the congregation, one of the first "friends" I made was a young woman named Gina. Remember in the cult I was raised in, the only friends I could have were people inside the church and nowhere else. Not school, not in the neighborhood, nowhere but the cult. You had to be friends with these people, forced friendships. Imagine that if you will. It is like a very poorly written science fiction novel.

Gina was shadowy and unwavering, at least that is how I saw her then, as a 13-year-old girl.

She wore the best clothes, was more mature than any girl our age and she did not take crap from anyone. Frankly, she scared me. She seemed like the girl that was either going to get me in trouble, keep me from trouble, or be trouble. She ended up being all three.

She was the eldest in a family of 6. She had one sister, two brothers and usually a butt load of cats at her home. Her father had been with Boeing for an exceedingly long time. I had never actually met anyone like her or her family. They were strong, opinionated, owned their own home, nice cars, and had this family dynamic that was less strict than how I was being raised. It seemed like a positive family dynamic. I did not know what one looked like, so for me, it seemed ideal. I remember being very jealous of her family, her parents, her possessions and jealousy was not an emotion I was used to. I was just used to being a kid.

In the church, at least from the places I had lived to this point, there were not many "successful" people. That is just how it was. The church discouraged higher education, and if you had grown up in the church then the chances that you would go to college, get a college degree, or do something bigger and better in your life, was slim to none. People just hopelessly slogged through life like Zombies, waiting for the end of the world. Doing nothing useful with their lives. It was a sad existence.

Most people I met in the church to this point were janitors, window washers, construction workers, tile layers, stonework, painters, etc. Not that there was anything wrong with those jobs, careers, but it really was the church's way of controlling your thinking, your finances and keeping you in a financial place that made it ridiculously hard to do anything fun or better with your life. You had no extra money, so you would spend your free time with the church rather than going on vacation. You had no extra money, so you would not be tempted to buy a fancy house or car. You had no extra money, so you would not be tempted to buy those expensive shoes. You had no extra money, so you would remain poor waiting for a new life that you knew God was going to give you any day. And as they teach, in the New World we won't need Doctors or Lawyers, but we will need Tile layers.

Those things and more were the church's way of making sure that everyone was "equal". But that equality came at a huge price. Jealousy and ignorance, and sometimes death. Mostly emotional death but actual death to many because the church stole their being.

But Gina's family was different, her father was successful at Boeing, her family had two new cars most of the time, they had a house that they actually purchased instead of renting, the mother did not work, and she actually seemed to enjoy being a mother.

I thought that they were the richest people I knew! Both financially and in the family dynamic.

Gina's parents were Hispanic, loud, fun and open-minded. They even used the word Shit on a regular basis, mostly to describe what their chickens did, but holy cow they used the word shit! MAN, they were cool.

Gina's parents were more lenient than mine. But let's be honest, whose parents weren't? My mother would not let me wear make-up until I was 16, yet all the girls both in school and the church were already doing it. I was not allowed to shave my legs, yet all my friends were doing it. I was not allowed to wear pantyhose, or wear heels, or pick out my own clothes, but all the girls were doing it. It is no wonder everyone at school and in the church made fun of me. My childhood was super fun.

My mother, as you will read later, always attributed things like make-up, clothing, perfume, and high heels, to a girl or woman's desire to have sex. Everything with my mother had a sexual ending. So, when the very painful conversations of wanting to wear make-up, for example, came up, well it must be that I want to attract the opposite sex, so I can have sex, that I want to wear make-up. When really, I just wanted to fit in with my peers. I just wanted to be a girl. I just wanted to feel normal.

When a mother says things to you like, red shoes are for hookers and babies, well you might as well throw your hands up because your life is about to be fucked up almost beyond repair.

Gina began to use my mother's crazy against me. She used every opportunity, real or imagined, to use my mother against me. She knew that my mother did not allow me to do certain things, so Gina would start to flaunt her preeminence in my face. Gina knew that whatever she wanted, her parents gave her, and she knew that my mother would never cave into me as her parents did with her. And she knew that my family did not have the money that her family had. So, for a while, Gina became more of my abuser than my friend.

The problem was that I loved Gina, I genuinely thought she was my friend and that she would never hurt me. Yet her odd passive-aggressive attitude toward my mother became her using my mother's abuse against me.

As the years rolled on, and I mean years, from 12 to 16, to 20, to 30, I still considered her one of my closest friends. Yet looking back it was obvious that I considered her more of a friend to me than me to her. It never occurred to me that she did not care about me, but only about her own interests. It never occurred to me that in my 50's she would not be part of my life.

I will add that my mother literally hated Gina. She hated how much she got away with, she hated her independence, she hated how she dressed, how much she talked about sex, she hated her, period. So that also made my life a nightmare.

Gina always seemed to be the Queen bee of the group. There were about 8 of us girls, all the same age, all in the same congregation, all trying to grow up together and all dealing with our own demons.

Gina had this unusual sex appeal about her. As she got older her skirts got tighter, her tops lower, she would go without a bra and underwear and not only wear dresses to church that showed it, but she would also brag about it, and most of the time, to my mother of all people. She would literally go out of her way to come to my house, dressed in a way that she knew would light my mother up and then she would sit on the floor, crossing her legs in a way that showed her pussy. It drove my mother crazy. In some ways it was fun to watch but in other ways that relationship was abusive. My mother and Gina were abusing each other with their own craziness. And I was caught in the middle of something that in the real world would be inconsequential. But in my world, it was everything.

Gina's relationship with her father was something I still think about today. I found it disturbing, very disturbing. I thought that I was the only one who thought that, but it was years after her father died, that it became a discussion among our small group of friends. And recently, and I mean the past month, it also became a discussion at my dinner table about her father and how his relationship with both his daughters was creepy and something people thought but never talked about.

Her father was buying her lingerie, tight skirts, bras and panties, perfume. He would call her sexy and even compliment her breasts. She appeared to find nothing odd about this. I even asked her several times if this was normal, and she actually defended him by saying that I was the one with the problem for thinking any of it was weird. Well make no mistake, it was weird then, and even years after Gina and I have not been in contact, it is still weird. And creepy, let's not leave out creepy. And the discussion also included Gina's sister and that her father was also doing things inappropriate with her. It is no wonder both of these women have huge issues as adults.

A man buying his daughter lingerie and complimenting her tight outfits and how nice her breasts look in something and how he can't wait to see her dressed in something in particular, is and will always be creepy not to mention downright gross.

Something that I did not know until years later was that most everyone in our little group of friends suspected that Gina had something going on with her father, but no one said a thing about it. And since Gina never mentioned it and treated it as if this was the normal way a father and daughter behave, well, we all just let it go.

Since her father was prominent in the church, no one dared discuss this subject, period.

Gina's father was very protective of her, in a very distressing way. You could not say a negative thing about her, without him coming to her defense. I remember one evening at church when Gina came wearing this incredibly tight sweater dress with no bra underneath it, and then purposely flaunted her outfit in front of me. When I took her outside and called her a whore, probably not my best ten minutes, it did not end well.

She told her father what I said, and he literally followed us home from church, came to our door, red-faced, started screaming at my stepfather, how dare you allow your daughter to talk to my daughter like that, shame on her, shame on you. Hands and fists in the air, loud voices, sweat pouring off her dad.

And Gina's father was a BIG man! My stepfather, not so much. Gina stood behind her father laughing at me and saying, "you got what you deserved", "boy is my father mad now!".

Gina's father's fists were rolled into a ball, and I thought he was going to punch my stepdad. I softened it all by saying that I was sorry and that my conversation was perhaps inappropriate and mean. Let's be honest, on that day, in my world, Gina not only acted like but dressed like a little tramp. She was always begging for attention from men and women. Though in the world I live in today her behaviors and clothing probably wouldn't get her noticed, in the cult world, it was noticeable, and it was unhinged. And I would not use the word tramp today to describe a behavior or person. But in the cult, that's just what you called people.

Good gravy, looking back on that incident, it was more than disturbing. Gina was way oversexed, not for the real world perhaps, but for the world we were all living in, under the thumb of the church. And for her father to continue to allow her to flaunt herself, made no sense to me. And she never got into trouble for anything, nothing, ever.

I was in huge trouble that evening, for calling Gina a whore. Yet I reminded my mother, if she ever took a breath from screaming, that SHE was the one who called Gina a whore all the time in our home. Why was it different if I told her to her face?

Gina's father was an elder in the church, and as far as financially, he was probably one of the most successful at that time. And I think people were afraid of him, literally. So, Gina got away with everything, and I do mean everything. I couldn't look at someone atypical without the elders wanting to chat with me about my supposed behaviors, or dress, or conversation. But Gina could come half-naked to church and brag about how her dad bought her lingerie, and no one batted an eye.

I have seen it too many times in my life, and I would bet the ranch that Gina and her father had an inappropriate relationship. I do not know if it was sex, or something different, but it was certainly something unusual, wrong.

I do not want to speak ill of the dead, because I had the utmost respect for Gina's' father. He died at the age of 57, on August the 30th, 1996 of a heart attack. I loved the man. He was strong and bold and smart, and my mother was made uncomfortable by him, for those very reasons, because he was strong and bold and intelligent. I think she almost felt challenged by him. She believed that any man who had a strong personality must automatically be an abuser. Gina's father was everything that I did not have. He was protective of her, he was kind when he needed to be, he was handsome, successful, bold, and he loved his family.

But Gina never cried, not that I saw. Not a single tear, not even at his funeral. She was cold and calculated, the deep mental state of an abused woman who was glad, sad and angry at the sudden death of her father. The none tears of a woman who no longer had her protector, her user. Every year that went by after that, not a tear, not a word. I remember that her conversations about her father became less and less until with me at least, they were nonexistent.

Gina's behavior began to get her into trouble. She started dating, within the restrictions of the church, but her definition of dating was much different than mine. Since she knew, she was never going to get into trouble for anything she did, so she just went ahead and did it, whatever it was.

I do not know that Gina was having sex with these boys, but I know that she was becoming the blow-job master. At least that became her reputation inside the congregations. The boys wanted to date her just to see if it was true.

And when you are brought up in such a strict religion that teaches you how sinful sex is, that blow-jobs are for gay men only, oral sex is sex only for homosexuals and pedophiles, and that the missionary position is the only godly position, then the thought of a young girl, giving away free-blowjobs, will literally and figuratively blow your mind.

Gina had this odd jealousy of me, though I was the skinny, crooked toothed, inexperienced one of the group, she always made our relationship into some sort of challenge. She and she alone turned everything I did into a challenge. I know now that it was her way of always controlling me, always being the one on top.

Whenever I would like a boy, she would try to take him from me. She did this with practically every single young man that I was interested in. She did not even have to like him or know him, she just had to know that I was interested in him.

I will never forget the first time that it really affected me and began to change how I saw Gina.

There was an incredibly nice looking new young brother visiting our congregation. His older sister was getting married, and he was hanging out for the summer. His sister was a very pretty, extremely popular girl in the congregation, who was getting married to an extremely popular, and nice-looking young man. It was going to be the wedding of the year. Weddings in the church were really all young girls had to look forward to because there was nothing else in life. No education, no self-worth, no imagination, no being who you wanted. Married, pregnant, miserable, dead.

This young man's name was Chad, and I thought I was in love. I had never seen or known anyone like him, and I had this crazy crush on him. And I thought, he had one on me. Gina could not stand that I had a crush on this boy, so she swooped in, in her way, and started making a move on him. She seduced him, in plain sight, at his sister's wedding. She danced with him, she flaunted her low-cut dress at him, she rubbed herself all over him. Literally! And then she told me, "He isn't interested in you, and I just proved it!". Oh my god! I was angrier at her than I had ever been before. I know this sounds silly to you the reader right now, but imagine my world at the time, young, naïve, abused at home, ignorant, alone. Trapped in a cult.

I think I must have cried all night after that incident. But then I began to realize that something was seriously wrong with this girl. She had claimed to be my friend for 5 years, yet nothing she did said she was my friend. And why, I thought then, as pretty as she is, as sexy as she is, much prettier and sexier than I, does she keep doing these things to me? Why does she care so much about the boys I like? It confused me deeply.

My stepfather made me stop thinking about Chad, he knew that it was never going to go anywhere. I thought it was because Chad liked Gina more than me, but as the years went on, I began to understand something in my heart I already knew, Chad was gay. I knew he was way too pretty and way too disinterested in girls to be straight. But even when Gina thought the same thing about him, she literally believed that her seductive ways could turn him. She did not really have an interest in him, she just did not want me to have him

All it did was turn my stomach. And start to turn me from Gina.

I still suspect to this day, that she gave him the best blow job he had ever had in his young 16 years. She bragged about her "relationship" with Chad for years later, but really all it was, was her way of trying to control a life that was spinning out of control, her life.

On the night of our high school graduation, there were 4 of us graduating together that day, June 1986, my parents said I could have a party, and a sleepover. Well, of course, I invited all these people to my house, and it was a great summer day. For some reason, that day still stands out in my head. Maybe it was because it really was a good day. No yelling, no fighting, just sunshine, friends and graduation. Even Jerry came to the party, at this time he was now interested in two of my friends. This time Gina was among them.

That evening, 4 of us stayed up and watched a movie, split a bottle of champagne and celebrated our graduation. Jerry stayed and hung out with us. This was kind of a big deal, especially since my parents rarely did anything to celebrate me. And they certainly did not like it when my friends stayed the night. As you will read my mother always believed that sleepovers meant surely someone was getting laid or molested. Her demons always took over my life.

My mother did not really believe in celebrations. She literally did not want me to have fun or enjoy life. It wasn't always clear to me, but in the end, her motto really was, if she wasn't enjoying life, why should I. But this was a huge deal, I graduated from High School barely, but I did it. And now my friends and I were going to get to have a little party at my home for once.

Well, Jerry was there, as he was still very much a part of my life, though we had ended our dating relationship. But as luck would have it Jerry fancied Gina, and it is pretty much for the reasons you think.

It wasn't because she was charming or smart, it was because he was a young man and he was oversexed, or should I say undersexed because of the guidelines of the church. And I might add that the church discouraged masturbation as well as sex out of marriage, so as you can imagine a 19-year-old young man was going to get whatever he could, from almost anyone that would give it.

After the movie, we all fell asleep on the floor of the den of my family's home. But not Jerry, he fell asleep on the couch. As the evening progressed and we were all asleep, where was Gina but on the couch going down on him, giving him a blow job. Right there, in my home, knowing my parents were just a few steps away. Gina did anything to get me in trouble, pleasure herself and as usual face no consequences. But let's get back to that blowjob.

Well, honestly it did not occur to me that this was really happening, though I have a faint memory of waking up in the middle of the night seeing it happen. No mistake, it was as happening.

Of course, I do not remember who felt guilty first, Gina or Jerry, but Jerry felt enough guilt to blab about it to my stepfather. I think he thought Gina would tattle first, so he was trying to hedge his bets. But knowing both of them, I do not think guilt was a factor. I think it was just cutting out the middleman. And as it was Gina's way, she denied the whole event. But then as if some memory just happened to come to her, she blamed my mother for giving her champagne. She said the champagne made her drunk and she did not know what she was doing. That she was so inebriated that she did not know she was giving a blow job. Can you hear me laughing right now? The 5 of us shared ONE bottle of champagne. She knew exactly what she was doing. I was certainly no fan of my mother. But Gina had to make up some excuse and blame someone else so that the congregation, when the word got out, and it would get out, wouldn't punish her for her behavior. And of course, the boy was not going to be punished because hey he just laid there and had no clue that a girl had her tongue on his dick. He must have been inebriated too. Oh please!

I do not know who blabbed first, but the news did come out in the congregation and once again Gina was renowned. I do not know if she ever really cared what people said about her, as long as she was still being talked about.

My mother was furious with Gina about this whole scandal. But then in my mother's typical fashion, she turned around and blamed me for what happened. Saying that I must have seen something or knew something or predicted something, and I should have stopped it. Yes, mom, I should have stopped her from giving my X boyfriend a blow job on our couch. Sure thing.

Oh brother, what a nightmare this became. Gina flaunting her triumph in front of me and my mother. And of course, Jerry wasn't going to say anything, because hey, free blow job. And now I became a pariah in the congregations because it was my house, my party so surely, I must have had something to do with it.

Jerry never confirmed or denied the incident to me, but my stepfather told me it was all true. My stepfather was not one to always tell the truth, but I know years later this incident not only happened but put our families more at a distance than ever before.

None of this would have been a big deal or even a discussion in the real world. But in the church, this was the scandal of the century. You would have thought we were all drowning puppies.

This was just another abusive action that Gina thrust toward me. She did not really want to be with Jerry, but because I had liked him and or dated him, well she could not resist getting her mouth around him, literally.

Gina was getting desperately close to getting herself into big trouble in the congregation. Or at least I had hoped she would.

Gina dated an older man for a while, named Barry. Barry was divorced and had two small children. Since Barry was a bit on the fence when it came to the church, he would be truly blessed that there was little gossip as far as his own life was concerned. But of course, Gina loved being talked about, it kept her relevant. Gina was free to date this man because he claimed to be a Jehovah's Witness, even though his actions did not show it very well.

Gina did not try to hide it; the assumption was that she and Barry were having sex. Or at least she was giving him one hell of a blow and hand job most days/evenings.

She used to sneak up to Barry's apartment, while having me wait in the car, to keep a lookout. It was so odd, she used to climb through his bedroom window some evenings, instead of just going in through the front door. Everything with her was about drama and secrecy all at the same time.

She would come back to the car and tell me how the condom did not fit right, or how quick the blow job went. I think she told me these things because she knew I would keep her secret. Or maybe she told me these things because she hoped I wouldn't and then she would be free to be with Barry openly or pursue more of the relationship than I think he wanted. I am not sure that he wanted to get married again. He was raising his two small daughters, from what I remember, alone. And Gina thought she would make an excellent stepmom. At 18 years old, I am not sure she would have made a good wife, more or less a stepmom to two small daughters. Make no mistake, Gina was a hot mess.

I kept her secret with Barry, and many other secrets, for years. But as was typical with her, she did not do the same for me. And I never learned my lesson. I honestly believed she was always my friend and that even her betrayals were part of the friendship.

There was a new family that moved into the congregation from New Mexico. They had a son that was our age. He was interested in dating me and he was so polite, he went to my stepfather to ask if it would be ok. But Jack knew that I was about done with boys. I had several short relationships, and looking back, they were all losers. And I was not about to date another potential loser.

But of course, Gina heard about this and swooped in to take the prize. She flirted with him, she rubbed herself on him, she essentially seduced him. I do not think she really liked him that much, but she was not about to let me have him, or him me. Fortunately, I was not interested in him, so it did not faze me very much.

They started dating and the sad part was, Gina had been Derrick's only girlfriend, ever.

As the rules of the church demand, if you are dating someone, then you must be ready to marry that person. The church gave little room for people courting more than one person. So, once you announced that you were dating, that was it, the end of the end, they would eventually have to marry. And especially with Gina's oversexed personality, I am not sure she would get many more chances to just date someone without all hell breaking loose in the congregation or at home. Her 9 lives were just about up.

The odd thing about the church, (well one odd thing) was that it emphasized marriage and marriage young. The disasters that that belief brought later in life to many women, especially, was more than disturbing. Women in abusive relationships, men miserable with the woman they met at 18 and now had to spend the rest of their lives with. The churches backwards view of sex, or sex outside of marriage, made for many a miserable household. Children being raised by parents who barely tolerated one another, loveless marriages, that, looking back, really should have been just a few nights of sex, nothing more.

Well Gina and Derrick eventually got engaged. But not everyone was happy about this. Derrick's mother even came to me in tears one day begging me to try and get this engagement stopped. She said that Gina was white trash who was going to ruin Derricks life. The fact that Gina had been Derricks only girlfriend, had not gone unnoticed by many. Especially his mother. I secretly wanted Gina to get married and did not really care if she was happy or not. I wanted her to stop, once and for all, trying to seduce the boys I was interested in.

They had a big wedding, remember weddings were THE event in the church. But if you were someone that was as they said, not in good standing, meaning you had been in trouble for something within your relationship, sex, oral, heavy petting, then getting married in the church was a hard no. But for some reason there was Gina and Derrick, her in her white dress, parading down the aisle of the church to become husband and wife.

What a fucking crock of shit. She was tossing it around like the paper boy and yet she was still allowed to marry inside the walls of the church. Friends and family, all teary eyed and well wishing.

And because neither Gina nor Derrick had more than a high school diploma, things were going to be rough. Very rough.

Gina got pregnant right away, and of course always said the birth control did not work. She claimed that the condom and the birth control pills were never enough to keep her from getting pregnant. Well, if you know the stats, that is pretty much bullshit. I think she wanted to get pregnant, so she did not have to work and that she could once again be in the spotlight. The first of our friends to get pregnant. Well, that's not entirely true, but let's just say, the first of our married friends who got pregnant.

Gina did not take particularly good care of herself while she was pregnant. She gained an enormous amount of weight and ended up with Toxemia. Her newborn son ended up with Meningitis, fluid on the brain.

I will never forget seeing that poor baby in the hospital, shortly after he was born. He was so tiny, a tube and needle in his head, to drain the fluid from his brain.

Gina never got emotional about things, everything with her was very matter of fact. But I saw her cry as she held this very fragile new human in her arms. I remember feeling sorry for her and wondering if she knew how difficult her life was about to become.

Gina and her husband proceeded to have two other children, along with a couple of miscarriages. I never understood why, as poor as they were, and now that their son would have a lifetime of health issues, they kept having babies. None of her choices ever made sense to me.

I think years later she may have found a purpose in life. Helping other families with children who had disabilities. Her Son never even spoke until he was much older. But as far as I know, as a 30-year-old, he still lives at home and still needs constant care. He is not invalid, but he certainly has so many health and mental issues that he will not ever be able to be on his own, have a family of his own, drive a car even.

Is Gina a good mom and wife? Has she been? I cannot say. I know she has had stretches of depression, but who hasn't inside that cult, it is almost a given.

I know looking back that she seemed frustrated with her choices, even as she was making them in real time.

I haven't spoken to Gina in 15 years. The last conversation we had was one I will never forget. She cried, she said she heard I was leaving the church, and that she hoped I would come back because I was one of the only friends she had. She sounded tired, weary, old. She told me she loved me. I loved her too; it was the last we spoke. I really did love her. My memories of her haunt me sometimes. Sometimes they make me weep, make me angry, make me confused.

But this time in my life was THE turning point for me. I was about to leave the cult, leave my family and finally get my life moving. I was about to do something I knew Gina would never be brave enough to do. I was about to be free.

So, our lifelong friendship ends as abruptly as it started. Gina and I grew up together. From the age of 12-38. We went to elementary school, Jr. High, and High school together. We got baptized the same year, got married the same year, and had children around the same time. Our families loved and grieved together. Gina was a constant in my life. She was one of the biggest game changers for me.

She was the Queen Bee, I was always the follower, the runt of the pack.

But her life never changed, she seemed to be in charge of it, but she never was. It was being controlled by the demons of her long dead father, the cult, her ill-educated life. She was never really in control.

I thought sometimes Gina was my rock, my protector. But she is just another sad story of a girl, a woman, whose life was taken away by that sad cult.

Her marriage and children have been a struggle. Her financial situation was miserable. At least for a while. After we lost contact, I had no view into that.

I know that Gina still thinks about me. How can you not when your whole lives were spent together? I know because she went so far as to tell her brother he could no longer be friends with me on Facebook. Come to find out she was jealous. Jealous of the new life I live, of my happiness, of my adventures, my bravery. I was now the Queen Bee of my own life, and she cannot handle that.

Gina and I had many disagreements in the years we were friends. But make no mistake, I learned many lessons from her. She was a huge influence on who I was and who I was to become.

In many ways, growing up, she was better than I was. She did not take shit from anyone. Even within the boundaries of the church she figured out how to work the system, how to stay out of trouble and how to stay ahead.

I wish she had taken a bigger leap and left that cult completely. I know she would have really been something outside the walls of the church.

But I do not know if she would have made it outside. She would have had to humble herself to the fact that she had a lot to learn about life, people, information.

Inside the church she may have been the girl who gave blow jobs. But in the real world she may have just become yet another person who knew how to give them.

I do not know if she is happy, I do not know much about her anymore. But I do know that without those years of her in my life, I would have been less complete. I have to take all the positives from my past life and see how they shaped me to be the woman I am today. And Gina helped shape me.

I will however never forgive her or absolve her for abandoning me when I really needed her. There is zero excuse for walking out on a friend in their time of need. We can disagree, but abandonment, unacceptable.

Cults ruin everything.

ALMOST MR. RIGHT

"You can never regret anything you do in life. You kind of have to learn the lesson from whatever the experience is and take it with you on your journey forward."

~ Aubrey O'Day

In my senior year, 1985-1986, of High School, I had "dated" a few boys by then. And because of the church my experiences were superficial at best.

My mother wanted me to get married so badly that she almost did not care who I dated as long as they were part of the church and as long as I could move out. She also thought that every time I left the house, surely, I was going to have sex. And she could think of nothing worse or more embarrassing for her than if her unmarried daughter was having sex.

As with most things in that twisted relationship between her and I, I thought surely getting married would let her or make her love me more, or some.

Though let's be clear, when I was ready to finally leave home on my own terms, at 18 when I wanted to move in with some church girlfriends, she shrieked about how would she be able to take care of her children and home and work full time if I was not there to be her personal full-time care giver, housekeeper, child rearing child, like I had always been. It was all very confusing and constantly toxic.

At this point I had known Jerry for many years. Since I was about 13. Our families went to church together, my parents did some business with his parents, and though he was a couple of years older than me, I was interested in dating him. Well as interested as I could be at this point in my life. He was a kind young man and he had work ethic, not something you always found in the church. There are and were plenty of lazy people in the church since they had no goals, then they just kind of hung around life.

He was immensely popular in the congregation, I guess it was mostly because he was fresh meat and any single girl would be lucky to have him, as my mother put it. Any girl, so I guess I had no choice.

I was far from in love with him, but I am not sure that people in the cult knew what love was. The love they taught was conditional love, period. It was mostly youth and lust that brought them together. And it was the cults rules that made them marry young just so they could have sex. Miserable marriages were mostly what you saw in the church, one after the other after the other. People who thought they were going to have to spend an eternity, LITERAL eternity with a person they now could not stand to be around.

I was 17 and Jerry was 19. He was mature, had graduated high school, (low bar) worked odd jobs, knew how to fix cars, and my parents loved him. He was soft spoken and kind. But not as kind as you would think, as it would turn out.

He had his own apartment by this time, and he was ready to marry. I think he was just ready to have sex but since it was forbidden unless you were married, here we were.

Since the church had such a tight grip on its young people, when you dated, you were barely allowed to hold hands without them pressuring you into marriage. So, as I have stated, people were in loveless and miserable marriages, because they married for sex not for love or companionship. They did not really understand the full weight of a marriage that would eventually be dead. These marriages were meant to be forever but for many the lust stopped quickly and reality set in.

The churches unnatural, abusive and disturbing views of sex made it impossible to have a healthy relationship with anyone. Sex is normal, the church turned it into something despicable. And to be clear this is not the only church or religion to do that, it just happened to be the one I was raised in.

Though as you have read, the church is particularly good at hiding pedophiles, sex offenders, and abusers of all kinds. And supporting them instead of the victims. And allowing the abusers to walk free among the congregations. And not reporting them to the authorities. So, this behavior also makes something normal like sex, become confusing. One minute it is a terrible sin the next they are covering over literal sex crimes.

Jerry and I started dating and it got awkward and heavy quickly. I had not thought much about the Me-Too movement until I started authoring this book and writing a few chapters, this one included, that made me realize I too was one of the Me-Too victims, not just once, but many times in my life.

I was still a kid, I was in an abusive household, my mother and I never got along and though I was not ready to get married, I couldn't wait to get out from under her roof. It was as if each day was choking my life out of me. Each day living with her, was killing me.

I was barely getting an education in high school; my mother was anything but supportive of education. My grades sucked and though I was a very social person, my interest in studying was nonexistent. Looking at my life now I understand that I have some learning disabilities but that was not something I could never bring to my mother. She cared about one thing, church and living forever in Paradise, period.

I knew I was not going to college, since the church discouraged higher education. I thought perhaps all I was destined for was marriage, cleaning toilets for a living and having babies. Perhaps I was right.

But dating Jerry taught me something, one especially important thing. It taught me that it was ok to say NO to someone. He was helping me to become a better person and he did not even know it.

During the time I was dating Jerry, I met a young man at School, Michael. He was a year younger than me, and I still find myself remembering his smell and his touch. I was madly in love with this boy.

Michael was fierce and intense and sexy and different from anyone else I had dated or really known. He was also not part of the church. Which made it a no-no to even think about dating him. But it made it wildly exciting to think about. My time with Michael changed me and scared me. I had never loved anyone so deeply in my life. I honestly believed that I would leave the church to be with this man.

Michael had dreams, college, the military, of one day being in the police force. Michael had seen rated R movies, he owned guns, he loved helicopters. I was in deep for this boy. He wrote 4 pages of goodbyes in my senior yearbook. Little things we shared, funny stories, secrets. Michael was everything I needed and wanted in a partner, husband, everything but a Jehovah's Witness.

And I figured no one would find out, I secretly dated Michael while still being with Jerry. It is not like Jerry paid me that much attention. He was just controlling me. He had to have me; those were his words.

But Michael needed more from me than I could give. I wasn't giving him sex, he needed me to. He never pressured me but when push came to shove, he found sex somewhere else. My heart was torn in two. I cried for months after Michael finally broke up with me. But my world had no place for Michael and his was no place for me, at least not yet.

But my love for Michael also saved me. It made me see that I did not love Jerry. And nothing Jerry was going to do was going to make him Michael.

Jerry's passion for me was real but scary at times. Jerry was forceful, telling me how much he loved me, all the time, buying me expensive gifts, and being sexually aggressive. Being in a cult that doesn't allow for sex or masturbation can create a lot of tension, and problems in relationships, married or unmarried. He would sometimes hold my hands to the floor, pinning me down while putting his hands down my pants or up my shirt, kissing me hard and violently, and it was all for his pleasure, never for mine. He would literally force himself on me and make me uncomfortable and treat it as if it was no big deal or that I was his property, so I needed to just welcome his unwelcome advances.

We never had actual sex but being sexual assaulted does not have to include actual penetration. It can be several things, and he sexually assaulted me on several occasions. I have learned plenty in my years outside the cult and one is that sexual assault comes in many forms and is never acceptable. You are not someone's property and it's always ok to say no. And any victim blaming, absolutely intolerable, always.

One of the worst times that he assaulted me was when my family was visiting friends in Oregon. Which we did a few times a year. Jerry began to go with us on these trips. I think my parents enjoyed his company more than mine. We all stayed at different friends' homes. But one evening he came over to the house I was staying at, with my best friend at the time, Karen, he brought me into the living room, and we sat on the floor. I thought we were just going to talk. But in a sudden move Jerry pulled me to him very violently, held my head while he forcibly kissed me, he unbuttoned my blouse and before I knew what was happening, he had his hands down my pants rubbing me until I climaxed. I tried to get away, but he was too strong. It was so fast that I did not even know how to respond. I do not know why he stopped there, I think it was because my friend came into the living room and saw what was happening. I remember her telling me that I needed to tell the elders in the congregation what had just happened. The problem was, I did not really know what had just happened.

But I do remember the next day Jerry telling me that my behavior was inappropriate, and it had better never happen again and that he thought about telling the elders what I did but would give me a second chance. And that his bible trained conscience bothered him that I would ever put him in that position to do lude things.

You see how he turned the whole thing on me? That was exactly how the church taught an abuser to respond. He assaulted me on several occasions, but every time it was I who needed to watch myself and stop teasing him and it was I who needed to confess my sins, not him. Oh no he was never to blame.

The other problem with it all was that I was not really interested in Jerry in a passionate way. And though I cared for him as a friend, I was never in love with him. His advances toward me always felt like assault even if they were harmless.

But I felt I was fated to get married to him. I almost felt trapped by this relationship, and I was trapped at home. Now I felt there was no way out of either situation. One was not better than the other. And Michael by now, was long gone living the life he deserved and desired to live, without me.

Jerry had this idea that he was in control of me. He started telling me how to dress, what to wear, what not to wear, how to wear my hair, what conversations I was allowed to have with his friends, that I needed to always act more mature than I was, and that if he did not like something I said or did, he would make it clear in public, that it was unacceptable, so that I would learn my place.

He told me not to laugh too loudly, and to always show respect and submissiveness to him as the head of the relationship. No independence would be tolerated.

I think that one thing that he did not understand about me, is though I was being held down by a cult and an abusive mother, I was fiercely independent and was going to make my own decisions and live my own life. It took me a long time to do it, but I did it, without him.

And with that, I was out. There was no way in hell I was going to spend the rest of my life in a relationship like this. Fuck, I was already in one like that with my mother, no man was going to keep me down too. I was not about to spend the rest of my life being told who I could and could not be, period.

I broke up with Jerry and though he cried a lot, literally, and even dedicated the Chicago song, Hard to say I am sorry, over the radio, a few times. Do not judge, it's what people did back then. But no amount of begging or trying to make me jealous was going to make me go back to him. And that was also part of the abuse, telling me there were plenty of other girls who wanted to be with him, he was such a catch, I do not know what I am missing out on. Fuck. Please just leave me alone already.

He really felt that I was making a huge mistake, and that I would want him back. He even said that I was too young to understand my mistake. Yet for some reason he felt I was mature enough to be a wife. Whatever.

In a last stitch effort to keep me, he bought me this expensive necklace and earrings. I said I couldn't keep it and he insisted that I do, no matter what my decision regarding him. I have a photo of him, and I when he gave me the gift and you can tell that I wanted to be anywhere but there with him.

My mother was furious that I broke up with him. She seriously wanted me out of the house, which is ironic since when I finally was moving out, she threw one of her famous pity party fits with me and even shrieked so loud that the neighbors came outside to see what the fuck was going on with the nut job neighbor, my mother.

My stepfather sat me down and gave me one of the oddest speeches of our short relationship. He told me that my friends would all be disappointed in me. That they had expectations of me marrying Jerry and that it would mess with the circle of things both in his world and in my own. That the church circles we ran with would look down on me for "leading a man on" without the intent of marriage.

He said that my circle of friends might change and be very judgmental about my breakup with Jerry. That my relationship with Jerry was my identity and I was ruining any chance I had for a future of happiness.

But then in the next breath, my stepfather told me that he supported my decision to not keep dating or marry Jerry. Mind blown.

Well, his little speech did not change my mind about anything. I still broke up with Jerry and he promptly got engaged to someone else a few weeks later and got married that next January. The break-up was in June, his marriage was literally 7 months later. Apparently to a woman who had had an interest in him for a long time, someone I never even heard of until I broke up with him. He had the nerve to flaunt her in my face, saying well if you do not marry me someone else will. Better her than me as it would turn out.

That speech STILL did not change my mind. I was not in love with Jerry and was not about to commit to something that literally made me sick to my stomach to think about.

Not because Jerry was a bad person, of most of the men I dated, inside the church, he was clearly one of the best. It simply was not right for me. He was very possessive and if nothing else, that was a huge turn-off.

His fiancé turned out to be a really nice lady. She was nice to me, but she was also condescending to me. I honestly had zero idea that she was just waiting in the wings to get with him should something go bad with him and I. And to be clear this situation would not be the last time something like this happens in my life.

I heard years later that their marriage had had many trials as I figured it might, not only because of the strict rules of the church, but honestly, Jerry hardly knew her. They were extremely poor for a long time. He wanted sex, she was ready to marry, and those things my friends are not exactly a solid foundation for years of happiness or even contentment.

And he had this feisty spirit that I never really saw come out in a healthy way. I believe that the church and his quick decision to get married really squelched his spirit.

Marrying only for sex is a terrible way to start your life. If you expect to be married for a long time, then you better know it is the right person and for the right reasons. Sex is not a reason to marry. Yet I saw it time and repeatedly with my friends, and now most of them are miserable. Still in loveless zombie marriages, just waited for the end of the world. Any. Day. Now.

Sex is normal and natural. And there is no reason that anyone should marry only for sex. Many churches teach this about sex. It is actually an extremely dangerous teaching. It leads to abuse, diseases, unwanted pregnancies, shame.

Many religions do not actually teach you about the years of marriage ahead, they just say you better marry before you have sex. They do not teach you about compromises, the trials, the ups, the downs, the children, the finances. It is just do not have sex until you marry. Pretty twisted.

But Jerry taught me a lot about myself. Though I did not appreciate it at the time, Jerry helped me to grow up a bit. You see breaking up with him was one of the hardest things I had done at that time. As far as my own future and happiness were concerned, me taking the reins and saying NO, was a huge turning point in the years to come.

Even with my mother and stepfather against my decision, I knew in my gut that it was the right thing to do. Looking back, it was one of the best decisions I ever made.

I knew that there was more for me in the world, and that marrying at such a youthful age, to a man that I did not love, was not only wrong for him but for me.

As much as Jerry told me he loved me, I knew that it would not be fair to him, to ask him to be in a marriage that I could not promise would be a good one.

It really was best for Jerry to move on with his life, and for me to move on with mine. Though the next few men that I dated, were layers lower than Jerry, I have never forgotten our time together, though brief, and the things he taught me both good and bad. They were all lessons for the next decisions I had to make regarding dating, and life.

I think about Jerry here and there and sometimes still feel bad for breaking his heart. I mean ladies I broke his heart.

I cannot see the woman I am today, married to a man like Jerry. I have run into him a few times as an adult and he seemed sad and bitter. But the girl I was, she could have been with Jerry had she not stood up and said, no. Many times, NO.

I still have that gold necklace that he bought me in his attempt to keep me. And Hard to Say I'm sorry, still reminds me of him.

He was just a small steppingstone into the life of this independent woman.

JUST KIDDING AROUND

"Life is measured in love and positive contributions and moments of grace."

~ Carly Fiorina

After dating Jerry, and my heart broken by Michael, I met a man named Delano through a mutual friend Karen Brown, who you will read about in a later chapter.

Delano was part of the cult, and he was the eldest of 6 children I believe. He lived in a place called White Salmon Washington with his family.

His parents were insanely dysfunctional, and his mother was a complete headcase. She was one of those women that you see that just keeps popping out babies and it seems her brain stops functioning. She was very rude to me, disliked me greatly and even called me ugly at one point. She said that it would take too many plastic surgeons working on my face and mouth to make me attractive enough to date or marry her son. Classy.

I thought Delano was handsome and mysterious! But thinking back on it all, he was also creepy, something about him was not right. I trust my gut these days, back then, not as much. Well maybe I did trust my gut, but I rarely followed through on that trust because I was being held so tightly by my mother and the cult.

We dated, mostly long distance for a while. I would spend what seemed like a fortune on long-distance phone calls. It was the days when you paid for every minute of a call, the price varied from approximately

2.00 for three minutes or more depending on where you lived, for every long-distance call that was not in your zone. I think there were months that my entire paycheck went to those phone calls. And looking back I realized that I was the one always paying for those calls, not the other way around. We talked all the time. He was charming and soft spoken, but things started getting really spooky.

He started writing me letters, every day practically, and always used the word "lover" in them. Calling me his lover, that he was glad we were lovers, and how he had always wanted a lover. It kind of creeped me out, but I was still in such a bad place at home with my mother, that dating again may have meant another opportunity to get out of the house.

Delano had more experience with sex. Or at least that is what he had me believing. Though we never had sex, he talked about it a lot more than any other boy/man I had been with. Even more than Jerry if that was at all possible. We dry humped a few times, but it was never for my pleasure, never. Let's be clear, he did have more experience with sex but not in the way you are thinking.

He had this creepy sexual vibe about him, the kind that you might find in your drunk Uncle. The kind that might get you molested late at night by the very person you trust. Like I said, creepy.

Mind you, Delano and I had zero in common. Except that we were both trapped in the cult. We did not like the same music, or movies or cars. We lived in two different states. He was a baker at a local Bed and breakfast. He taught me to break eggs with one hand. Otherwise, nothing. I do not remember a single thing that we shared except his desire to marry me and my desire to leave home.

Well, the letters just kept coming, sometimes it was just an I love you letter, but then they started getting really outlandish. The letters were long, page after page of his desires. Animals, sex, masturbation, other women.

He started talking about how much he loved animals... yes animals. Not the kind of love you have for Rover, but the kind of love you have for say, a girlfriend.

He began telling me how he used to have sex with animals. How much he liked it, how it made him feel alive. Correction, how he WAS having sex with animals. Take all the time you need with this.

He said that sometimes he would walk out into open fields, take off all his clothes, and sleep in the field. He said that waking up naked in the field made him feel like Christ. Then he said he would go door to door, naked, preaching about god.

He also said he would find various animals to sleep with, goats, chickens, dogs. Find them in the fields, neighbors' pets, whatever animal he felt like having, he would just take it.

Ok now thinking back I was not sure who was crazier him for fucking animals or me for staying with a man who fucks animals. Seriously what was wrong with me?

There were so many red flags. His abuse became very public. Telling me I was not getting a wedding ring at our wedding because a ring was something I had to earn. I would not be allowed a telephone in the house until I earned it. No television until I earned it.

And I was getting mixed messages at home. My mother disliked him but still went through the motions of helping me plan a wedding. Like sorry your fiancé is a goat humping nut bag but here is a wedding magazine for planning. Nice.

Though I will add the side note that she was not about to pay for anything or do anything nice for me for my wedding. She was borrowing other people's wedding gowns and veils and having me try them on. They were hideous. They were outdated, yellowed, some smelled like moth balls. Nothing that I pictured my wedding being.

And why are there so many stains on used wedding gowns, yellow stains, what the fuck was that about? I did not want to think about it.

My mother said I did not deserve a new gown and to just suck it up because unless I paid for it myself, I was not getting a new gown. Nor was I having fresh flowers, and it would be a potluck because she was not about to pay for meals. But please take what she was so generously giving me and be fucking grateful about it.

Remember a wedding was the ONLY thing a girl in the church had to look forward to and I knew that all my girlfriends were going to have supportive families who were going to throw them big parties with amazing wedding gowns, and here I was getting moth ball gowns with yellow stains. And I was supposed to be so appreciative. I was supposed to fall at my mother's feet because she had forethought to ask her friends for their hand-me-downs. Fucking please with that.

Well, my gut did finally kick in and after several months of dating and weeks of his creepy controlling abuse, I broke it off.

I spoke to my stepfather about my decision to break it off. And he was pretty supportive of it, and he did say that he was also pretty creeped out by Delano. Thanks, that is literally information I could have used yesterday.

Delano did not take the breakup well, at, all.

He went kind of nuts. He started going to bars and getting drunk every day and night. Picking up women even prostitutes. He would come to my home with a knife, drunk, sitting in my front yard screaming about how much he loved me and wanted me back.

If memory serves me right, he even got arrested one night at the bar, for, picking up a prostitute who was actually a police officer. Fuck. He called my stepfather to bail him out of jail. Which as you can imagine made my mother both irate and happy.

Since my stepfather was an elder in the church, he had to tell the other elders about Delano's bizarre behavior. These behaviors would or could get you removed from the church. I mean even in the real world; these behaviors can get you removed from society.

Delano was also stalking me. What story isn't complete without good old fashioned creepy boyfriend stalking? He would show up everywhere I went. My job, with my friends, the mall, church, everywhere. And it wasn't the days of social media, it was not that easy to just know where someone was or was going. I mean it took serious work to stalk someone every day.

One evening I remember after the jail, the bars, the prostitutes, all of it. An elder came to my house, I thought to help me out. Help me get rid of this nut bag for the last time. But no, he was there to scold me. SCOLD ME!

This elder was a rat bastard and the worst elder in the congregation that I attended. I was 18, 19 years old. Though things would get worse when it came to the elders in my life. This elder had an exceedingly high opinion of himself. Not that that was a rare quality in an elder inside the church.

He sat down on the couch next to me in my parents' house and told me that I had NO choice but to marry Delano. That an engagement was a contract, and that god would not approve of me breaking things off.

This elder also told me that he was sure that Delano had not only been picking up prostitutes but that he had gotten one pregnant. And that it was MY fault that she was pregnant because I was going to deprive Delano of the one thing he needs and that is sex. And that if I had not broken off the engagement Delano would not be acting this way.

I could not believe what I was hearing from this man. A man that was supposed to be a trusted man in the congregation a man that was one of my best friends' fathers, was literally sitting in my living room telling me that my Ex-Fiancé had gone to bars, gotten drunk, picked up prostitutes, went to jail and perhaps became a baby daddy to a prostitute because I did not want to spend eternity in that abusive relationship.

Sit the fuck down man. If I was the women then that I am today, I would have had plenty of words to say to him and I would have kicked his sorry ass out of my house.

I did however plainly tell him that I was NOT going to marry Delano and that he needed to stop with that crazy thinking. Not protecting the victim is unacceptable. And if you want to push that crazy ass thinking on your own daughters cool, I will not tolerate it.

As it turns out he encouraged all of his daughters to get married at the age of 16, 17, 18 years of age. You know because his wife was 16 when he married her, and they have spent the rest of their lives literally hating each other. So, I guess if he wasn't happy then no one else should be either.

Now I do not know if Delano got a prostitute pregnant. I am still in contact with Delano, and it is not something that he ever mentioned. However, I do believe that that elder, Larry, was just fucking with me to try and force me to take the blame and feel responsible for the behaviors of a very unhinged man.

Side note, in no way do I condemn prostitution, when a woman or man is of legal age, and in the sex trade because they choose to be, fine. However, in the church prostitution was not something people talked about, ever, at all. Unless they were trying to shame you for something you were wearing and called you names like whore, hooker, slut, tramp. So, for the elder to use it as a tool to try and get me to return to an abusive man, nope. And odd, very odd.

The church rarely takes the side of a woman, they love blaming her if her husband abuses her, must be her fault, she must not love god enough. And though I did not fully understand that victim blaming is not only a huge problem especially inside churches, I knew that I was not going to stand by and be victim blamed and shamed into marriage.

Delano eventually stopped harassing me and the elders after a few more visits stopped harassing me too. But Larry the one elder who tried to make me feel responsible for an abusive man's behaviors, brought it up to me almost every time I saw him.

When I first left the church, I was mad at so many people and I send Larry a message online telling him what a horrible human he was and how I would never forgive him for what he did to me and how he shamed me and felt that it was acceptable to shove me into an abusive marriage. How dare he not support the victim.

He literally sent me back a message saying that he can see that god is still not in my heart and he hopes god forgives me some day for what I did to Delano. And that I needed to take responsibility for my attitude and that my bad attitude is what made me leave god. Blah, blah. It was just rambling from an old man who spent his life trying to control every woman in his life. And using the church as his excuse to be a dick.

Mother. Fucking. Christ.

Delano married a woman about 6 or 8 months after our turbulent relationship and break up. I went to the wedding and found it odd that she had a wedding ring. I thought how did she earn that, but I never did? I tried not to think about that too much because I was done with him anyway. But I was worried that she was getting herself into something that she was not quite prepared for.

She really loved him. She had actually loved him for a long time. I do not really remember why he dated me and not her. She was ready to spend her life with him, she seemed to know who he was, and she did not care.

They have now been married 35 years I believe.

But it has not all been fun and games. They separated a few times and their son, their only child, committed suicide. I actually felt bad for them over that.

Delano came to find out he has some serious mental health problems. I know it seems like a duh after reading my story but honestly it was not something we talked about in the church. He was not on medicine for a long time. My understanding is, he is now.

Side note: The cult frowns on helping people with their mental health. They frown on getting proper help, therapy, medication. Delano has had mental health issues for as long as I have known him. Obviously. His behaviors with animals alone were a huge red flag but since the church does not support mental health then he was left to flounder his way through life actually being an outcast. He lost jobs, friends, almost his marriage many times. It's unacceptable for any church to not take mental health or addiction problems seriously. Its why many people kill themselves in the church because they need proper help. No amount of praying to god or reading the bible is going to get them healthy. Looking back, I feel a bit ashamed that I did not take his situation more seriously. But I was also still in the cult and was also taught that mental health issues did not exist. So, I was not going to be able to guide or help him in any way. But it's shameful for me to see that he was crying for help, and no one seemed to care.

When Delano is off his medication, he will message me once in a while on Facebook. I had not heard from him in a long time, but he will send me things like "I still love you", "I did not understand you", "my heart always saw you".

He also sent me a message that said, "I hope you are proud of me; I haven't thought about fucking a chicken in over 22 Years."

Cool man. Sigh.

I do want to shout out to his wife of many years. I cannot imagine what she has had to put up with or what she has had to handle being married to him for so long. The instability, his mental health, his family. Losing their son. I am not sure how she has done it.

But please do not judge me it was a different time; I was a different person. Living in abuse can make you do crazy things. Sometimes even jump from abuse to abuse.

Still, I cannot help but cringe when I tell this story.

Its cringe worthy, go ahead judge me.

JUST TO LEAVE HOME

"Family is supposed to be our safe haven. Very often, it is the place where we find the deepest heartache."

~ Iyanla Vanzant

Have you ever had those clarity moments? This is one of those. Or we can call it a, WTF moment. Maybe a moment that lasted more than a moment. Mine lasted for over 10 years.

At the age of 19 I had been ready to leave home for at least a year now. Truth be told if I could have left at 12, I would have. But because of the strict demands of my mother and her abuse, I hesitated to ever breach that conversation. I knew it would be hell. But I should have just pulled that band aid off. I had been waiting since I was 12 to actually give my mother the finger and live life without her. But I was too much of a chicken shit to actually confront her. I kick myself today thinking back on all the times I should have just told her to fuck off. She made my life miserable, and I allowed her to do it. I had ultimate control of my life and my future, but I was literally frozen with fear over what my mother would say or do should I actually stand up to her. I cannot emphasize enough how abusive she was to me. And her love, or what I perceived as love from her, was the only emotion I knew I wanted. But that was burying me, smothering me, killing me. My need for her to love me was paralyzing my life.

I had had a conversation about moving out once before with my mother, at age 18. I told her that a friend of mine, Christine W., had room for a third roommate in her apartment, and that she could use the rent money, so I was going to move out and move in with her.

I thought this might be a wonderful thing for my mother, she hated me being at home, we fought all the time. And when I say all the time, I mean there was not a single moment in the day that my mother and I did not fight. Or rather she screamed, and I took the brunt. The truth however would be that she could not have me leaving home. I mean who would clean her house and raise her children and do the laundry all while she worked? Isn't that what parents are supposed to do? Go to work and take care of their families? I guess it did not really occur to me that she needed me more than I needed her. And in some ways, she was holding me hostage with these demands. She was having me raise her children and take care of her home, because the financial demands of a household of 5 and the demands of her job did not fit together with raising her children.

Today I look back and ask myself why she kept having children if she could not afford to care for them. She hated being pregnant and she seemed to vehemently dislike being a parent.

That initial discussion of me leaving home led to a lot of screaming, you would think I would have been used to it by now. There were a lot of words about me being ungrateful, that I was not mature enough, that living on my own was my way of having sex with boys and not getting caught, doing my own thing, independent thinking, which was a mortal sin in the church, etc. That I did not love anyone but myself, I must want to try drugs or alcohol, that I would surely die outside the home. The kinds of ramblings a sociopath screams at her victim.

Actually, not being an expert in the field but living through my mother's constant episodes made me later in life do deep research into her behaviors. My offspring and I have had hours and years of conversation about my mother's behaviors. They took the brunt of her crazy many times. I believe her irrational moods were mixed, Unipolar, Sociopath, PTSD, Depression. She may also have had serious thyroid issues as I remember some of her health problems that duplicated in me in my 40's that were easily remedied by thyroid medication. But mother would most likely not have asked or been diagnosed because that is how she always managed her health, by not managing it. By barely speaking about it, until it was too late.

I know that it may have seemed easy to just leave home. And for many it is, was. But for me I was trapped in my abuse, I was so petrified of my mother that it froze me in place. That deep pain and fear inside me would keep me from breaking out of my abuse.

After this very painful exchange with my mother over what seemed like a normal and natural thing, I could only think of one other way. The only way to leave home was by getting married. She seemed to have wanted this anyway. Every single time I was interested in a boy, a man, her hopes were that I would marry and get the fuck out her house. But as soon as I wanted to leave on my own terms, nope, she was having none of it. Sociopaths do this.

As a side note she even forced me to color my hair bright blonde since I was 13 years old, because she said men only marry you if you are pretty. And pretty is all you need to be in life so you can marry. You do not need to be educated, or well-read or well-traveled, just pretty.

Well, I finally met someone that was a serious contender for marriage. But he was not part of the church. So, this was a wicked and terrible thing to do. Marrying anyone outside the church was almost one of the worst sins you could commit. Well, I guess outside of masturbation, but I digress. We started dating secretly. I met him at one of the first big jobs I had at an insurance company in the town I still live in, Bellevue, WA. This was a respectable job, good pay. A job that Gina helped me get as she worked there as well. This man worked in the accounting department. He was exciting and funny and nice looking. He offered me a world I had never seen or really knew anything about. He was three years older than me.

We started seeing each other at work on our breaks. Then we started going out to lunch together then I started sneaking out to see him at his house. I would sneak out to movies with him, to play tennis, to go to the park. I made up more excuses in those few months than I ever had before.

I was older and had my own car now, so leaving the house occasionally was easier and it was not the days of smart phones, so being secretive was incredibly easy.

He was excited to be with me, because he had never met anyone like me. Naïve, a virgin, a woman/girl who had never ever actually experienced life. I had no college experience, no travel, nothing really. Not even a good drunk night in the bar.

It was the naughtiest thing I had ever done. It felt dangerous and exciting and scary and my ticket out. I could literally smell my freedom.

I would have tried anything, except true confrontational bravery at this point.

We dated for several months without my parents knowing anything about it. We eventually fell in love, and he bought me a promise ring. A ring I still have, small, 14k gold, with two small diamonds and a large garnet for the center stone. I love that ring. It was one of the only things he purchased for me out of pure love and selflessness. Something that he thought through and gave me without reservations. A ring that I told my mother was a gift from my friend Lisa, who I rarely saw because she lived quite a distance from us.

But eventually Chris asked me to marry him. It wasn't very romantic. He actually said, "hey I have May 23rd open, how about we get hitched". And we were in a parking garage to boot. Aw how sweet and awkward. Now how to break the news to my family.

Actually, I did not really have to. Come to find out some woman in the local church with us had been spying on us, following us around and she saw us hold hands one day at a restaurant, so she immediately called my parents and all the elders in the congregation to tattle on me. PS tattling is what Jehovah's Witnesses do best. She totally flipped out as if it was the worst thing she had ever seen in her life. Two people holding hands, you do not say?

Well, I just went ahead and did it. I told them I was getting married and to a "worldly" man. Someone who was not a baptized member of the church. Someone who let's face it, knew nothing about Jehovah's Witnesses. And why would he, he lived a normal life. He actually lived his life.

Holy hell broke loose in my family. My mother started quoting bible scriptures to me about marrying someone who did not love God. My stepfather called all the elders in the congregation and made a colossal show of it. He liked being a drama King anyway. They started laying out church books and bibles opened to scriptures, all over the living room floor showing me what a horrible thing it was that I was marrying out of church disapproved by their god. And I literally mean that I came home from work one afternoon and the entire living room was covered in open books and bibles, about why marrying this man would make god so angry and that I would never get back to his good graces. You could not walk on the floor because it was covered in open books. And honestly, I did not know we owned so many copies of the same bible. Good grief, this mayhem went on for weeks.

And the elders started coming to the house, one after the other, sitting down with me, shaming me, reading me scriptures, pretending to cry at the awful thing I was doing. They held my hand and said I needed more prayer; I need to fix my relationship with god. How terrible I was, how I was breaking my family apart, how the congregation and my friends would never approve of me again. Literal abuse and guilt. This droned on for a couple of weeks.

As it was in the church the women would call and gossip to each other about their lives, their children. They had nothing else to do and nothing else to talk about. Gossip was the grandest communication one could have in the church. My mother was a gossip and busybody, and she was calling everyone she knew about what I was about to do. She called every friend, every elder, ever elders wife, old friends. Thank goodness we did not have social media in 1988. I cannot imagine the damage she would have done. But the phone calls were bad enough. Her drama made it worse; her ignorance made it embarrassing.

She was not actually concerned about me, let's make that crystal clear. She was never concerned about me. She was concerned about how she would look to the church, to her friends. She did not actually care if I married, she cared that she was not in control of the day-to-day happenings inside my marriage and yes even inside my bedroom. She cared that she was about to lose all control of me.

Finally, it was time to actually move out. I had got myself an apartment, with the help of Chris, my new fiancé, and I told my mother I would be moving out that weekend. I had not slept in days because the screaming and abuse would not end inside my home. I was sick and tired of both those things. I had terrible stomach issues and I know now that it was all because of the abuse I was enduring.

The day of moving came and my mother screamed, and I mean screamed at me all day long. She called me a whore, called me a loser, said I would never amount to anything, that god would never forgive me, that I would never have any friends again. She said she hated me and that I was making a fool out of her to her friends. That I get what I deserve in this marriage. And to never come to her or ask her for anything ever again. And if my marriage is bad, or if he is abusive, that I must live with it, that I am never allowed to ask for help or get a divorce because I was going against god already and there is no way god would give me a second chance. That I had better never make a fool out of her again by divorcing this man.

She was screaming so long and so loud that my sisters were bawling their eyes out. I can still see them in the den of our house, right by the door frame, hugging each other and crying begging me not to leave, begging my mom to stop yelling at me. They were so young, so sensitive. One sister was just 6, the other 10. To this point I had been their mom, their protector, their day-to-day world, and now their world was about to change as well as mine. Though I could not explain it to them then, I had to go, I couldn't stay another minute in that abusive household.

I was allowed to take whatever I could fit in my car. No furniture, no bed, no stereo, just clothing. I took everything I could in my car, a 2 door Ford Tempo, I shoved it to the rim, and I was out.

My fiancé had shown up with his car and a friend to help me move, thinking I might have furniture. And as luck would have it, my crazy mother came to the front door as I was loading one last thing. Screaming so loudly that the neighbors were coming outside to see the commotion.

This was it I was almost free, but not until my mother got in a few last shouts at me, outside, in the yard for all the neighborhood to hear. "What if he wants you to give him a blow job?". Those were the last words I heard my mother say to me for an extraordinarily long time. The church vehemently discouraged oral sex, and since my finance was not part of the church, my mother's biggest fear was that good grief, I might give or receive it. The church had this odd obsession with homosexuality and oral sex and pedophilia. So, to her screaming that at me, was kind of a big deal, to her at least. Looking back on it, it was the most absurd and abusive turn of events.

It was as if it was her once last attempt to keep me in gods' graces, or rather to keep me controlled by the cult and in turn by her. Everything about my mother was how to control. Who she controlled, and how. She had lost control of her own life years ago and never regained it. And not being able to control me was eating her alive.

It did not occur to me until much later, with many years of maturity, education, experience and clarity under my belt, that that incident damaged my relationship with my sisters, and really damaged my middle sister. She always thought I had left home because of something she had done. We talked extensively about it just a few years ago. She has even to this day spent years in therapy trying to figure it out, trying to understand that one day in April 1988 and why her life, the family and life she had known, was in an instant, gone. How my heart was broken. I think she still isn't fully clear about my reasons for leaving home. The relationship with my mother was so different between the three sisters. Mine was the most volatile.

And make no mistake I blame my mother for this, for forcing my hand and forcing me to change the fragile dynamics of the family because of her stubbornness, selfishness and abuse. I had to make drastic choices because she was so abusive. She was so selfish and so angry and stubborn.

My fiancé and I set a date of July 1988 to get married. His family was not happy that he was marrying me, but he did not seem to care much. We had a few bumps in the beginning. His father was going to jail for embezzlement, his parents after 25 years of marriage were divorcing, and Chris felt really embarrassed by all of this. But to me, I did not care much about that. I just wanted out from under my mother's hand. And I think I had a fairy tale dream of how my relationship would end up, or how it would go along the way. I knew nothing of marriage, I only knew that a wedding was the highest honor a young girl could have in the church, even if the church disapproved of my relationship. My mother's marriage was not the best example for me and most of the people in the church were marriage zombies. Just going along day to day asking no questions just doing what they are told. Marriage was necessary, not something you could choose. It was just a matter of when, not if. And people married so young. Even one of my friends being forced to marry at 15 because she had gotten pregnant by an older man in the church. Delightful.

Now mind you, I was working, and I did not have to marry once I was out of the house, but I felt it was the right thing to do. I think that I was always programmed to believe that that is just what you do. You marry. And I did love him, he was a decent man, he loved me too, but life would change us, age would change us. Our two wholly different backgrounds would end us.

As young girls many of us have that buy a dress, pick out flowers, get bridesmaid gowns, have champagne dreams when they get engaged. Show off your engagement ring. Pick out colors. Dreams of doing these normal things with our mothers and sisters and friends. Ask one of your friends to be the maid of honor. None of those things ever happened for me because of my choice to marry someone who was not part of the cult.

Not even one of my friends came to the wedding, not a single person from my church, not even my own family. Think about that, you have grown up with people your entire life, and not a single person comes to your wedding, and they stop speaking to you as well. My mother tried calling me every day up until the wedding to try and talk me out of it, but I would have none of it. A few elders tried calling me every day to try and talk me out of it. Even trying to bribe me into coming back to the church. I should tell you, with no big shock to you I am sure, that my mother called to scream at me about what a horrible human being I was and how I would never have another friend in my life. How no one would accept me back, that the church would always judge me and that god would never forgive me for my choices. Same speech, different day.

We got married on a sunny, hot, summer day in July, at Snoqualmie falls, surrounded by his family a bunch of his friends from his life and some new friends I had made outside the church, along the way. He had a big family and most of them were kind and supportive. At least to my face. They helped make the wedding fun. They helped me decorate, they paid for most things because he and I had zero money. And since my parents were not involved the only way to have the wedding that I thought I wanted, was for them to pay. Which also meant that Chris's mother got to make a lot of decisions about the wedding that I was not happy with, but what was I going to do? Elope I suppose but damn it I wanted a wedding. I was 20 years old and the only dream I had was of a wedding.

His sister, Mindy, (name changed) had just gotten married a couple months before us. She had a fancy church wedding to a Marine. It was a wonderful day, she looked beautiful. Looking back, I remember how much I wanted to be part of Chris family. How much they all seemed to love each other. How close they seemed to be and how they seemed to support each other over everything.

144

But in the end his family, not all, but some, turned out to be the kind of people I would never have in my life. They had zero integrity and they were backstabbers and honestly just rude. They only saw the world through their eyes and had truly little tolerance for differences. Though they had plenty of secrets between them, they certainly felt comfortable judging me.

We got married outside, as I was not allowed to marry in my church because I was now considered "bad association". Anyone who spoke to me or attended my wedding would be punished inside the church for their choices to associate with a person who was deliberately going against the teachings of the church. I had only one church in my life and one belief. I knew nothing else. I only knew that every church but mine was bad. That's what I was taught my entire life.

I always wanted a big fancy wedding. Lots of bling, huge gown, my mother and sisters there with me. It was really all you wished for as a young girl in the church, because that and that alone was your worth. All the girls tried to outdo each other, because, well let's face it, there was nothing else to live for but being slaves to the church, and soon slaves to your husbands.

As a side note, all the friends I had growing up, Leah, Gina, Kelly, and a few others, we all got married the same year. They were all perfect specimens for a church wedding, following all the rules on relationships, the bible etc. Well, you have read about Gina so you know that is not true, but she was allowed to marry in the church and I was not.

My wedding was nice. It wasn't fancy, my parents contributed nothing to it. Not a dime, not a well wish, not a gift, not a phone call, nothing. I did not have the wedding gown I wanted because I had no money. But I had one given to me by a friend. It was acceptable and pretty and all I had. I was 20, in love and so happy to be away from my mother, not much of the other things mattered at this point.

I do remember however Chris's mom being absolutely hammered all day. She apparently was not as happy with him marrying me as she let on. Or maybe I just ignored her rude jabs. And Chris, well he threw up all the way to the wedding site, out of the car, because the night before he had been our partying with his friends and stayed up until like 5 in the morning. He did not even answer the phone when I called and called and called because we needed to get ready for our photos. I had to go pick him up and get him out of bed. That was my first warning sign of things to come. Not even married and yet the signs were there that this was not my forever marriage.

Chris and I had fun at first. He was charming and his background was so exciting for a girl who grew up in such a closed, and at times abusive environment. He had gone to college, was in a fraternity, his parents loved to travel, he smoked, he had done drugs, he had slept with plenty of women. He was the jock of the school, the hot guy, the guy everyone wanted to be with. And he was not part of the church, so it made him exciting. And he wanted to be with me. I felt honored and almost superior to those friends inside the church who were stuck with those zombie unintelligent boring man boys.

As you would guess but not understand in the normal world you probably grew up in, I was a virgin when I got married and to him and all his male friends that was the what every man wished for. I knew nothing about sex except some of the abuse I had been through. I did not know it was supposed to be enjoyable, fun, exciting, sensuous, anything I wanted it to be.

Most of the boys and men in the church, were boring and controlling. Uneducated and desperate for sex. They had done nothing with their lives, had no plans, no ambitions, did not want to be better or do better. They lived and breathed the church, that was all there was for them.

But as time went on, my mother's control once again popped up its ugly head. She was insisting that my husband start being part of the church. I had been married long enough and played enough games with my relationship with god, she would say. My parents had not really spoken to me since I left home, but if Chris would just come into the church, then they would consider bringing me back into the family and accepting

Chris. They would consider loving me again. Let me say this again for those in the back. THEY WOULD CONSIDER LOVING ME AGAIN! What kind of fucked up shit is that? That's the kind of fucked up mess this church weighs people down with. Conditional love.

Chris reluctantly agreed and started studying the bible with a few of the members of the church. Getting in his "bible knowledge" so that he could become baptized. Honestly this just made our life more miserable. Chris did not want to be part of the church, he did not want to stop smoking and hanging out with his friends, the friends he had known his whole life. He did not want to stop celebrating holidays or birthdays like he had done his whole life. Who would? But I insisted, I thought surely this will bring my mother around and she will begin to be that person that I needed her to be. Things for me always seemed to be about my mother's love or lack thereof.

In many ways my thinking was flawed and entirely selfish. I was thinking only of what I wanted and needed, not how he was feeling or would feel about it. I think I just assumed he would come into the church. But I think it broke him, broke us, broke his family.

Him coming into the church just made things worse, for us and for any kind of wished for relationship with my family. If we did not show up at church for one night, mother would call us yelling as to why we were not being good Christians, why were we so selfish. She held the church over our heads and was constantly reminding me that I deserve all the misery I was getting because I disobeyed god. It got tiresome and eventually Chris was done with her. But not done enough to stand up to her, just done enough to watch me be miserable with her but not to help change things.

He was baptized in the summer of 1993 and that afternoon it was like my mother had changed completely. She hugged me and told me she loved me and how excited she was to have me back in the family. That excitement and acceptance was, as usual, temporary.

Eventually Chris became a man I did not know any longer. The man that I knew that had spunk, he seemed to love life, he used to tell jokes and tales of his youth, he seemed smart with his money, he was no longer any of those things. I think the things I was demanding were breaking him. It wasn't fair to him, but I did not know anything else.

Someone recently asked me was he really all those things, or did I just make it seem that he was because the alternatives in my life were so much worse. Good question.

When I became pregnant with our child, in 1990, his selfishness surfaced hard. He said he never asked for a kid, did not ask to be a father, did not want to be tied down, wanted to keep having fun. Even though he was perfectly happy not wearing a condom while we had sex, and not working a good enough job to provide health insurance so I could afford to be on the pill, but hey let's argue about a baby already on the way. And he never even thought about changing our life, or his habits so that we could have a decent future for ourselves and our offspring.

I started to pawn things, my wedding ring, my beautiful 12 string Hummingbird guitar that my step father bought for me. Chris' wedding ring, my class ring, I even stole some of my mother's jewelry and pawned it. He refused to work, I was pregnant, we had no insurance and I was cleaning houses sometimes 4 a day, in the heat of summer by myself to barely make enough money to pay our bills. And some months we did not pay them. The power got turned off many times. And he always got upset with me about it. Even though he usually refused to work or keep a job.

One of the oddest things, and I tell people this today. Is that Chris thought that if for some reason I was not working, maybe I got laid off or was you know 10 months pregnant, then he would just quite whatever job he had because he would say "well why should I go to work when you get to just sit at home and do nothing?" We had zero money coming in, a baby on the way and he would literally stop working because he thought I was just sitting in our rat-infested apartment, having fun, I guess.

Here I was in a marriage that I had bet the ranch on, and it was quickly turning against me. I made the decision; it was on me. I know my mother would never let me live that conversation down. To be clear I was never going to have that conversation. I would never let my mother know that things were not working out as I had planned.

But looking back I remember the first time my husband's behaviors took me by surprise. We had only been married a few months. We had no money to take our honeymoon. Which we were taking in September of 88. A honeymoon his parents had paid for with his fathers embezzled money. Staying in a condo in Hawaii that his parents owned, also paid for with his fathers embezzled money. Plane tickets purchased with his father's embezzled money. A very dark pattern of behavior. I began working a second job to save enough for our personal expenses on our trip. I had saved all my money from my second job and I was feeling less stressed about our upcoming trip. One afternoon I went to the bank to make another deposit into our savings account, and the money I had been saving, was gone. I was literally sick to my stomach. What had happened to it, where could it have gone? But not only was the money in our savings gone, so was the money in our checking account. It was about 1000.00 in all. Mostly savings. But all of it was gone. There was nothing for food, gas, rent or our trip.

I confronted my husband that afternoon and without hesitation or remorse he said he took it out and spent it. On what?? Oh just a few things, cigarettes, lunch out with friends, drugs, porn. I was like WTF man, that was the money we needed for our honeymoon. He gave me all these excuses and some asshole conversation about how he was not going to be told by a wife how he could spend his money. I said what the hell are we supposed to do now? He said it was my problem to figure out. And said he never wanted me to question the money again. That he would spend the money how he chose to spend it. This, THIS was a sign of unbelievably bad things to come in our marriage. *This* was when I should have packed my shit and walked away.

I should have known at that point that this marriage was going to be more difficult than I had ever anticipated. And mind you, this was only

2 months after we said I do. Only two months after I had bet everything on this.

Please do not get me wrong, Chris was/is a nice man. When I met him, he was exciting and new. He had a world experience that I knew nothing about. I was so excited to be married to this man. I was excited for him to show me a world that I was lacking. I was excited that marrying him pissed off my mother and that I was in some ways, I thought, giving the finger to the church.

But as luck would have it, there was a huge push and pull in the relationship. I wanted him to be accepted by my family and church and he wanted to just be left alone to love me and keep the life he was used to.

I was so young and had absolutely no world experience about anything. I was ill-educated and ill-equipped to manage the life I was now in. I wanted this life, but I was not prepared for this life.

Chris did his best to try to fit into the mold of the church. But years after our divorce I realized that he never would have fit in. It was not who he was, it was not in his make-up to be put in a box of rules and principles.

It also did not help that his family had gone from a deep Catholic background to a crazy Pentecostal mind set. They were heavily into pushing their beliefs on us, and they even thought speaking in tongues was some kind of calling from god. They would not let up on us. They wanted to argue bible topics day in and day out. And they mixed their political views with their church views. Which never makes sense to me. Even though I do not believe in god today, it makes no sense to think that Jesus or god would somehow want to have anything to do with the politics of a certain religion. As if Jesus was choosing our president and forming our government's. It was nuts. And they were nuts in their deep brainwashed way.

Not that the cult I grew up in was not also brainwashing people. But the push on both sides became too much for me to handle, so I just stopped handling it all together. I think his family began to realize that they were a bit trapped in religious crazy. They eventually moved to a 4 square born again kind of church, thinking. I think it is still the church they attend today, I think it is more of a congregational type of church. But let's be honest it is not really any better. It is still mixes god and politics and it is still incredibly judgmental about the LGBTQ community, immigrants, blacks, brown, transgender etc. All in the name of a so-called loving god.

I think in some ways all this broke him. But what really broke him, I believe, was the death of his father. In November of 1995 at the age of 54, Chris's dad Jim, died from complications of cancer.

Chris would never be the same. Never. And even to this day, 28 years later, Chris still struggles with his depression. He even tried to take his own life in 2008 and still talks about dying even today. And his personal behavior regarding his health shows that he really does not give a shit whether he lives or dies.

He spoke fondly of his father from day one. How much he loved him and how involved Jim was in Chris life. Being a coach for certain sports while he and his sister were growing up. It seemed his dad was supportive and loving. But honestly, I did not know Jim that well. He was quiet and he died young. The youngest of three children himself, with demons of his own. I mean one doesn't just wake up one day and embezzle money for years. There must be some kind of reason, or desire that is not obvious.

Jim had been embezzling money from many of his companies, for years. He would eventually get caught and spend time in jail for this. Embezzlement is both a federal crime and a state crime. And Jim did pay for his crimes, but I think in the end it cost him his life. All the things Chris cherished, vacations, material things, huge holidays, all paid for because of his fathers' crimes.

Growing up in the church there were so many rules that it was sometimes hard to actually live your life. But many of the rules, or beliefs, were things that other churches found to be sacred. The celebration of holidays, birthdays, politics, voting, family time etc.

The church I grew up in did none of those things, but Chris' family was very into those things. It was as if those things had defined all their years together as a family. And knowing what I do now, those memories do shape families. Memories of holidays, of vacations, of birthdays. I had none of those things. My memories consisted of working, the church, moving from state to state, a lot of abuse, screaming and sometimes an occasional camping trip, where you guessed it, mother screamed about everything. We did a couple of road trips, and we camped almost every summer in WA state, but as I got older those things were more stressful than fun. My memories were dark and burdened and his were filled with fun and good times, mostly.

I remember seeing a lot of his family photos of vacations, holidays, they were always smiling, laughing, hugging. My family photos had a lot of forced smiles. Even some of my mom that I look at from time to time, just a fake smile in most

As the years went on, I think I was happy, but in a way that said I knew I had made my choices when marrying him, I was away from my mother, not fully, but at least I did not have to live with her. Though I still took the brunt of her verbal abuse.

Chris and I had some fun times, we were very poor but we loved music and one thing we used to do was buy CD's at the beginning of the month with our paycheck, there was a time when we only got paid once a month, and play those CD's on a Friday nite while having a beer or having over a few friends. Those small things were who we were, I smile thinking about those fun days. But they were few.

But our relationship was never solid. It was broken in many ways. He had a huge addiction to porn that now that I am who I am today, doesn't seem like a big deal. I do not think it would have been a problem or addiction if he had been allowed to just be a human without all the rules. But in the church, porn was a disfellowshipping (shunned and removed from the church) offense. And though he felt guilty about it, he continued to do it and he kept us poverty-stricken in the process. It was in the days when not all porn was free on the internet. You had to buy most of it either on the net or on VHS tape.

But Chris also had a backwards thinking in regard to money. He spent all the time, even though we had nothing. We had no savings, no home, were deep in debt to the IRS, we lived paycheck to paycheck and sometimes could not even pay our rent. Our cars were always shitty and broken, but yet he kept spending. Yet he would spend money we did not have, sometimes I did not even know where the money was coming from or where it was going to.

I worked all the time. Sometimes I worked two jobs and yet we were always broke. He had no sense of finances, of saving, of paying bills before fun. Wants vs. needs. To be fair I was not much better. In the beginning I was trying to manage things so that we had savings, that we were not living paycheck to paycheck etc. But it did not matter, every time I had money in the bank, he wanted to spend it on something useless or just spend it in general.

Chris' father had set a very poor example for his children. Chris told me how he grew up with everything. Every time there was something new on the market, his family had it. A new car, VHS, microwave, they even put an addition on their home, they had boat slips, and a condo in Hawaii. They traveled, both Chris and his sister went to college. But things began to crumble in 1988. That is when Chris' dad had been caught embezzling money from his company. It would explain why a man, Chris' father, who was a simple accountant could provide such a lavish lifestyle to his family. And his mother was a secretary, or an assistant, yet they lived a very good material life.

Chris was devastated by this revelation, and it rocked his family. His mother divorced Jim and began selling things to the family or whoever else would buy them. Their condo in Hawaii included. She kept the house, the possessions, the car, her bad attitude.

His mother seemed so upset over the revelation that Jim was and had been embezzling money. She made a good show of being upset and angry.

She cried a lot, made some real drama out of it. She tried to pull me onto her side. Crying on my shoulder. She wanted me to be supportive, to take sides, when she went crying to the family about how shocked she was by this horrible revelation about her husband.

Do not get me wrong, it was embarrassing for Jim and for the family. But I cannot emphasize this enough. There is no way that a woman, married to a man for 25 years, does not know that something suspicious was happening. She knew how much money he made, yet she was enjoying the lifestyle of someone who made 5 times as much money. She enjoyed every trip, every convenience, every new car, every piece of jewelry, every bragging conversation about these things.

But when push came to shove, she was not about to take the fall with him. She would divorce him, throw him under the bus and talk about how tragic and embarrassing it all was. Yet she wasn't complaining in all those years when her life was top notch. She never complained when the things and trips were freely rolling in.

She was not going to stop it because she wanted to flaunt her "wealth" in front of her family and friends. To make it seem as if she had more than she really did. And so, when the shit hit the fan, all she could do was pretend that she had zero idea that anything was wrong, or illegal.

Even her own family, sisters, brothers, they all seemed so shocked by the revelation. Come on man, it was so obvious! How could a man with his salary provide so many things of comfort and it not raise eyebrows? I simply think that Chris' mom wanted so badly to not be looked down on. She grew up poor, the eldest of nine children. She wanted a lifestyle that she was prepared to toss her husband aside for once the truth came out.

That's a huge blow to a family, to people's egos, to trust.

But those financial behaviors really rubbed off on Chris. Chris could not make a decent financial decision to save his life. Here he is today, 58 years old, never finished college, two wives down, not a penny in savings, not a home, doesn't travel, defaulted on all his bills, got evicted from his apartment, had his car repossessed, lived in one his cars for a while. I cannot understand the dangerous financial thinking he has. He will die, perhaps soon, as he has already had 2 or 3 heart attacks, and he will be penniless. He will leave nothing to his offspring, he will die a sad lonely man who had so much potential. So much.

Though he has said that because of COVID and being stuck at home for over 1.5 years that he has nothing to spend his money on, he has finally, at 58, built a small savings account. I am not sure whether to laugh or cry at this statement.

Chris was always into get rich quick schemes, which never went anywhere and always wasted money we never had. He felt that money just grew on trees, people are just wealthy because they are. He never really sat to think that people are financially successful, most people, because they make good financial choices. Savings, 401K, frugal spending, etc. I do not think that ever occurred to him, still doesn't.

Or that people work very hard for their money. Sometimes two jobs, sacrificing many things for a long time so that eventually they can get or have the things that they desire, like a home, car, travel, maybe even an education, depending on their life's circumstances.

Looking back on some of the jobs he held, retail, accounting jobs, and Microsoft, he ended up losing or being fired from all those jobs, for you guessed it, stealing money from them. Embezzlement seemed to run in the family. Though he refutes the Microsoft accusations, but not only did he lose his job there, he is never allowed to return to Microsoft for work. So, I am pretty sure, because of years of his pattern regarding money, that he was also fired from there for the same reasons he was being fired from other places.

Chris never wanted to sacrifice anything for me. Even at times just up and quitting a job because he simply did not want to work, though we may have been down to our last penny and or no way to pay rent or keep the lights on.

I do not think he has ever come to terms with the loss of his father or how his father left this world. Divorced, penniless, ashamed. Jim even had to spend time in jail and work two jobs to pay back the money he stole. Please understand that Jim was a kind man. He was quiet but kind. In the brief time I knew Jim's parents, I can tell you they were elitists. And they had zero reason to be. But they were judgmental of everyone and everything. Every time I was with them, I was made to feel uncomfortable. I did not have much of a relationship with Jim either, except for the mental mess he left his children, I have nothing bad to say about him. He and I never had a meaningful conversation. Though you know me, I tried. I think Jim was already a broken man when I met him in 1988.

But looking back I also think this is one reason Jim did what he did, stealing money and living a lifestyle he couldn't give his family. I think his father had huge expectations of him and he simply could not meet those expectations, so he did whatever came next, he committed crimes to make it happen.

I remember being there in the room when Jim died, it was heartbreaking and awkward. People wanted to grieve but I think their shame took over their grief. Most people had already written him off, yet he was leaving behind children, grandchildren a wife of 25 years and a legacy that did not show what a good man he was, could have been.

Chris' sister was the only one I had hoped for. She was always kind to me, though I am not sure she really liked me, she was kind to me. Still is today. She was married to a military man turned police officer. A difficult man to say the least. A man whose depression or as she recently explained it was more anxiety, took over his entire world. But he worked hard, and he provided for his family. He took incredibly good care of her and them as she put it. I believe he was more verbally abusive to her and his family than was ever spoken about outside their home. Chris's family would never speak of things like depression or mental illness. Everything with them was hush hush, even after a tragedy. I saw Kevin's anxiety take over everything he did. He and I even had a few blow outs that made no sense to me, but I recognize it all now as anxiety or depression of some sort. And in 2016 he took his own life. I was saddened by this, but not surprised.

The family, however, was so embarrassed by this, they barely speak of it. Chris and Kevin never really got along. Though both men had tried to commit suicide and one succeeded.

I was shocked to find out that when Chris tried to take his own life his family were beside themselves because they had a belief that god would never forgive Chris. That he would burn in hell and that god would forget about him. But when Kevin took his own life, the family celebrated his relationship with god and had a funeral for him and though they do not speak of it much, and did not put it in the obituary, their utter hypocrisy for Chris vs. Kevin made me absolutely incensed. Why is it that their god loved one but not the other when they were both suffering from depression/anxiety? Oh, that's right because one of them was stepping to your own beliefs and your own god so he gets to be in your heaven while the other gets to be an outcast.

And Kevin's parents were some of the most arrogant, selfish people I have ever had the displeasure of knowing. These people did not even come to their own son's funeral. I have nothing nice to say about them, period. They were always too busy, or too good for any of us. In the 30 years I knew them I literally saw them ONE time. They rarely came to gatherings, and if they did, they sat in a room alone never socializing with anyone. Cannot come to your ONLY son's funeral, fuck you. Though I know now that his mother was terribly ill, it still does not excuse their behaviors in the past or that the father did not attend. I just cant wrap my head around this.

To be fair I was a strange kid, woman. I had a lot of my own demons and a lot about life to learn. But being thrown into the deep end, though it served me well when learning to swim, it did not serve me well in acclimating to Chris' family. And they were determined to not accept me.

Chris and I had not been married very long when one evening at the dinner table in his parents' house, his mother screamed that she would rather her son be a homosexual than be married to me. Ouch. And of course, Chris never said a word, did not stand up for me. That would be our marriage.

His family had so many secrets and kept so much to themselves. My family was a fucking mess. Nothing about these two things was ever going to go well. My parents and his parents, in the 14 years we were married, never even met. Not once, even though we all lived in the same towns.

Their worlds were opposite. And there was no way my mother was ever going to get along with his. My mother had zero desire to get to know anyone that was not a Jehovah's Witness, period. Family or not.

He and I spoke recently and in some regards our mothers were the same. All they wanted was to control their children. And if they couldn't have control, then they did not want much to do with you.

If you had meet Chris' grandparents on his father's side, you would understand some of it. His grandfather was a total asshole. Literally a pretentious dick. This guy treated his family like trash I never liked him, not one single second. He would even tell me how to act in his home. How to hold my fork, when to say please and thank you, what subjects I was allowed to talk about and not. I disliked him deeply. Even when he was on his death bed, he treated others poorly. His words always cut people to the core. But the family seemed to worship this man. I think it is because he had some money and they knew if they were nice to him, he would leave them some. Which in the end, he did. Not much mind you but some. Enough for my husband to spend on useless things, instead of paying off our bills as we should have.

But let's be clear, not everything that went wrong in that marriage was his fault. There is plenty of blame to go around.

I was young, and inexperienced, I was rude, and selfish, I had my demons and I did not know how to manage them. I was on the defense all the time, and that was one of my biggest faults. That would take me until I was almost 50 to resolve, or at least get under control. To recognize why I was the way I was and to know that it was no longer necessary. I did not have to defend myself anymore, to anyone. I was allowed to live and be me. No excuses necessary.

I was allowed to educate myself and be able to defend my views with facts instead of trying to just prove I was smart, when I wasn't. But nothing Chris taught me or being with his family taught me about being a better person. At least not while I was in the family. But seeing it all from the outside, I can see why they did not like me and why I did not like them. But even today we have very little in common. My own offspring has nothing to do with them because of their judgments and their constant god speak.

Chris treated me well for a while. We had some laughs; I remember some good times. But there came a time when I was tired. I was tired of working and never having anything to show for it. I was tired of carrying the marriage. He was unreliable, and selfish. Chris usually only thought about Chris. There were very few times when he put my interests first. Or even his child's interests first.

Chris was rarely present in his child's life, even though we were still a family. He always made excuses as to why he could not spend time with them. Or come to their concerts or help with homework. Even when I worked all the time, he couldn't be bothered to bathe them, feed them, put them to bed without some kind of woe is me attitude. It really was his undoing when it came to their relationship. He wanted to be anywhere and do anything but be a father.

I was tired of being disappointed all the time. ALL. THE. TIME. I used to look forward to going out or doing things with friends and he rarely if ever kept those arrangements or promises. He always had an excuse as to why he couldn't go, a headache, a football game to watch, too tired. It got old very very quickly. But it lasted until the day we were no longer living together. Even today if he says let's talk or let's meet, I still get that old feeling that he won't keep his word and show up or even call to say he isn't coming.

He never even picked out my wedding ring or made a proper proposal. But since we were rushing because of the caustic situation I was in, it did not seem to matter much, back then, considering the way our relationship had started. But those little things matter. They are memories that stand out in people's minds. And they matter.

He never put his child's interests first. Everything with Chris was Chris. He always talked about how he wasn't happy, he did not want to be told how to live, he wanted to just be who he was with no concern for others. But when the marriage finally ended, he seemed visibly hurt, affected, and confused that it was over.

I remember he said to me that I should have thought about others when agreeing to marry him, that I should have thought that marriage was forever. Which at the time made me laugh because to be fair except for a few times of small affection, Chris never thought about anyone but Chris.

And if he recalls, I gave up my life and community to be with him.

I suppose the conversations were not frequent enough. I was in this marriage, and I was not about to leave it. I was not about to give my mother the satisfaction of seeing me get a divorce. But to be fair I do not think I was brave enough to tell Chris that I needed more. I guess it did not occur to me that he did not care enough to offer more. Or perhaps I knew he was not equipped to give me more.

There came a time when I needed more. I needed more hugs, more love and a more certain financial future. I needed to be first, I needed to be respected and I needed it badly.

Chris was never going to give me any of those things. And though I cared for him, I still needed more. But what and how was I going to get it?

At the age of 27 my life began to change, and it affected everything that was about to happen next. Our life was predictable and now that I was making changes, saying no more often and distancing myself from him, it all took him by surprise. But it also made him think that he was losing control of me, which he was. And he wanted to keep some kind of control over me, but it was too late. I was already headed down another path.

I know that he thought I was attractive. And sometimes he would make snide remarks about me being a trophy wife. That he could just polish me and put me on the shelf and that was all I was useful for. Mind you I did everything for this man. Everything. He couldn't even be bothered to change diapers on our new baby or pick up his dirty clothes off the floor. Or keep a job or pay the bills, or clean, or cook, or shop, nothing.

It took another 6 years for the marriage to come to its end. After his father's death Chris went into a deep depression. There were lots of factors involved. Chris still did not want to be responsible; he did not want to help me care for a home, he did not want to babysit when I had to work, he did not care that we were still poor, still living paycheck to paycheck. He wanted a bank account of his own, money of his own, decisions that were his and his alone. And his porn addiction was out of control. Mind you I did not care that he watched porn, I cared that he was ashamed of it and kept it from me and that it became a wedge between us.

This part still sits clear in my mind. I had saved up enough money to buy us a new car. We never bought a new car together because his choices in cars were impractical. We had a small child, a janitorial business and he said he would only approve of us buying a big truck. Nope. I was having none of that. Mind you it would be a truck he picked out and drove. I would never get a chance to use it.

And since my money was ours and his money was his, well this was a bit of a challenge. But I picked out the car, saved my down payment, and when I excitedly told him about it, he looked at me with this blank stare and said, "I want a divorce". He told me he had already spoken to a lawyer, and he wanted out.

He said that it was too hard to be a father and a husband and that he did not want to do any work in the yard or around the house. That he wanted his life to be his life without responsibility. Mmm k.

Then for some odd reason he kept talking about all the things in the house that he wanted and did not want and all the things he did not want to pay for, like alimony and child support etc. It was as if he wasn't part of this relationship at all. As if he had not seen what was going on, as if he was living a different marriage than the one, I was living.

Mind you, at this point in the marriage, we had nothing but debt. We owed over 73K to the IRS, we had two cars, one was over 12 years old and barely ran and one that was 15 years old and barely made it out of the driveway. We did not own a home, we had CC debt, we were still living paycheck to paycheck and though my new job was paying well, his was not and he was still spending money like mad. On what I cannot tell you.

But I can tell you that he no longer felt the need to contribute financially to the household. He kept more than 50% of his paycheck for himself and even reluctantly put the rest in our joint checking account.

He had this crazy idea that I should pay off his CC debt for him because he had bought me a new dryer, a 330.00 dryer. And somehow that translated into a 8K dollar cc bill. I said NO way. I will take half the IRS debt, and nothing more.

He took the downstairs furniture, the large tv, some plates and glasses, his personal belongings and that was about it. OH, and do not forget he wanted the car that was in the best working order. Which looking back, was neither of them. But he did not care as long as Chris got what Chris wanted.

And guess what he did with it? Go on guess. Yes, he traded it in, got 150.00 for it, and bought himself a brand new, fancy, truck. He even forged my name on the title. A big truck. One that eventually got repossessed because he couldn't make the payments on it. And somehow this also had something to do with me. Nothing to do with his mentally unstable view of money and bills and how the full process worked. Nothing to do with Chris and his warped view of money.

My child tells me that they vividly remember the night that Chris told them that we were getting divorced. They said he cried and played up a good act as if he was sad that he was leaving. When the reality was, he had not been part of that marriage or family for a very long time.

Before Chris moved out, my friend Gina came by the house to check on me. It was an odd exchange. He was packing up some of his things, and she cried a bit. She told him that leaving your family was not something that people do. She had this long, almost tender conversation with me about how was I going to make it on my own, how sad she was for me, would I be ok, what was my husband's problem, etc.

I did not think much of it at the time. I always felt like Gina just liked to stick her nose into my business with no real plan in mind, except to get all the latest gossip.

I believe looking back on that moment that she was both sad and jealous. I think that she saw the new found freedom that I was about to get. Being single, not tied down to a man, and calling my own shots. But also, sad because her father, he stayed with his family. I do not know that her mother and father were always happy, but he was there, always. Until the day he died. Maybe she was already unhappy in her marriage, in her decisions and had hope for some kind of out. But that was an out that to this day, has never come for her. Though I believe she loved her husband, she knew she was trapped by her forced decisions of the church.

And mind you Gina was unsupportive when I married Chris. She stopped speaking to me and she did not show up for my wedding. But now suddenly she was worried about me.

Chris left one afternoon, with very few items. I do not remember feeling particularly sad about him being gone. But in some ways, I was sad. Maybe not for the marriage ending but for the fact that I had put so much effort into this marriage, that I had pissed off my family and friends to almost no recovery, and now after 14 years I had allowed it to end. Honestly, I was tired of carrying it, him. I was tired of all of it. His fucking family, the bad financial strain, the lies, the distrust, the disappointments.

I did not manage my marriage very well, I admit. I could have been more focused on him. But I wanted to be focused on me and my future. I knew there was more to me than what I saw in the mirror each day. I knew that life held more than I was ever going to get from this man, from this relationship.

My child also tells me about the things he did once he left, spending money on things like a guitar for me, and a puppy for them. The guitar apparently was his way of saying that he was sorry that I had to pawn my very beautiful guitar that my step father bought me just so we could pay the power bill. That of course was very early on in the marriage. So, he bought me a 50.00 guitar, after he moved out, to I guess say he was sorry. All it did was piss me off.

Then he bought a very expensive puppy for our child. Left the dog with me, made me train it, feed it, etc. I had zero money to do such things. I had zero time to do such things. I was now a single mom, raising a child, working two jobs and every single child support check he gave me bounced.

But also, I could have stood up for myself more and told Chris NO more often. No more stealing money, no more blowing money, if you do not like it here with me you are free to go. I think about a lot of conversations I should have had with him very early on in the marriage.

I was so frightened when I left home, so afraid of what was going to happen when I decided to marry outside the church, out of my mother's approval. But I did it anyway and thought it did not last and did not end the way I had thought, or had hoped as a young girl, it was the right thing for me to do at the time.

Chris is still floating in limbo. I do not hear from him much anymore. He has pretty much isolated himself from everyone. Which seems so odd to me knowing the man I met 30 years ago. He was funny and bright and exciting. But I guess we never know what someone else's demons really are, even if you live with them.

I know that Chris blames me for the marriage ending. At least he did in the beginning. He told me shortly before it was over that I should never make a promise to someone if I am not going to keep it. Well though that may be true, people change. People grow, circumstances become our destiny and sometimes promises are impossible to keep. It doesn't make us bad people, it just makes us human.

When we divorced my mother and a few people in the church made this huge scene about how much they loved him and how they were going to miss him and how they could not believe that it had ended.

But truth be told no one really showed me they cared that much. They were never actually involved in the marriage unless it was a way for them to control every move we made. They were not there to help or to build us up. So their fake tears when it ended, were ridiculous and hypocritical to me.

Lets be clear, I know people think that I ended the marriage. I did not. Chris filed for divorce and he is the one that left his wife and child. He wanted no more responsibilities, none. Even getting him to pay child support for a child that he would eventually ruin his relationship with, was nearly impossible. I eventually gave in and up on collecting money from him. And it was not the money, it was the principle of it that kept me hanging on.

Maybe I should have had more grace with him. Maybe I should have seen that I was trying to change him as much as he was trying to change me. And that his heart ached for the situation with his father and his father's death. But back then, I couldn't give it to him. I was too tired to care anymore.

I do not regret my decision to marry him. I look back and see that I learned a lot from this man. And from his family and from the years we were together. I learned who I was and who I was not. I learned what I did not want and what I wanted. I also learned that people have potential and if they do not use it, they will surely lose it. And those people can grow even from a bad situation, into something grand.

I am sure I should have been sadder when he left, but truth be told it was a blessing and it was another path out of something that I deeply needed.

The next few years would bring me a path that I could have only dreamed of, but was about to come true. The next few years would literally change everything about my life.

LESS THAN UNEDUCATED

"Tell me and I forget. Teach me and I remember. Involve me and I learn"

~Benjamin Franklin

Along life's journey we might meet people who are educated, clever, well read, brilliant, fascinating, quirky. Or perhaps we meet people who are just plain dumb. Or those who claim to have knowledge, maybe even bragging about this said knowledge, yet it seems they cannot put together a declarative sentence, nor defend an idea or stance on something they might hold with great passion. In this country we recently had a President who fits this description. Arrogant beyond words, spouting nonsense every single day and yet people fell at his feet as if he was a god.

My mother was one that claimed, or projected in most conversations or situations, that she surely knew the answer to most things. She would parade her ignorance with the lack of realization that she looked like a fool. Especially to those who were educated or well read. After 17 years of being out of the cult and my mother being gone for 13 of those, I still catch myself saying something or believing something that she said or proudly preached, even though I now know it is totally false.

Growing up in the cult is bad enough when it comes to education, as you know they disapprove of higher education, and they treat basic education as something to be ashamed of. My Uncle who decided to go to college and live in another part of the world is being shunned by his mother because she has some absurd idea that education is bad, and stupidity should rule. It is the most backwards way of thinking that I know of. And she believes that people should just be happy being stupid and poor and that only rich elites have educations and that they are terrible humans. How and where she got this idea is beyond me. She has spent most of her life around the cult as well. And honestly, she has been one of those poor but showy people who parades her ignorance like a shiny crown.

I went to elementary school, Junior High, and High School. But I struggled a lot in school. I wanted to be part of the education system, I wanted to pass tests, and learn new things, and rise up in the academic world. I had a feeling in my heart that I was bound for big things. My first thought of a career was to teach. But I also wanted to be pretty and popular and fit in with the "it" crowd. My life was torn because I was never going to fit in in school or in my church circles. Neither with the educated or the pretty. I would always be the left out, the loser, the last picked, the gangly snaggle toothed awkward dumb kid.

As my luck would have it, my mother would have none of the education conversation. She was so steeped in her own ignorance and the gut-wrenching hold of the cult that she did everything in her power to make my trip through the education system as miserable and useless as possible.

I never fit in and I never had a real education. I was in limbo most of my life. Always in the middle. Neither bad or good at things, but my financial struggles were both because of the cult and its lack of acceptance to education and because of the fact I struggled with learning new things. It would not be until years into my adulthood that I realized I also had Dyslexia. Not as bad as some but enough to prevent me from doing simple things, like sitting down to read a book. My brain transposes words in such a way that an entire sentence can be read by both you and me and I will see it with an entirely different meaning. It is very frustrating for me and it sometimes causes me embarrassment even in my closest circles. As the world progressed around me, I seemed to stay still. Living paycheck to paycheck and living in a social world where it seemed everyone was content being poor and stupid.

My first brutal experience in school was the 2nd grade. Because of the cult we were not allowed to celebrate any holidays. So, we were not allowed to participate in any kind of celebration at school. That included not being allowed to make pictures of things like Christmas Trees, or Pumpkins or Hearts at Valentine's Day. We were not allowed to eat cupcakes brought in by other kid's moms for their birthday, or sing songs that had to do with anything holiday or birthday related.

It was a school day, 2nd grade in Tucson, Arizona. It was Valentine's Day and all the kids had those little paper valentine's day cards, the ones with little hearts and cute characters, and they were writing on them and giving them to other kids in the class. There were little valentine's day gifts for all the kids, there was candy and cake and cupcakes and there was a big valentine's day celebration. I could not partake in it. I had to sit in the corner of the classroom and watch all the other kids having fun. I cried all afternoon. When I got home from school still crying, my mother asked what was wrong and when I told her how sad I was that I could not partake in Valentine's Day with all the other kids, and how embarrassed I felt, she literally grabbed me by the hair and started screaming at me. She slapped me and grabbed me by the arm and started kicking me. She screamed at me about how horrible I was and how god would never forgive me for my behaviors. I was sobbing and she threw me on the floor in my bedroom, and told me I was grounded for being such a fucking baby who did not love god. I was 8. I will never forget or forgive my mother for that day. It has haunted me my entire life. Haunted me because I was a kid, who wanted to be a kid. I could not for the life of me understand how my mother could be so cruel to me when all I wanted was to celebrate something fun with my friends.

Shortly after that incident I was being bullied at the bus stop. This older kid was throwing rocks at me and another girl. He picked up a huge one and threw it at her, I was trying to protect her and I stepped in front of it. It hit me square on the back of the head, splitting my head clean open. If you are not already aware, a head bleeds, a lot and quickly. I had to run crying to my mother, and by the time I got to the apartment my entire clothing and hair was covered in blood. She immediately took me to the hospital where they cleaned me up, shaved some of my hair and put in a few stiches. I was so traumatized but she insisted I go back to school that day. Of course, I got the lecture, you know the one, terrible things happen to little girls who disobey god with things like wanting to celebrate holidays.

So she blamed the incident on my desire to celebrate valentine's day with my school mates.

Way to keep fucking up your kid. Oh yes in case you are asking, no my step father never stepped in and protected me. He never took her aside, he never apologized for her and he rarely took my side.

However, there were a few times when he felt some guilt, those were times I ended up getting huge bags of toys or a new bike. Like the time I fell out of bed and hit my face on the window ledge, cracking the bridge of my nose. But that was an accident, so he was kind, it had nothing to do with my mother's abuse, which he never intervened in, NEVER.

I did not go to kindergarten, why is something I have never been clear on. I was doing well in school when we lived in Arizona. I was going to top classes, passing my tests, having great days in school, I had friends, I loved doing activities like art and science and music and math. I had great teachers who helped me along the way, who seemed to have my best interest at heart and even my mother was helping me succeed. I had a book published in the school library in the 4th grade about the ocean and whales. And my mother willingly helped me put that together. I was actually immensely proud of myself and proud of the things I was doing in school. I looked forward to going to school every day. I had a few friends and at one point I was being bullied by a much older girl in the school who would smack me when she saw me in the bathroom, or she would call me names. But as I recall, that situation did not last long. She either left school on her own or got suspended, or simply moved away. But her bullying was nothing like I was going to get in the next few years.

Things were not great at home though. There was a young man living next to us. And I was alone all the time. Even as a young girl I walked to school alone, came home alone, spent most of my days alone. This young man was nice to me. His family was part of the church. He used to come to my family's trailer and talk to me. Ask me if I wanted to go listen to his records, swim in their pool, go to the park. I was 9 he was 19. I was so neglected at home that my thoughts regarding this boy were totally unnatural and naive. He started molesting me very soon after he started grooming me. He knew just how to get me to trust him. Every day after school I would go to his trailer, his parents were never home. He would put on an album, mostly Heart, the band, other albums, and lay me on his bed and molest me. He did this for about a year, if I remember correctly. There is an ending to this incident that I do not remember. My brain to this day will not let me remember. It was the last time he molested me, I remember the afternoon, the music, the heat, the smell of his room. And the next thing I remember I was waking up in my bed at home, my genitals covered in a heavy sticky crusty substance. I was so freaked out I ran to the shower and cleaned myself up before my parents arrived home. I do not have a memory of what happened from the time I left his trailer to the time I woke up and showered. Even years in therapy or in my writing my brain has never let me remember what happened. I assume it was too traumatic for my brain to allow me to remember. Though I can guess what happened, I am not sure it really matters if I know. I am ok with that, I am ok that my brain is protecting me.

I never felt shame or guilt about this until I was much older. I never spoke about it with anyone. And it was not until I was well in my 30's that I told my mother of the incident. And in her abusive dismissive way, she said I must have been doing something to encourage him and that the blame rested solely on me not him. "Abusers only abuse because they are led on by little girls", she said. And in her own words she told me to get over it because kid's memories of trauma usually are worse than the actual trauma. Right, I mean I guess being molested really is no big deal, just move on and forget about it. This shocking reaction is why I told her nothing about any sexual abuse ever again. Or told anyone really. Fuck her seriously.

Imagine saying this to anyone who came to you with this heavy weight of an experience. And imagine being so cold-hearted, especially to your own child. Even if an adult friend came to you now to tell you of such an experience would you not feel compassion and love for them? Would you not want to help them, embrace them?

I had my struggles early on in school, math was never my best subject, and I can even tell you now that as an adult, it is still not my best subject. But I had a few great teachers and they really helped me to make the most of my years. At least that is how I remember it in Arizona. I was heartbroken when we had to move. And I say had because that is exactly how it happened. School was the only thing I really liked in my life, and I was scared that it would never be that way again. As my luck would have it, I was right, school was never a positive experience for me again.

When we moved to WA state, I started school right away. It was my 5th grade year, and the class sizes were huge compared to what I was used to. And they combined classes, 5th and 6th together for example. We had a few teachers teaching different subjects, but we never really left the single classroom unless it was for PE or Music class or of course recess.

My new school was hard. I got made fun of for the way I dressed and the way I did my hair, on the very first day of school until I graduated. As I remember it, my first class was music class, the class had already started, I walked through the front door and before I even spoke the kids started laughing at me, calling me ugly and asking if I got my clothes from a thrift store. It was horrible. I was so looking forward to going back to school, but I never had another good day in school. My grades slipped, I struggled with my identity, the bullying got worse and worse. Did I graduate, yes, barely.

My mother had this peculiar obsession with how I did my hair, it was something that she screamed at me about most of my life. Even as an adult with a child of my own she would say things to me like, "when you can be so pretty why would you pay to be ugly?". She made me dress in slacks and blouses instead of jeans and T-shirts, she did everything in her power to make sure the kids would always make fun of me and that it would be a huge distraction from my education. She never let me pick out my own clothes and always made me dress as if I was going to a job interview. Everything with her including clothing had some kind of sexual connotation. It was not until a couple of my church friends finally said something to her that she started easing up on letting me choose my own clothes. Mind you, I was already in my high school years.

My first couple of days of school in Washington, we had a few quizzes. The one that sticks out in my mind was to name all the presidents from George Washington until now, 1980. Shit, I had no fucking idea. I did not even know that Abraham Lincoln was the 16th President, that seemed to be the one everyone knew. From that day on my teachers were nothing but rude to me. Asking where I got my education before this and did, I need to go to special education classes to get caught up with the "normal" kids. I was humiliated.

Because in my household education was not something that one strived for, I had no support system to help me improve. To help me study or be better. My mother wanted nothing to do with my education. She told me to just pass high school then I could get married and have babies and wait for god to bring an end to the world. As you read this you are shaking your head thinking that cannot be true, that sounds ridiculous. But in my world, at the time, it was exactly how we lived. The world was going to end at any second and there was no need for an education.

God was more important than education and education would be our downfall. If you are educated you ask questions, and asking questions in the cult was considered taboo. You just move along, dredging and dying.

Junior High was better but still brutal. I was so very much into music and as usual was in a music class. I wanted to be part of plays and recitals, but of course many of those had to do with the holidays, so I could not participate. I was not even allowed to sing holiday songs in class as part of my grade. I loved music so much, and still do. But I had little confidence and it held me back. My junior year my teacher came to me and said if you cannot participate in most of the things we do in this class, I am asking you to drop out. He felt it was not fair to the class to have me just sit there most of the time not being part of the group. He was right, and I was heartbroken. Now of course I could have just sung the songs, who would know? But I was so afraid of my abusive mother that if she found out, I do not know what she would do, and I couldn't take that.

For someone who did not give a good god damn about my education my mother sure had a lot to say about it. She would even come to school and embarrass me and talk to my teachers about things she thought I should not be learning because of our god. Looking back, it was some of the reasons the kids bullied me. At least some of my friends in the church who had the same beliefs, their parents minded their own business and let their kids make decisions without too much interference.

I got through junior high with decent grades. I was still bullied a lot. There was one girl, Tiffany. As I write this she is now literally dying from ALS. She tortured me for 5 long years. There was not a day in school that went by that she did not bully me. Her abuse still haunts me today. And seeing her dying has made me conflicted about my feelings. She used to push me in front of the bus, throw my homework into the street in front of cars then push me in front of them hoping I would get hit. She threw eggs in my hair. My hair was long and eggs, well they do not easily come out. In music class one day she lit my clothes on fire with a lighter, I had coke poured in my hair, I was punched, kicked, spit on called names, teased, even grabbed sexually and traumatically. My grades suffered but not as bad as they should have. I couldn't get away from this girl, her very presence changed my life. She stole 5 years of my youth. Seeing her photo today and watching her friends and family talk about how wonderful she is and how much they will miss her when she goes, almost makes me want to scream. I do not wish pain on someone but honestly, I cannot think of a reason to feel sorry for her death.

My mother refused to help me with homework, and I was not allowed to set aside my chores at home or babysitting my sister or sisters for homework. Everything, literally everything came before my schooling. My mother was so self-absorbed with her own bad decisions in life that she was taking away every part of my childhood. Including what now I would understand to be the most important thing I would be lacking, education.

When I was 16, I was brutally attacked on my way to school by a dog. The dog jumped from its 2nd story balcony and came at me. He bit me on my right leg, then pushed me down, tore off my clothes and began biting me on the leg again. I screamed for help and was in such shock that this dog, the one I knew, was going mad and I was so scared that this moment would never end. My stepfather heard me screaming from the house and ran out and rescued me from the dog. My neighbor whose dog it was, and her daughter also tried to get the dog off me. My stepfather immediately drove me to the ER. I was in shock and pretty eaten up by this dog. My mother did not join us at the ER, looking back I cannot really remember why. I lay on the cold table with doctors all around me, poking at my bites and cleaning my sores, and stitching me up. I had to get a tetanus shot and my wounds were deep. I went home with bandages and medicine and amazing trauma.

My mother let me lie on the couch for a few hours but then said you will be going to school tomorrow and you will get over this and just move on. She said she did not want to hear any more about it. I said how I couldn't stop feeling and hearing the dog attacking me and I was in pain and the trauma was so real I even remember it today. I told her with tears in my eyes that I could even hear the dogs' teeth biting into my flesh when I closed my eyes. She said, suck it up, get over it, go to school, stop talking about it.

I went to school the next day, in pain, blood from my wounds seeping into the bandages, and when I told some of the kids what had happened, my bully Tiffany laughed and said I deserved it and that it was too bad the dog did not do more damage.

I have physical and emotional scars from that incident. I hated my mother for not being nurturing, at all, not even a tiny bit. Everything in life was a distraction from my education.

High School should have been good, fun. I even thought perhaps my parents would let me go to the prom, as we were not allowed to attend any dances in school because of the church. But alas they did not. I was not allowed to be part of anything, no groups, no sports, no clubs. I was still being bullied. I did join some fun classes that I did exceptionally well in. Graphics class, Yearbook class, the school newspaper, photography. And I took English and or literature class all three years in High School and I aced those classes. As long as I did not have to stay after school, I was allowed to do some extracurricular activities.

There were, however, tons of books we were required to read, and you guessed it, my mother always interfered and would tell the school that I was not allowed to read those books. You know books that would shape us like 1984, Dante's Inferno, Slaughterhouse Five, The Bell Jar, Lord of the Flies. To be fair, I could have done without that last one. She would come to school and tell my teachers that because of my religion I was not allowed to read books that she somehow found against what the cult was teaching.

My mother even went so far as to get me out of classes that were *required* for graduation. She had me removed from debate class because she said that in the new world with god as ruler, debating politics was not a skill I needed. She had me taken out of government class because as Jehovah's Witnesses we did not get involved in politics therefore it was inappropriate for me to take a class that taught me about how the government ran. As an adult who no longer believes in the nonsense of the church

I was raised in, let me tell you, a high school government class is exactly what I needed in life, I could have used in life.

I still have a lot of gaps in my education because I never had a chance to make up for those things. Once I was removed from class, and put in something else acceptable for graduation, well the only thing left for me to do was get married and have babies. There was no talk of college, none. And though I just wanted to get away from my family, if I had some of this to do over again, I would fight like hell for my education. No matter the cost. College was never going to be part of my life, until I was much older.

I was not sure where to put this part, but it is a huge part of my senior year, well a huge part of me. It is something that rips at me emotionally, I think one because I had no one to talk to about it, and two I felt I should have been much stronger. Victims always feel that way. And no matter how long you have known me, chances are this will be the first time you have ever heard me tell this very deeply personal story. I almost cannot tell it, it is so painful.

Because discussing sexual violence was not something I was allowed to talk about in my home, when it happened to me, I just went about my days as if it did not happen. And a few things, well I just pushed them aside. Who was I going to tell? Who would believe me? And in my home, my life, sexual violence was always the victim's fault, always.

My senior year was one of the hardest for me as far as sexual violence in school and my personal life. It seemed as thought the violence would never stop.

There was a young man named Chuck Gross. We were in the same graduating class. He was obsessed with me. Not sure why, maybe because I was naïve, pure. Who knows? But we were friends. I mean I talked to him and though looking back I should have been way more cautious with him than I was, I guess it did not occur to me that what happened next, would happen.

He asked me to meet him in one of the classrooms that he knew would be empty, at the end of the school day. I was never afraid of this young man, it never occurred to me to be. But that summer afternoon I went to that classroom and before I knew what was happening, I was on top of a desk, with him holding me down by one shoulder and unbuttoning my blouse with the other. I screamed "what the hell are you doing". He told me to shut up, he started unzipping his pants, he put his hand up my blouse onto my breast, still holding me down. Mind you in high school I was very petite, 110 lbs. maybe. Chuck was not a large man, but it was his quickness and strength that took me by surprise. Before I knew it, I was almost totally topless, and he was almost inside me. I screamed and slapped him to get off me and asked with tears in my eyes what he was doing! He did back away, tucked his penis back inside his pants and zipped up and said, "you are such a tease all the time I thought this is what you wanted BITCH". This event, not as brutal but similar happened twice with this young man. The second time he followed around the school and laid in wait inside an empty classroom for me so he could once again attack me. I was more prepared this time, I did not let him undress me or get a hold of me. The incident ended quickly but again he called me names like whore and tease and then told everyone in school that I was the one stalking him and begging him for sex.

I was a tease? How in the world did he interpret anything I did as teasing? I was not even allowed to wear shorts to school because my mother thought that boys thought shorts or skirts were an invitation to have sex.

I will be honest for a long time that event haunted me but more so when I realized that Chuck was telling everyone in school what happened and that I teased him then left him with "blue balls. You guessed it I did not even know what that term meant. Blue Balls, what?

I never saw Chuck much after that he did not try to come at me again or follow me around. But he has tried to friend me a couple times on social media and it was those few times when I was reminded of this behavior from school. I honestly had put that incident far behind me. I guess mostly because I knew no matter who I told, they would not care.

So, it was the first of many burdens of sexual violence that I carry in the back of my mind today.

That same year there was more violence, more ways to tamp down my soul.

And I will preface again that no matter how long you have known me, this will also be a story you have never heard me tell. The pain of it is almost too much to write about. But it is part of the things I learned to survive. With no support, no one to tell, no one to take my side.

My senior year, again, there were these boys who bullied me all the time. And not just in a teasing taunting verbal way, but in a sexual way. They would find me in the hallway and push me up against the locker and push their groins against me, grab my breast, say disgusting things to me. They would say that one day they would rape me or torture me. This was a weekly occurrence.

I had no one to tell. These boys were powerful in school. One of them was the top drug king in the school and everyone knew to stay away from him. And I had no safe place at home where I could talk to my parents about any of this. There was no safe place in the church either because the elders always blamed the victims, always. My mother would have blamed me for it and suggested that I must have done something or worn something that made those boys think their behavior was ok.

We have recently set up a new computer lab at school. It was filled with brand new computers, and it was a huge deal for that time, 1986. One evening someone broke into the school and stole all the new computers in the lab. The principal offered a 500.00 cash reward for anyone who knew anything about the incident. And it would all be anonymous.

I overheard the boys who bullied me, talking about how the leader of the group and his brother had set the whole thing up. They broke into the school, stole all the computers, put them on a truck and traded them for drugs that they were now giving out or selling on school grounds.

I struggled with what to do. Should I keep my mouth shut and just let what I knew go, or as a not so popular girl at school, tell the principle what I had heard. I finally went to the principal and told him what I had heard, and who I had heard it from. I needed to make sure that he was going to keep his word about not telling anyone where he got the information. He assured me that no one would know.

Not one day later, I was in graphics class by myself after school finishing a project and these boys came into the room. They asked me about what I knew. I said, "I do not know anything". They said that the principle had told them that I was the one who ratted them out. I was shocked, would the principal really do this? Surely, he had to know what kind of trouble these boys were.

I assured them I was not the one who said anything about anything. And as quickly as the conversation started so did the violence. There were 5 of them, they dragged me by my hair into the dark room on the other side of the classroom. They shoved me to my knees, it was very dark, only a red light overhead. One held my hands behind my back, one held my head back, and the other boys took turns putting their dicks in my mouth. I begged them to stop, but they just kept pulling my hair and laughing at me. It was pure torture. It went on for about 45 minutes. They grabbed one of my hands and had me touch each of their dicks. And the leader said that I was lucky he was not going to kill me that day. Then as quickly as it started, they pulled up their pants, threw me on the floor and walked out. Leaving me crying and in physical and emotional pain. What had just happened, how did it happen, why? What do I do now, how do I just go on with my day?

It was not much later that one of the boys was arrested for the incident of the computer theft and to this day, I have no idea where he or his brother are. Yet I do know that the oldest of the boys did spend time in jail. But they were nothing, but trouble and I feel lucky even with that incident, that violence, that I was not hurt more, or raped more, or tortured more, or killed. They were terrible humans.

I was horrified and ashamed and scared and I knew I couldn't tell anyone. I had no allies in school or at home or with friends. Imagine that the people you surround yourself with who you believe are your friends are not even people you can turn to for help or guidance in a situation like this. So, I kept that secret most of my life. Even when my mother was dying, I never told her anything about it.

I never spoke of it until about 20 years ago. It did damage to my psyche regarding men and trust. I do not think I ever even mentioned it to my therapist when I was seeing one. As it turns out, the principal never did tell anyone how he knew who robbed the school. But he did call the police and two of the boys were suspended from school and arrested and put in jail. But not before they went around telling everyone else in school that I was the rat and that it was my fault they were going to jail. As if my school days could not get any worse.

I did, however, get the 500.00 reward from the principal as promised and I kept that money a secret and to myself. It was one thing my mother could not take from me, though I was essentially raped for it.

I look back at myself as a young girl. I do not recognize that girl anymore. I have spent so much of my time trying to be someone different. I have educated myself; I have changed how I respond to things and people. I ask questions and I surround myself with passionate amazing humans who have taught and given me so much.

If I was the person today during my school years, I would have told my mother to fuck off. I would have treated my education like gold. I would have found a way to keep the bullies out of my life and I would have seen what the future would hold for me and done everything in my power to educate myself.

The only thing I wanted back then was to be popular, to be seen. And yes, all my report cards say, "Angela talks too much in class". I laugh when I type this because that's still me. I love to talk, to converse, to share ideas and stories. To offer my opinions. Shocking I know. Though now I try to be a better listener than a talker. My husband will tell you that sometimes I fail at that. But he loves me for it anyway.

I honestly do not know how I graduated high school. I had some great teachers, some who were so confused about why a child's family would not take education seriously. Some who lost their patience with me. Some who recognized that I had some learning disabilities. Disabilities that I have learned to manage in my older years. But in the end, I managed to get my diploma.

Though I still have a lot to learn, I no longer feel like that fool at the table. I can carry on a conversation with the best of them. Now I may not fully understand some things, but I have filled my brain with enough knowledge, and I keep up on events every day. I can be part of the conversation and I never feel awkward or afraid.

And since COVID I have taken many college classes, met amazing people who have helped me to fill my brain with the kind of knowledge I only dreamed of as a girl.

I now bring more to the table than just my elbows.

My school years left me haunted more because of the abuse than the things I was lacking. But I suppose I like many things in my life, because of the amazing love and support of my husband and friends, I have overcome many things in my past so that I can build a great future.

Education is key. Religion can be poison to those ideas.

JOBS NEVER A CAREER

"For a long time, I was very naive and very trusting. I Just did not think anyone would want to do anything to harm me, but I learned through trial and error that that's not the case."

~ Margo Price

Depending on how you grew up, chances are you were asked, what do you want to be when you grow up. Or perhaps your parents encouraged certain studies, or career ideas. Or your parents were educated career people who you might want to follow in the footsteps of.

Maybe growing up you found a single interest that got you excited about what your future career might be.

Or perhaps someone along the way inspired you to do something in a certain field or study.

Either way, while reading this I assume you have had or have now a career of some kind. You most likely went to college and became something. A lawyer, doctor, teacher. Maybe you went into tech or started your own business. Whatever it was, most likely it was encouraged by your friends and family, and you had support and money or student loans to pay for your career path, your college choices.

I would have no such path. And there would be no such thing as a career or career path for me. Growing up in the cult there would be no talk of college, or what kind of career I wanted. No talk of how to support myself outside of a menial low paying job.

Mind you I did have big plans. I wanted to teach, I wanted to be a flight attendant, or I wanted to be a lawyer.

But not only would those things never happen, there would never be a conversation in my home about college or a career.

You see higher education was, as I have spoken before, frowned upon. Anything that would open your brain to new possibilities in life, outside the teachings of the cult, was considered a no, full stop.

Even if I wanted to be a flight attendant, which I had considered, was something scandalous. Flying from city to city, being with tons of people who were not part of the church and not being able to attend every weekly propaganda church meeting, was considered wildly inappropriate.

So, I did what I could because I had to work, to earn money of my own, because I would eventually have to move out of my family's home.

But as most women in the 80's and before, who had no educations, and no experience, I went into the secretarial field.

Remember according to my mother I did not need to have an education, all I needed to do was be pretty and things would just come to me. Jobs included.

The first time I made money working, outside of babysitting, was one summer between my junior and senior year of high school. I was paid 12.00 an hour, which in 1987 was a huge amount of money, to clean up construction sites.

I learned a lot that summer. I cleaned up sites from the debris left behind, nails, drywall, tape, dust. It was hot and it was dirty work, but I would get up every morning at 5:00 and go with my family friend Steve to these job sites.

During my time there I learned how to plaster, how to sand, how to use a nail gun, how to calk, how to frame a door, how to sand drywall and how to paint. I loved that job, and it taught me skills that to this very day I have used and use.

But it was also the first time I really realized that men on these job sites were very handsy. I almost got myself into a few positions, literally, that were dangerous. I had men call me into empty apartments, and put their hands on me, try and kiss me, put their hands on my breasts and other parts of my body.

I did not want stop working so I just let it go and each day tried to make sure that I was not alone at any given time with another man on the construction site. Eventually the word got around that I was there working sometimes alone, and the men would just not leave me alone. It was like I was their toy.

I was so ashamed that I stopped doing that job. Of course, I could not tell anyone why I stopped because if I told my mother she would have blamed the victim, as she always did in these situations. I loved that job so much, but I also began to realize that being attractive would also get me in trouble. (Side note in no way did I ever think I was attractive. But looking back on my life I can see that I was not the worst looking and I was young, thin, and naïve)

The second job I had was working at a Deli/restaurant. It was in downtown Bellevue in a glass high rise, and it was on the bottom floor. It was the first time that my job had me being with and or serving what I perceived at the time, the wealth of the city. The restaurant was called *Gretchen's of Course*.

The building was filled with attorneys, CPA's and other professionals.

My job was to stand behind the counter as people picked out premade foods, salads, sandwiches, espresso, drinks, and serve them what they pointed to. I was called a behind the counter hostess. I was paid 4.25 an hour for this job.

I got up at 5:00 am every day and went to work. I made salads, muffins, and I got incredibly good and fast at making espressos and using the cash register. This was during the days that you had to push each button on the register to ring in a sale. We did not have scanners or computers.

I worked with some fun people. One lady who had been at this job for years. She was, I am guessing, in her 50's at the time. Her name was Claudette. She was a truly kind but odd woman. She would come to work almost every day in tears. Come to find out her son had just recently taken his own life. And her husband had left her because of that and other factors. I felt so bad for her. Every month she would go to her son's grave to lay flowers and talk to him. She was so heavily burdened by her sons' suicide that I think it drove her crazy, literally. She was deeply depressed, and no one really understood her.

But she taught me a lot about the business, and it helped me get promoted to baker at that job, eventually making 4.50 an hour. I liked the job, and I believed I was good at it.

However, the men who came down to the restaurant were always flirting with me. Which was exciting and scary at the same time. They would give me their business cards and want to call me. I was still incredibly young, just 18 years old and these men were not only in a world I knew nothing about but much older than me.

Growing up in the church, and not yet really being a part of anything outside of it, except my school experiences, my rape and my molesting, I was unprepared for anything regarding relationships, men, flirtation, etc.

I supposed I should have been flattered but the amount of flirting and aggressiveness of some of the men made it almost impossible to work there any longer.

I quit this job. And of course, at the screaming of my mother, I had to find something else quickly.

The next job I applied for was at a place called AB Dick. (from Wikipedia)

The company was founded in 1883[1] in Chicago as a lumber company by Albert Blake Dick (1856 – 1934). It soon expanded into office supplies and, after licensing key autographic printing patents from Thomas Edison, became the world's largest manufacturer of mimeograph equipment (Albert Dick coined the word «mimeograph»).[3] The company introduced the Model 0 Flatbed Duplicator in 1887.[4] Later on, the flatbed duplicators were replaced by devices using a rotating cylinder with automatic ink feed. Basic models were hand-cranked while more elaborate machines used an electric motor.[4] AB Dick model 350 and 360 small duplicator presses, paired with Itek Graphix plate makers, were instrumental in the beginnings of instant or "quick" printing shops that proliferated in the 1960s/70's/80's. These early plate makers first used paper plates and later used polyester plates made by Mitsubishi. They revolutionized plate making for small press printers with the introduction of digital plate makers in the early 1990s. A. B. Dick also produced machines using the competing spirit duplicator technology. Starting in the 1960s, xerography began to overtake A. B. Dick's older mimeograph technology.[2]

John C. Stetson was president of A. B. Dick when he was appointed Secretary of the Air Force in 1978.[6]

In high school I had become obsessed with and very good at printing, as in using a printing press. In those days we did print out things like business cards, stationary, notices, wedding invitations, thank you cards, all things that we can now print for ourselves in some cases, or get them printed for us at a print company. I also learned silk screening in high school in the same class. Silk screening t-shirts, pants, uniforms with logos, names, school years, etc. I could silk screen and print just about anything.

And learning to use those machines was not easy. The process was quite difficult and time consuming. Taking a photo, having it developed on a metal plate, placing the plate on a large machine and adding colored ink to the machine. Adding paper and sometimes having to add the paper just right because if you had to print more than one color, you guessed it, you had to use more than one metal plate. And you had to make sure the plate was placed exactly right on the machine so that it could print multiple times on an item and always strike at just the right place, therefore making an entire picture or wording of some kind.

So I thought I should go into the print business. The job I applied for at AB Dick was for a parts and shipping clerk. It was a great job. I had my own desk in the office and I had my own phone number and books filled with parts and orders. I would answer the phone all day and place orders for shipment locally and all over the country. I was good at this job. It paid well as I remember about 6 or 7.00 an hour. That was almost double minimum wage at the time.

I learned more about the print industry in my year at this company than I had anywhere else. My manager was good to me, patient and he taught me quickly how to do the job.

I met some great ladies there and I had fun. I thought this was the job or even career for me.

As my luck would have it, there was a General Manager, Dan. He was suave and handsome and wealthy, or appeared to be. He was always flirting with the women in the office. He had a huge office of his own down the hall from my desk. And he was in there most days, with the door locked.

His secretary was a beautiful Polynesian woman who I admired for her beauty and the fact that her job was considered one of the most sought after prestigious in the office. The head secretary of the General Manager.

I wanted this job; I thought it was a job that was impressive and it paid more than mine for sure. I also thought I would be more respected if I had this job instead of the one I currently had.

But I found out quite by accident that I did not want that job.

I found out in the months I was there that the General Manger was a misogynistic dick. He would threaten women's jobs if they did not sleep with him. He would bully and harass them and he was the one who for the most part had a say in what women could and could not be hired based on their looks alone. Because I was not really part of the team that was on the frontline, he did not interview me. But he did take an awkward interest in me.

He would come to my desk most mornings, sitting on it, asking me very personal questions about my personal life, if I had a boyfriend, if I ever thought about dating a married man etc. I just brushed it off most days and went about my day. But the more aggressive he became the more uncomfortable I was.

One afternoon he called me into his office. Fortunately for me my direct manager had his office just behind my desk. He heard most the conversations the GM was having with me. This afternoon I had gone to the GMs office and he quickly sat me down and closed the door behind him. He sat on his desk and began grilling me about whether I liked him, if I had ever been with an experienced man, and how he would promote me if I got a little friendlier with him.

I was scared shitless. I immediately got up out of the chair and begged him to stop and let me leave. He did not object and I thankfully got out of his office quickly and safely.

The next day my immediate boss called me into his office. He said that he had no choice but to lay me off. I was SO upset. What had I done, or not done? I loved this job so much, I loved the work, the office, the people. Tears welled up in my eyes and I begged him not to let me go and I promised I would do better.

He said to me look it is not the job, this is painful for me to do but I think it is for your safety. I did not understand a word he was saying.

He just flat out said to me, " I am letting you go because I cannot hold the guilt of knowing one day you are going to be laying on your back looking up at the ceiling, wondering how you got there".

I had no idea what he meant. But I took my letter of recommendation and quietly left the office. It was not until a couple days later that I realized this man was protecting me from the General Manager. And his only way to do that was to let me go. In some ways I owe that man more than he knows. And I was so naïve that I had no idea that these things happened. But they were happening and I was quickly protected from the sexual abuse and abuse of power in that office.

But these things would continue almost until the day I stopped working. My next job was working in a printing facility. It was of course dominated by men. These men were so vile. All I wanted was to be part of the industry, it was literally one of the only things I was good at. But from the second I walked into this shop it was nonstop harassment. Comments about my ass, my boobs, my frame. How much sex had I had, did I give good blow jobs, where was the best place I had had sex. One guy, my manager, was one of the vilest people I had ever met. He could not stop touching me, like all day every day. I asked him once to stop and he said that it was his right to do whatever he wanted because he was a man and men own women, that's just how it is, according to him. One afternoon one of my X boyfriends came by the shop to say hi and this manager threw a fit. Like who is he, do you love him, do you have sex with him. I did not last in that job for more than a few months. I literally felt like I needed a shower every time I left the place.

After this I went into the insurance business. And this office was female dominated. But then I quickly realized that these women were having nothing to do with me. They were smart, educated, had life experiences.

I was a young, attractive, naïve, smart ass who thought I could just get by on my looks. Things I was taught but did not realize until I left the cult, were simply not how to get by in life. This job taught me discipline but it also taught me that you can get fired at the drop of a hat.

However, this job if I had gotten my head together, I probably could have been very successful at and stayed for many years. But I was still young and I was itching to still live my life.

This is the job where I met my first husband. He was in accounting I was in claims.

This was a hard job, I was the one who got the calls when someone had died. A husband, son, mother. They called me to ask me about their insurance policy, what the pay out was, when could they expect it. I had to look up the information regarding the kind of policy someone had, if at all. Get all the information on the persons death, a death certificate, reasons for the death, as some policies were for accident and some were just for natural causes.

I learned a lot in this job about customer support, how insurance claims were filed, and how to work in a large office where there were people with tons of different skills, education etc. All working together daily for a single cause.

The women in this office were brutal. They were all experienced and smart, as I remember them. I was, putting it plainly, dumb, just flat out dumb.

But instead of teaching me, or helping me as the days went on they just berated me and made fun of me. They teased me and laughed at my life. They laughed at my ignorance and did not seem ashamed about it.

There was one woman that I worked with, she was 30 years my senior. She began to help me, guide me, teach me and she was very patient with me. She never made fun of me and she even told me to ignore those other snotty women, they were just bitter and mean and to pay them no mind.

This was the first job I remember where the HR person called me in their office several times to ask me if I was SURE that I did not want to sign up for the 401K program. Though I was not super clear on what a 401K was I did know it had something to do with savings. I went home and asked my mother about it, she said absolutely not, we do not get involved in programs to save money, since we were confident that the world would end any day now and why would we need savings. Mind you I was a 19-year-old adult at this time. But I went back to my HR rep and said no thank you I did not need savings. She could not understand anything about that conversation, but she let it slide.

As it turns out, 30 years later, and with much of life under my belt, that was a huge mistake. As you see the world has yet to end.

I ended up quitting this job for a few reasons. This was a hard job, answering the phone every day listening to person after person crying and telling me they had lost a loved one and could I cut their insurance check right away. One of the last calls I took that really took a toll on me was from a young woman, she was pregnant with her 4th child and her husband had just been killed in a freak accident. She had no money and had no job and now that her husband was dead was unsure how she would pay the rent. She cried and cried on this call. As I held her on the phone and looked up her husband's policy it was with great regret, I had to tell her that her husband had very recently cashed out his policy and that there was no money left for her to receive. Sadness turned to anger and anger turned to abusive words at me about how I must be a liar, I was trying to keep her kids from eating etc. I had to escalate this call to my supervisor. It haunted me for many years and I was not sure that I was the right person for that job. Also I did not really fit in with this office, the dull, and very rule oriented way this office was run.

You were not allowed to have anything personal on your desk, like a photo. No coffee cup, no water glass, nothing. Pens, pencils, paper, your phone, that was it. Your breaks had to be exactly 12 minutes long, nothing more nothing less. And if for any reason you missed a break or did not take enough or too much time, you heard about it.

Also there was a woman I worked with Jerri, she was older and very overweight and she was constantly making remarks to me about how it must be nice to be pretty and young and thin. Everyday was some kind of constant remarks about my looks. Which you would think were exactly what I had been brought up to love or need. But it really was just abusive and it interfered with the job I was doing.

There were several Jehovah's Witnesses who worked at this company with me. One was Gina, who helped me get this job. But working with her just as it has always been in life, proved to be too much to handle as she was always up in my business as to who I associated with, went to lunch with etc.

And since I had secretly started dating my first husband after I had met him at this company, every witness had their nose in my business. One witness was the one who tattled on me to my parents.

I had also met a woman here who ended up for many years being a very close friend, not a Jehovah's Witness. We had been in touch off and on for many years after this job. We had our kids about the same year, got married the same year, just got along well. But as with many things in my life I ended that friendship quite painfully because I really loved her. My husband had insisted that I end it. If he was going to become a Jehovah's witness and end all his friendships, then I had to do the same.

Many years would go by until I met up with her again, social media helped with that. And we had very little in common after 30 years. I tried to keep that friendship going but it was apparent because I had moved forward in life and she had not thought that it was going to end again, and it did, badly. The first time it was about money the second time about her and her families dangerous and non-chalet attitude regarding the COVID vaccine. They are so ignorant they were allowing and letting their own friends and family die instead of just getting vaccinated. This time I was out for good; I have zero desire to have her back in my life.

After this job I got married and went from one bad job to another. Answering phones, cleaning houses, cleaning buildings, waitressing. For a while owning my own janitorial business with my husband. Then working for my mother in her business. That was a daily disaster.

None were paying the bills, and none were offering me a future. Most of them dead end jobs. And I hated janitorial work, hated it.

I would never have a career. Now mind you I had the time during all this to change my tune, go to college, figure out my next step. But because I was still so deep into the cult, it never occurred to me to try. And my first husband was more than I could handle. He was never supportive and everything was about him, always.

I just did whatever came next, and next was always hard and unrewarding. And offered me no future as far as my financial situation was concerned.

I finally took a great job at Victoria's Secret. This was after many years of working in janitorial with my mother and her business and my husband and my small child by my side. But with zero retail experience, Victorias Secret offered me a job as a sales manager. I think because I had owned my own business for a few years and because they were desperate for someone to take the job.

My offspring was young and though it did not pay very much it was a good steady job with a good company. It took me a while to figure out how to manage my schedule while having a young child at home and having zero support or assistance from my husband. Also, I was ending my janitorial business so that I could take this job and for a month I had to work both jobs. So, I was keeping my home, managing my duties as a mother, working full time during the day and working every evening until late. And going to church 3 to 5 times a week. As you guessed it my husband did zero to help or even offer to help. He did not want to babysit, or clean or shop or even take over the business at night just for a short time so that I could get acclimated into my new job. He wanted nothing to do with any of it.

In the 5 years that I had this job I was promoted several times each time with a decent raise. The company was very good about training its managers. We had seminars, outings, classes, required reading, etc. I loved this job and I was good at it. I had gained the respect of my employees, had been recognized by my bosses as a top performer and respected manager. If I had stayed at this company, I probably would have gone all the way to district or regional manager. But as my luck would have it, my husband kept losing his job and the money I was making at Victoria Secret was not paying the bills. I even left there for a bit to manage a Motherhood Maternity and Liz Claiborne store; both offered me more money. But I was lured back to Victoria's secret each time with the promise of better pay.

But eventually I had to leave the retail industry one because my husband refused to babysit our child on nights that I had to work or weekends that I had to work. He was simply too busy playing Xbox or sleeping to help me out. And two because the money was not enough to once again pay the bills.

With the help of a friend, I ended up interviewing for an Administrative Assistant job at a large tech company. They pay was double what I was getting in retail. It was normal hours and the health insurance and other benefits were too good to pass up. Even though I loved working in retail I had to make a hard decision for my family's sake. It is not like my husband asked me what I wanted. Or that he would ever get or keep a steady job so that I could do a job that I loved. Or that he would get a job that would pay enough to help pay the bills.

So, after days of interviewing, I was offered a job at the tech company. Mind you I knew nothing of what I was about to take on. Of course, I was familiar with administrative jobs, but this was a whole new ballgame to me.

I took the job with excitement but very shortly into my roll I was, without being aware of it, assigned to work for one of the worst managers I had ever worked for. He immediately started making comments about my looks, and everything went downhill from there.

And this is the same job where my hiring manager literally told me that the only reason that I was offered the job is because the day of my interview I was wearing a see-through blouse. Here we go again.

I was being trained by another Admin and though I was learning a lot my job became almost too big to manage. I needed an assistant to help with this ever-growing job. But the manager I was reporting to too did not care. He was cruel and he hated me. Why? Not sure I know even today, why. It was almost like he got off on seeing me fail. I was harassed, yelled at, teased and belittled. Day after day. I went to HR for a long time to report about my manager and to let them know how I was being treated. I of course was unaware that this HR rep was going to my manager to tell him the things I was saying about him. But the HR person kept encouraging me to come talk to them because you know, they are there to help me. But instead of HR helping me they were participating in making my life more miserable. The more I spoke to them, the more they discussed with my manager, the more abusive he became. It was a vicious, brutal cycle of abuse.

Because of HR my life inside the company became progressively worse and with every passing day, as I worked my ass off trying to please my manager, my team, other mangers, my job was eventually going to come to an end. Hindsight, I should have left the company way before it put my future on hold.

It all ended in quite a terrible way. One afternoon, I was working with my assistant in her office (finally got an assistant) and as we were changing the furniture around, we pushed a desk against a wall and one of the very heavy metal hanging bookshelves fell off the wall, coming undone from its attachment, and landed right on my head. Absolutely brutal feeling. As I would later find out, fracturing my skull. A two-inch fracture on the left side of my head. The fall also bruised my shoulders and arms, pinning me underneath the bookshelf. I was helped up by some other people who heard it fall. But it was at that moment that things about my life for many years were about to change. And even today the after affects of that injury still haunt me sometimes.

I was having massive headaches, I slept all the time, I had a concussion and a fracture that also left with me a hematoma. I had many years of health issues after this. Even some today that you may not notice or may not know as left over from my injury.

However, when the headaches got too much to bear my doctor wanted to put me on medical leave for a while so that I could rest, heal, go to physical therapy and get my life back. But 72 hours before taking medical leave, the company fired me. That piece of shit manager, fired me, or should I say one of the other abusive managers that worked with him, fired me. And in that very moment they took my badge, my keys my corporate Amex card, locked my office door and had security escort me out the front door.

And that was that. I was out of work, a single mom, with a small savings that eventually would be drained and a head injury that caused me many health issues for many years.

Here I was once again, without a job. And because of the way I was raised it was just another job that I would lose. I had had no career, no formal education and honestly everything always seemed hopeless.

Day by day, paycheck to paycheck the years rolled out. One shitty manger after another and an unsupportive spouse for everything in my life. One more job, gone.

My husband by this time had left me so I was down to one income or by now, zero income.

I did get unemployment for a while but that eventually ran out. I couldn't find work mostly because of my health. And before I knew it a year went by and I was literally down to one more unemployment check. I had used all my savings to pay bills and live. And someone offered me 11.00 and hour to answer the phones at their office. I took the job because 11.00 and hour was better than no money an hour which is where I was just about headed.

I also was in the middle of suing the tech company for unlawful termination and sexual harassment.

Shortly after my receptionist job, maybe a year in, I took a job at a boat company as a loan officer. This job was Tuesday through Saturday. Which kind of sucked because I used my weekends to spend my time with my kid. And it's when most of my friends wanted to hang out, go places. As you do on weekends. I did not keep that job very long because not only did I have zero experience at this job but the men I worked around, were you guessed it, absolute misogynistic dick heads. They did not want to train me; they just threw me in the deep end. And the women it seemed were just there to see how many rich boat owners they could bed.

My manager was an abusive dick who literally yelled at me all the time. And told plenty of sexist and racist jokes. He even told me how to decorate my office and what kinds of clothes to wear. If my blouse was cut lower then surely, I could sell more boats or more warranties or get more business. He used to ask me all kinds of personal things about my sex life, and he was just a vile human who I literally hated being around every day. I would have done anything to get just a small break and have an opportunity for a better job.

It was then I did get that small break. When the attorney I had used to sue the technology company had sent out a mail saying that her firm was looking for an office manager. That seemed right up my ally. But would I be allowed ethically to work for her?

I replied to her mail and yes, if I was no longer her client, then I would be able to work for her. So, I turned in my resume like everyone else and then I interviewed and got the job.

This was a really great job. It paid well, had great benefits and vacation and it was in a small law firm. They would train me and for a very long time, I loved this job. I loved the people I worked for and the things I was learning. I loved working in law. I loved getting out of bed every day to go to this job. The firm was unemployment law, civil law, divorce law and estate law.

I got along well with most everyone in the office, but when two women attorneys decided they did not like me, for different reasons, then things became tense. One woman did not like me because I did not have a college degree and she simply couldn't understand how anyone could go through life and not have been to college. Mind you, she was an attorney, and I was the office manager, why it mattered so much to her so as to make my life miserable towards the end, baffled me. She used to make snide comments to me about my life, my choices. Though she did not actually bother to get to know me or why my life was the way it was at the time. She felt that she was in many ways far superior to me. And she wanted to make sure that I knew it. She felt like one of those phony friends you have in high school who stabs you in the back all the fucking time. Yeah her.

The other attorney was a young new attorney who had just passed the bar. She at first was fun to work with but in the end her own personal bias towards me was no longer letting us work together. She was a hippie that had been raised by hippies. (literally) She had a lot of opinions about a lot of strong topics. I was not yet quite out of the church but just dangling on its edge, so I still had not opened my mind to new views or educated myself on the world around me. It seemed that every week she had some topic to talk about that she knew would tweak me and she got me riled up over things. It should not have mattered as we were from very different backgrounds. But in the end, it was our undoing. I even at one point thought we were friends, but she was way too self-absorbed in her own life dating and dating and dating and trying to bed some sports figure that she had no time for me outside the office.

However, I will add that looking forward she taught me a few things and got me to see things that I had previously not understood. Some about politics, some about racism, some just about life. She also taught me about a few things I did not like about humanity, how we treat men, how we treat each other. But all in all, they were good lessons, ones that I did not take lightly. I think in some ways she was a transition person for me as I was leaving the cult and getting ready to really change my life. I think about her often because she was right there in my life both personally and with my daily job. I am not sure she even remembers me today, but I can thank her for helping me, sometimes with irritation, to transition from one life to another.

I was very shocked when I lost that job. My husband's X wife said that it had something to do with her and his divorce and how she magically ended my job because she was in victim mode all the time. Looking back, I think it was just the tension in the office with the other attorneys. I mean to be honest, even to this day I do not really understand it. I know they wanted me to have a few more skills than I had, but they had trained me, and we all seemed to work well together.

And it was the first job in a very very long time where I was treated with respect and was not sexually harassed. Seems like things that everyone should have in their careers, but that was never part of my experience.

But that job helped me move on to better things. I say in some ways it saved my life. I was able to go back to the tech company but just as a temporary worker. Which was perfect for me because I was experienced, knew the company, knew all the internal systems and yet if I ended up working for an abuser I could just walk away from that job and the company I worked for would find me a different job, no questions asked.

I then went into family law working with a friend and then working with the friend's larger firm where she became a partner. This law firm had only women, no men. It was a large firm and though I answered phones and filed, they also taught me a few things about being a paralegal and to be honest it was the first job I had had in many years where everyone just worked well together. No yelling, no backstabbing, no messy office relationships, at least not that I saw or heard about. I mean yeah, a few people were not the best of friends, but it worked, and I loved working there.

I think that perhaps if I had had the proper opportunities in life that law may have been the way for me to go. But I had dreams, big ones. I wanted to teach, I wanted to be a flight attendant, I wanted to be a lawyer, maybe even a judge. A writer though, I knew one day I would be. But instead, I was stuck with many terrible jobs working for the worst of humanity. I was living most of the time, paycheck to paycheck, squeezing out a daily "living" to barely put a roof over my head. I had no hopes, no prospects and each day was filled with anxiety as to how I would pay the next bill or feed my kid.

Not that these jobs were bad. Not that they did not teach me things, or introduce me to good people sometimes, but they brought me no hope, no future. Not that some did not teach me discipline and maturity. However, outside those jobs, those dead-end experiences... there was a different world.

In my new life most everyone I know has a career. And they have a long story behind it. They went to college, chose a path and made it happen. They had supportive parents and friends who shared the same or similar paths. Of course, it was not as easy as that. One of my friends worked as a server while paying her way through college. Some of my friends had scholarships, some just worked and paid their way. Some of their parents paid for all or part of their college. But in every case, they each had a career. Not that they did not do small jobs here and there as they aged to pay for things. But a career is the key. The key to a future. A future of paying bills, saving money and literally doing normal things. Like buying a home, a car, traveling, going out to dinner, buying groceries, keeping the lights on.

I am not sure, looking back on my life, my ignorance, my confusion, my lust for something more, if I thought the world was going to end. Did I believe it? Did I think that no education would serve me well?

Oh, that's right I thought if I was pretty, then nothing could harm me. My bills would be paid, my future set. God would keep me alive in a world where money was not needed. So, I was set! Saying this shit out loud even all these years outside the cult just makes me sound like a ridiculous person. Yet people still live like this. With this insane mindset.

And as it turns out… one doesn't always stay pretty. One ages and with that age comes reality and sometimes heartache. With age comes a gut punch sometimes.

If I had a choice, to do it all again, the only thing I would change would be taking my education seriously. Doing well in school, going to college and planning my career, my future. No matter my disabilities, or lack of support, I would have buckled down and gotten my education.

Of course, that may have taken me from my cult a lot sooner than when I left. Though I am certainly not unhappy with my life today, filling my brain with actual information over the last 17 years has in some ways been overwhelming.

The things I did not know and the dangers I put myself in because of my ignorance. And I blame all of this on my mother. Each and every god damned thing. Well, when I started this book, I wanted to blame it all on my mother. I always seemed to have my hands raised in hate and frustration for her. And though I hold her deeply responsible for my years of ignorance. I take full responsibility for the time when I became old enough to look at my life and say I am not going to take this shit anymore. Angela out. I take responsibility for waking up every day and saying do not worry Angela as long as you are pretty everything in life will work out fine. And you are going to be 25 forever so there is zero need to fill your brain with actual information and experience.

Being brought up in a doomsday cult is deeply toxic. And it fucks with every decision you make. It steals your youth, your education, your dignity, your life, your family and your fucking reality.

I cannot thank my community enough for gently guiding me forward from the cult to reality. And never ever looking at me and saying "were you always this dumb?" The education I have gotten from my years outside the cult, with a community of amazing friends has given me the foundation to say that perhaps now I have chosen my career. And most of it comes from the love and support you have all shown me.

Being a writer was all I really wanted I think, and my life experiences, education or not, brought me to a whole new world, where it did not matter if I was pretty, it only mattered that I was genuinely me.

FALSE DYNAMICS

"The other night I ate at a real nice family restaurant.
Every table had an argument going."

~ George Carlin

When you grow up in a family, you have a role. A daughter, a son, a middle child, the eldest, the youngest, a twin. The mom, the dad, the grandparent.

Perhaps your family is a Brady Bunch style of family, with stepparents, and stepchildren. Or it might have half-siblings.

Perhaps some of the kids in your family have a large age difference. Or all the kids only have a couple years between them. Perhaps there are twins, or all girls or all boys. Families can be unique to you or like those that you spent time with growing up. Perhaps because of the generation you grew up in, or the town or the church you attended. I specifically remember many of my friends growing up had many siblings, one family up to 13 children, most having 4 or more.

I grew up with families that had problems and lots of them. An abusive parent, very poor, a child who had died, a divorce, illness, a mother who had mental issues, a father who was sexually abusing his daughters or children, you know normal stuff. As I look back on my life before I left the cult, I remember very few families that did not have some kind of major issues. Was that normal? I thought it was. I thought that every family in the world lived in a toxic abusive household. Unless of course you were a television family.

I watched a lot of television as a kid, mostly to escape the world I was in. Most of the family shows I watched had good, wholesome, and loving family dynamics. Usually one working parent, a mother who stayed home with the kids, she cleaned, and cooked and whenever her family came home there was laughter and kindness and hugs and communication.

Whatever the family dynamic is, it may seem unique to your life, but it probably is not. Most likely there are thousands of families all over the world who have a family dynamic like yours.

My family dynamic was at first one way. A mom and a daughter. Then a mother who remarried, making it a mother, a daughter, and a stepparent.

As the years passed the family would change to myself and two half-sisters. One born in 1977 and one born in 1981. One born in Arizona and one born in Washington state.

As the oldest of the children in the family, 9 and 13 years apart in age, I always felt a responsibility and was also forced into responsibility of being a caregiver a housekeeper, a teacher, a child raising someone else's children.

My life was forever changed, not so much when my first sister was born in 1977, but when my second sister was born. I was 13 years old, and had only been living in Washington state one year.

It quickly became my responsibility to raise my sisters, at 13 my life would no longer be mine. Why my mother continued having children was beyond me. She was not, to put it bluntly, a good mother. Nor was she an especially happy mother. Nor was she someone who liked raising children. Her behaviors about being a mother were always heavy with a responsibility she clearly did not want.

When my mother had her 3rd child with her second husband, life was already a heavy burden for her. She was SO upset about becoming pregnant with her 3rd baby that she cried most every day thinking about it.

I remember sad long days where it seemed she would never come out of her depression. And it did not help that her pregnancy made her very sick physically. She had to work full time and she was very unhappy. She was 33 at the time. About the same age as my own child now.

We were also living in a new state, town, place, where she was trying to fit in, make friends, and though she knew a few people, those who had come to Washington with us from Arizona, she was having a hard time, especially since we were so poor and most people here, were not, even in the congregation.

I also remember when she became pregnant with her 2nd child while living in Tucson. You remember I told you that she became very sick during that pregnancy and I was burdened with taking on a ton of responsibilities in the home. Nothing changed much after that. I would forever be burdened with heavy responsibilities and much of my childhood, day in and day out, would become nonexistent. Every day that went by, I saw fewer and fewer of my friends and became more and more loaded with the responsibilities that my mother and her husband should have taken on.

As a child raising children, not babysitting mind you, raising, you have no clue what you are doing. You take one step at a time and you fill in the blanks when you can, with what you can. And you hope you get it right, but in the end, you will find that there will be someone who loves to tell you about all the things you did wrong. And then you hear those very children that you raised, as adults, tell you how you messed up their lives.

I was not a mother nor was I equipped to even play one on TV or in my home. I wanted to be a child, I wanted to hang out with my friends and spend summers at the beach. I wanted to ride my bike and lay in the sun and have iced tea and picnic and listen to music.

Now I was stuck at home, all the time, bathing, changing, bedtimes, story times, and bringing up my sisters.

My time raising them was something I took very seriously. They were little girls whose mother was rarely around and mind you even when she was, she wasn't. Her mental state made her unfit to properly raise children. And why did she need to, she had me to do everything for her.

It was not my sisters' fault that this was their life, but I know that at least my youngest sister, later in life, blames me for all the things that went wrong in the family. And without knowing facts or taking anything, I said seriously, even as we aged, she for the most part thought it was hilarious that our mother always threw me under the bus, always made fun of me, always lied about me to them and to our friends. She found my mother's abuse of me to be hilarious. She knew nothing of the 13 years before she was born. She did not care that I was abused, that my mother was toxic to me. She thought it was funny. Her behavior is incredibly toxic and it has played a role in why my youngest sister and I do not speak today. Thirteen years have passed since we have had a single spoken word, in email, phone, text, anything.

I remember trying to talk to her one time about some of the things I had been through as a child, sexual abuse, abused by mom, and she just said, "yeah sure ok".

In my family it was as if I had become a stepchild instead of the other way around. As if I had interrupted their peaceful and happy home. As if I was the stranger in their lives. The reality was my sisters had come into MY family, with MY mother. They had interrupted everything about who I was and who my mother was and who we were together. And my youngest sister as she got older would manipulate this dynamic to her favor. It was psychotic.

My youngest sister and my mother had the best of relationships. My middle sister and I both had difficult relationships with our mother. Toxic and abusive.

It was not until much later in life that I began to realize that one reason mom and my youngest sister, Loren, had it better together was because mom was tired, and Loren was a manipulator. And a very good one at that. Mom just kind of seemed to give up on being a mom. Or else she was just tired of hearing herself scream at us all the time, so she just kind of stopped.

I look back on all the years that I missed after I left home, watching Loren grow, and all the years at home and how my sister Loren grew up. I remember how she was given everything she could ever want, with very little consequences. She dressed how she wanted, she was given a car, she dated who she wanted, she was friends with whomever she chose, she listened to whatever music she wanted. She went out, she partied, she had sexual experiences with whom she chose. And as I recall my mother said very little about these things. Even though my sister was also being raised in the church. I mean hell my sister's now husband was practically living with her in her bedroom at home. Do you think anything was said? Nope.

She wrecked her car; she got a new one. I wrecked my car, it was tough shit, take the bus or buy your own. I needed new clothes, nope. New shoes, nope. But my sister, yep, she got whatever she wanted.

I remember the subtle way Loren would manipulate my mother. The way she would change the conversation or giggle in a way that mom would see as dismissive but never questioned it. It was as if mom was in a trance with this kid. She rarely got upset with her, and she let her run the household and let her manipulate her way through it.

I would not be able to get away with half the stuff Loren did, even now in my 50's, if mom was still alive.

I also remember Loren became very good at manipulating others as well. Her friends would even fall into this odd trance around her. But they allowed her to manipulate them.

I think the first things I remember were how she took advantage of her friends financially. She would pretend to not bring her wallet or that someone owed her something or that she could not afford the food or the drinks at the restaurant she was at. Or her blatant actions of making those within her circle who had more money than she did always pay for things.

I do not know how she did it, or why she did it or how her friends continued to put up with her behavior.

When she tried it with me a few times, I fell for it quickly but then I remember her sinister laugh, one that said, you are a sucker. That laugh that she always used to hurt me.

I wondered how her life was all those years after I left home, being raised by her mother instead of me. How did it differ for her. And how did she become so ungrateful for all I had done and sacrificed for her.

The hard part for me looking back on it was that I had been in that family with that mother for 13 years before Loren came along. Thirteen years is a very long time for a family to run, develop, function, dysfunction, grow, become strong or weak, good or bad. Thirteen years and in one afternoon, that kid changed everything.

And everything in the house now changed to be about her and her alone. Even my other sister Melody became kind of a second-class citizen. She was ignored and made fun of. And to my deep shame, I also ignored and made fun of her. I played along with whatever the family did and that's what they did.

So now here we are a 13-year-old, a 4-year-old and a newborn. A mother who was miserable in her life and father and stepfather who was always checked out.

I left home when she was 6 and our relationship was never the same after that.

To be fair to the situation I was now an adult, and I was on my own defying everything about my upbringing, my church, my family. I was an ignorant kid who had zero life experience and now I was out from under the control of my abusive mother and as I recall my own self, I was kind of a little asshole. I had a brave arrogance about who I was and what I wanted in life, though nothing about that girl or women would be anything like the person I am today.

As I was doing research for this book I went through some old photos and old letters and cards that I have saved all these years. And there was this very sweet letter from my sister Loren about how much she missed me and loved me. A few cards here and there with her sweet handwriting about how proud she was of me for being a good mom and getting though some challenges in my life and how much she loved me. I admit I wept when I read those, mostly because we have been estranged for so long, I had forgotten that we did have a small tight bond at one point. I even keep one of those cards right here in front of me on a board behind my monitor and I can see it every single day.

As my mother was dying, literally dying, my sister still found it funny to laugh at me, it was a subtle bullying of kind. I remember going to my mother's home shortly before she got very sick and went into hospice. My mother was selling everything she had, at a garage sale. Every memory, every trinket, every piece of art from my childhood. As I was talking to my mother about why she was selling everything, especially since she had not told me that her cancer had rapidly progressed and that she probably only had a few months or years to live, my sister stood in the corner giggling at me. Like actively giggling and laughing at every question I asked my mother. She never actually said anything to me, but it was like a bully on the playground. As if something about me was SO funny that she couldn't stop laughing.

At hospice my sister would not leave me alone. She followed me around the facility and every time I would ask a question to a nurse, my sister had to be right next to me making sure I did not ask the wrong questions, or say something that she considered inappropriate. She even would give me permission to see mom in her room or tell me what I was allowed or not allowed to say or do while visiting.

Sometimes she even hesitated to leave me alone in the room with mom.

I am the oldest of her children, leave me the fuck alone, is what I wanted to say every day that I was there. But I was still a bit trapped in the cult mindset and the place was crawling with self-righteous Jehovah's witnesses who thought they knew my mother better than I did. Trust me, they did not.

My sister angered me more in those few weeks than she ever had in her life. Her husband having the nerve to get in my face about how the family dynamic will now be him in charge of the family and he will make family decisions and that I had no say in things because I was no longer part of the church. And let's be clear he also thought he somehow understood the relationship, time, years I had with my mother. He knew nothing. To this day I doubt he even thinks twice about me or how fucked up my life was with his mother-in-Law.

What I should have said to him is fine you little asshole go ahead and take over this dysfunctional family, no one wants that job, it is all yours.

MIND you there were two other sons-in-laws who were older than him. Not sure who he thought he was but obviously looking back I know that he knew zero about my mother, her past, her mental state and her lies. Nothing. He knew the tired, checked out woman, and nothing more.

The abuse and bullying continued for the entire 23 days my mother lay in that bed. My sister was always manipulating, always trying to make it seem as if somehow mom was dying from cancer because of something I had done. As if I had control over my mother's health.

She even said to me that her and my other sister Melody would go through moms' things after she died and take what they want and then give me whatever "trash" was left over. Even after I had begged for things like jewelry that belonged to my grandmother or pieces that mom had when I was just a girl, she gave me nothing but some old crap and a few scarves.

She even said that mothers will did not provide anything for me and that it was all going to them. NOT that my mother had that many things really. No home, no antiques, just a few things that I wanted but my sister was having none of allowing me to get anything.

My stepfather even told me that in the will that mom specifically said I was to get nothing. My sister Loren thought somehow this was also funny. Ha ha another joke on me.

So, I had to hire an attorney to get a copy of this so-called will that everyone thought was so hilarious. And as it turns out, it said nothing. It was signed on her death bed and simply said that I got the pieces of jewelry that I bought her over the years. And even then, my sister only gave me a couple pieces of that. I literally had to take the rest from my mother's jewelry box when my stepfather was away one afternoon.

My sister was so hateful and rude to me when mom was dying, it took me years to stop thinking about her words to me. Her abuse and her bullying and toxic behaviors were unacceptable. And 13 years later, looking back at all of it, especially when mom was dying, I should have told my sister to STOP. Stop thinking you are in control of anything or anyone in this situation. I am the eldest and you will respect me and will cease with the bullying and manipulation. And stop thinking you know ANYTHING about my relationship with mom, you clearly know zero. And please STOP thinking you know the woman you see dying in that bed. You do not know shit about anything because all she did was lie to all of us our entire lives.

My husband used to say to me, honey, in a few years none of this is going to matter. Try not to waste your time thinking and being angry about something or someone who obviously doesn't care about you or your feelings.

Well now 13 years have gone by, and life has certainly changed for me and for her. She has two children now, that I have never met. I can only assume it is because of the church that I no longer want anything to do with. Some of it could be this false narrative she has about what kind of person I am. But who knows. I have sent her a couple of emails and texts in these 13 years and have heard nothing from her. I assume she has blocked me from her life.

To be fair we did not get to grieve the loss of our mother together. We went to mom's memorial and then we went our separate ways. There were a few angry emails exchanged but then it all went dark. I have heard nothing from her since.

I know that she must still grieve for the loss of our mother. She is the youngest of 3 children, the one who seemed to take it the hardest and yet not the hardest.

I remember when mom told us that she had cancer, I had a family meeting with my sisters, and both pretty much told me they were doing nothing to help with whatever mom needed. And that as the oldest it was my job to take care of things.

So, it was my job as the oldest, wait for it, to work 2 jobs, since my first husband had just left me, raise my 10-year-old child alone, keep a house, and then take care of everything for mom. WHILE mind you my youngest sister still lived at home. And my mother was still married to that useless 2nd husband of hers.

But as the oldest I was to get no say about anything, or to have any opinion about anything when mom was dying.

I guess I cannot imagine what kind of awful and hateful things my mother said about me to my sisters after I left home. But whatever trash it was, my youngest sister fell for it then proceeded to treat me like garbage.

Never grateful for my sacrifices or had any sympathy for my years of abuse at our mother's hand.

I do remember my mother telling me the things she was saying to my sisters about me. How I was evil, I lied, I was selfish and cared for only myself. One specific memory I was supposed to go as a chaperone on a field trip with my sister and her class, I think she may have been in the 4th or 5th grade. I worked evenings and sometimes I would work until like 5 or 6 in the morning and I had a young child. I was not going to be able to make this trip to help with the class. My sister called me early that morning to make sure I was still coming and before I said I couldn't make it she said, "well its ok if you do not come, mom always says your word means nothing and that you never do anything for anyone but yourself." You better believe I got out of bed and went on that field trip.

But those words stuck with me for years because it was really then that I knew my mother was in her way, STILL abusing me through my sisters even though I had been away from home for years at that point.

You see the toxic in this dynamic, all of it, every single fucking day, nothing but toxic behaviors.

Look I love my sisters. Deeply, they were basically my children. I would have done anything for them. But in the end one sister should be deeply ashamed of how she treated me. She had zero idea about the abuse I was sustaining in that house, at school, with friends, in the congregation.

And she did not bother to get educated on it.

My family dynamic was a hot mess. And it ended badly with the death of a toxic mother.

A family deeply split. A step father remarried, three sisters who barely spoke or speak today.

A toxic mother dead.

The oldest sibling tossed aside like trash. Left to pick up her own life and move forward without her sisters.

I am not sure that my youngest sister will ever understand the deep abuse that I sustained at the hands of our mother. I am not sure that she will ever care. But perhaps one day, if we ever meet again, as adults we can talk it out or get to know each other again.

I hope that years of her own marriage, being a mother herself, and age will soften her and educate her.

Before I end this chapter, I wanted to throw out that after all these years it's time I give my sister Loren a bit of grace.

She was only treating me the way my mother treated me because she really knew nothing different. She was just a child herself when I left home, and she had zero idea what hell I had gone through for 19 years living with that toxic woman.

And how could she and why would she? My mother treated her very differently because my mother was living a different life. At least that is what she wanted to do, live a different life. But in the end, she was still the abusive toxic woman she always was to me.

I mean come on her own grandchild, my offspring, was so affected by my mother's abuse of me that they wanted to go to therapy for it. I mean. For. Fucks. Sake.

And how is it that my own child understood and saw the abuse, but my sister did not?

I do not get why anyone would protect an abuser. It makes zero sense to me. Even if their dynamic is different, it still never excuses abuse.

It is amazing how a parent can fuck up their kids so badly. How they can turn their own kids against each other.

I think this is why therapists are wealthy and why we have so many reality shows about messed up families.

Tonight, I looked out my home office window while finishing this chapter and the sky was pink with an amazing winter sunset over the lake, I thought about my sisters and how much I loved them. How I missed being the oldest in the dynamic and how I wished sometimes; things had ended differently for us. But differently how? I know that toxic families rarely make it out whole.

But I can no longer carry the burden of their decisions, as adults. Good or bad, right or wrong, in the end they are who they are and they in some ways must live with their hate for me and the lies they listened to. And the abuse that was heaped on me. At least one sister does as I think things might be mending a bit with my other sister.

My mother's demons always haunting everyone else around her while also killing her slowly for years.

Three sisters, living different lives, never grieving together, abuse or not. My mother leaving this earth without shame of how she separated and cracked us, and broke us apart, and shamefully pit one sister against another just for her own pathetic abusive agenda and cult of lies and hate.

She ended her time here and did not give a second thought as to how she broke us along the way. I wonder to this day if she cared about the mess she was leaving behind. And the damage she did to three sisters.

As the years roll by, I imagine a world where we try and mend our broken relationships. But as the years roll by quickly, I fear that we are becoming more and more separated on this planet and perhaps even if we were to meet again, we might not be able to mend the years that have gone by.

I do hope to one day to meet my nieces if only to ask them if their mother was a good mother and if they were happy. And maybe even, if they would like to get to know me.

Perhaps they would like to hear stories of their grandmother and the life she had lived since they were born years after her death. Stories that only I can tell because I alone was there from one tragedy to another.

Stories that are different than the ones their mother tells. Important stories about how she got where she was and how they got where they were.

My family dynamics were complicated daily, and the broken pieces may never be glued back together.

Once my mother died the family was irreversibly broken. Sisters split, friends divided, lie after lie, tear after tear. Now years gone that we will never be able to get back.

I suppose I wonder if my sister thinks about me at all. If she understands the sacrifices, I made for her because of the dysfunction of the mother that she clung to even at her craziest.

And if she ever sits back to understand that what she experienced was not what we all experienced and much of it was very bad, very hard and very abusive.

I think she should give me grace for the things I went through, and she should be ashamed that she walked away from the one person who literally sacrificed her youth to raise her while her dysfunctional mother could not.

Either way, I am around and will always open my arms to her and her family and will not throw her away like she did me.

If your family dynamics are even close to mediocre, embrace that. Even your most ridiculous brother might be the soundest human in another family's dynamics.

DIXIE LEE LEVERETTE

"Periods of kindness, no matter how short, bond the victim to her abuser."

~ Jess Hill

As I wrote this book, I realized that I did not take the time to say many kind things about my mother. And I was scolded by someone who said that surely, I could think of a kinder side of the woman. Food for thought.

Her abuse and disdain and disrespect for me clouded most things that could be considered kind or good.

But I will say a few things. The years have taught me to give more grace to people than perhaps some of them deserve. I surely did not always think my mother deserved grace. I remember as a child, up until I was about 12 years old, that I had some good, happy memories of my mother. Fun times, times that make me smile.

She was funny, and beautiful. I thought she was the most beautiful woman in the world. She had a beautiful singing voice, she was an artist, creative, put together. She took great care in how she dressed, did her hair, and appeared to others.

I remember laughing with her, shopping with her, baking with her. I remember her having matching clothes made. I remember her comforting me when I hurt myself or just when I was sad.

I remember her hugs, how her hair smelled sweet. Her white shoulders perfume. Her mauve lipstick. Mauve was her favorite choice.

I remember her friends and how she always loved to dance and have fun. I remember the smell of alcohol and soap, Georgia pine, red clay and moth balls.

My mother was young, just 19 years old in 1968 when I was born. And until 1974 when she remarried, she was still young, just 25 years old. And though she had been broken, was broken, she seemed to keep enjoying life. Seemed to be.

I now have a few photos that some of her old friends sent me, when they knew I was writing this book. A young beautiful woman who eventually died young and broken.

I stare at them sometimes. Just to look at her and wonder what was really going on inside her. She had so much of her life left to live. And yet I can see into the future when I look at those photos and know that she dies lonely and sad and heartbroken. Not alone, but lonely. I think she missed out on so much of her life. And she let others dictate to her how she must live. She did whatever came next, I suppose. Not really thinking too far into the future or what consequences her decisions and actions might cause her.

But my mother was also a very hard-working woman. There is not a day in all the years I remember her, that I remember her being lazy. She worked, always worked. And she was industrious.

When there was no job, she found one. When she had no skills, she learned one. When she had no money, she started her own business. A highly successful business I might add, that lasted for over 30 years until she passed.

As a young girl, with mom being single, I remember her stories about how she worked and saved to buy things on her own. The years she worked at MaBel and saved and saved to buy herself this small gold pinky ring with her initial "D" on it. The one thing I wanted so badly when she died that my sister refused me.

In one wedding photo of mom and my stepfather, you can see her wearing that ring. She wore it all the time. It was engraved into my memory.

She saved to buy us a new and better trailer to live in. As a girl those places were my home and I never thought we went without or that we were poor. We were poor, but mom never showed it, at least not to me. The things I needed to survive, I had. Food, water, shelter, clothing. Sometimes hugs.

I remember two mothers. One before 1979 and one after 1979.

The one before, who laughed, danced, smiled, shopped, hugged, partied, dated. And one after, who cried, screamed, threw things, abused me financially, physically, emotionally and religiously. One who loved doing her hair, wearing nice clothes and putting on makeup for every outing. And one who went through the motions of life and most days not very well. Painful step by painful step she weaved her way through.

I learned a lot from both of these moms. What I really learned was who I did not want to be. Though my mother had some qualities that I admired, she mostly just made me livid and sad.

When I started writing this book, I was still so angry with my mother. I loathed her to her core. And my tears stung my face as I cried for days at a time for the person, I needed her to be. But as the years went on, and I aged, life changed, I remarried, my offspring grew into an adult. I guess I learned to forgive my mother. Not forget mind you but forgive her. The more I learned about her past, her choices, good and bad, the more I understood her. The more I processed her choices, the more confused but open minded I became towards her.

Though some days my heart deeply aches for a mother. Not my mother necessarily, because she did not give me what I needed. But aches for a mother. I realize that we do not all live a Disney dream. Not all families are good and not all families are good for us. Sometimes they are just plain toxic.

Though as children we do not have many choices, as adults we can choose to not forgive the behaviors of those who were supposed to love us, nurture us, hold us, teach us.

I choose to let myself love her in my own way. To forgive her for her abuse. But to not forget the horrible things she said and did to me. Not to forget the hate she oozed for me every day in her words and deeds.

I also understand had it not been for her decisions along the road of her own life, that I would not be here today, who I am today. I would not live in this beautiful state, with the most amazing friends and loved ones that a humble, uneducated, bent but not broken person could ever ask for.

This place that changed me, helped me, saved me.

The place I hated and did not appreciate. The place I detested because my mother loved it. The place I wanted to run from so many times.

It is not only a physical place but a place of mind and heart. A place that transformed my heart, my education, my politics, my family, my community and my ideas.

It is the place where I was meant to be.

However, I will emphasize that It is OK to not forgive an abuser. No matter who they are. A spouse, a parent, a friend. Abuse is not acceptable in any way, period. I was told recently that I HAD to forgive my mother. That not forgiving her would eat at me until I died. And that not forgiving was not fair to her.

Why I thought, why do I HAVE to forgive the one person who was supposed to love me and instead abused me and hated me.

I do not , I wont and not forgiving, in my opinion still gives me control over me. I can honestly say from my personal experience, that forgiveness is not necessary to move forward.

However, that is my take, my life, my choice.

I respect and love anyone who takes a different path in their journey of leaving abuse no matter how small, large or long.

Some days I miss my mother so much, I simply cannot breathe. Some days I do not think of her at all.

Some days I thank her, some days I question her. Some days I curse her.

Today I thank her for her terrible choices, her forward movements that allowed me to be a better person even if by chance.

That allowed me to look at my past and see that every single step she took put my life on a path of absolute happiness and freedom.

My heart is content today with how things ended with her and I. I am not sure that even if I had to do it again that I would have the courage or strength to do things differently. Would I ask the hard questions? Would I tell her how I really felt about her while she lay dying for days in hospice? My answer is, I do not know.

Each day I recognize that life is very short, and I do not have time to waste on hating her.

I hope wherever she is today, she has found the peace she so desperately needed in her own life.

I suppose I can see the positives she left behind, even if that was never her intention. For me to be happy, made her angrier than how I got here. Leaving a cult, remarrying, leaving her abuse. For me to find peace in her death, she would not understand. But I do thank her for pushing me away into the arms of a better place, better people, better companions, better choices.

The positives outweighed the negatives, once the years passed and the scales tipped in my favor. Once she was dead and gone, I was free to live my life the way I wanted to live it. Without her.

And that beer that we always had; it now stands for her selfishness. Her absolute idea that I was never as important as anything or anyone in her life. That I was easily dismissed and tossed aside, like an empty beer can. The beer always filled the fridge, always offered to friends, always there even if food was not. The beer had more say in our household than I ever did.

I do miss you mom, but I missed you when you were alive and it takes more than one beer to wash away the ache in my heart.

THOMAS EUGENE ROBINSON

"We have to live a life with a sense of urgency so not a minute is wasted"

~Les Brown

There once was a man, one that I never knew. Not until I was in my early 30s. He was a man that my mother never or rarely spoke about. A man that even when he died, I did not really know.

I had no photos, no videos, no way of even knowing if he was alive or dead. What he looked like, sounded like. It was not the days of social media so anything I knew, which was nothing, was all in my imagination.

This man was my biological father.

Though you know from my other chapters that my parents were married, in 1967. Though all the research I have done I have been unable to find a marriage certificate to prove it. But in the Alabama vital records in 1967 there is a sign in in the register that says Mom, Dixie and my father Eugene were in fact married.

My legal name was always Robinson, so married they must have been.

All the conversations with friends, old friends of my parents, my uncle, other family members, no one could tell me why they married, when they married, how they married. I did not see a single photo from that time that showed them married, or their marriage, wedding. I tried my best the past 10 years to find any photo of them being or getting married, nothing. I think that was more for my personal ease than for sharing.

When I finally met my father, the conversations before that with my mother were very awkward. She was always hiding something from me yet I never knew what. Mostly what she was hiding was her own lies.

When I got the call in February of 2021 to tell me that my father had died of COVID in his assisted living home in Georgia, things that I previously did not know about him, or that my mother flat out lied about were about to come to the surface. (Figure 12 Thomas Robinson death certificate)

My mother always told me that my father had been adopted. But he was not. His mother and father, were his biological mother and father. (Figure 11 Thomas Robinson birth certificate)

When he was buried, he was buried next to his parents in the Kennesaw memorial Park in Marietta, GA. The very town I was born in. His parents had purchased plots for burial when Gene was a boy. His parents having been married in 1932 in Alabama. (Figure 16 Dana and Mildred marriage certificate, Figure 22 Dana and Frances gravestone, Figure 23 Thomas Robinson grave stone)

His cousin Glenn and his wife sent me a box of whatever things he had left when he passed. It was not much. Photos of his parents, photos I had never seen. Photos of him after the accident. A few photos of the band. Friends. No photos of my mother as I recall. I have just looked through it all again, and nope not a single photo of my mother or of me in the whole box. A few stuffed animals, a pillow that he had at the home with him. A plaque that had his name on it and said Veteran.

Other things I did receive were his discharge papers from the military. (Figure 13 Thomas Robinson Marine Discharge) And divorce papers from him and my mother's divorce. (Figure 14 Dixie and Thomas divorce judgement) I had seen one thing about that after my mother died and I went through her old papers while no one was hovering over me making sure I did not steal anything. (eye roll) But those papers were more about her keeping custody of me than her divorce from my father.

I do not know why she never shared this with me, though she did later in my life mention to me that she had fought in court to keep custody of me, as I have previously written.

My mother told me one time that she had taken me to the hospital to see my father when I was a baby, after the accident and he had come out of his coma. So, my guess in this puzzle is that I was about 6 months old at the time. And that when she went to his room to bring me to him, he sat up in his bed and slapped me really hard. And that was the last time she ever took me to see him. That was the last time I saw my father until I was well into my adult years.

I never understood his behavior until 2021 when I received all his papers, there were papers in there about him being honorably discharged from the military because he had emotional issues. And that the Military was going to let him work on those issues then perhaps come back to join them. And this information was according my uncle. But that never happened because the accident was in August of 1968. And after that Gene's life was pretty much at a standstill. No more band, no more wife, no more daughter, no more military.

However, there was also a letter in there, from 1967 about a year after he entered the military, from the naval Hospital in Memphis (Figure 15 medical eval for discharge Thomas Robinson) which talks about how he had mental issues and had stayed in the hospital for a while. Now putting together what I could over the years, and since his death I can tell you I know no more now than I did when I started this book. I still believe that he was being abused sexually by his mother. All conversations over the years point to that. BUT I have zero proof of that. All I know is that he was being treated for something, in a hospital, and that it was so disturbing that even his treatment was not working. So, he was released from the military and sent back home to be with his parents. A few months later he was married to my mother, because I was born in May of 1968.

I reached out to a friend who works for the White House to help me try and get all his medical records from 1966 to the time he was discharged but it seems that no one, even having his social security number, no one can find any of those records. Not at the hospital, not on the bases, not in the homes where he eventually spent the rest of his life. And none of it was in his personal effects.

It was kind of fortunate that he was still in the military when the accident happened as it was the VA who paid for his care up until the day he died. I think Medicaid took over some expenses too in the end because his newest assisted living home was way more expensive than the VA would pay but it was an approved VA home.

He was never able to work again and his parents, who he lived with both passed away. (Figure 17 Dana Robinson death report, Figure 18 Mildred Robinson certificate of death) Leaving him to live in their home with a private nurse, until that nurse died in approximately 1999 leaving Gene to have to be moved to a VA assisted living home. His cousin Glenn and his wife Delores were helping transition him and apparently Glenn was making sure that Gene was being properly cared for by the VA and the home and that his bills were being properly paid by the VA. And that his needs regarding clothing were met. Glenn had POA over Genes affairs, medical and financial.

There were also more legal papers in that box, papers where my mother got the court to deem Gene unfit to care for himself or his own finances. And he had to prove and beg the court that he was not unfit for that. This was based on the fact that he had anger or emotional issues, his dismissal from the military and his abuse of me, though brief.

It was called the Petition to Restoration of Sanity, and it was 6 months after the accident. (Figure 19 Certificate of Restoration of Sanity 3 months after he came out of a coma.

It looks like in 1970 the court did finally grant him the power to manage his own life, finances, medical decisions, etc.

Not sure why my mother seemed to think that it was her place to take such control over Genes life, especially since she was divorcing him. And social security benefits had already started to be paid out. It seemed to be a pattern with her later in life to always be in control of others' lives, decisions, etc.

But the very year Gene and Mom married he was deemed so unstable or abusive or depressed, that he was released from the military. I can only figure that she married him because she was pregnant. But I have no proof of that and in all my years of research, I could not find the facts regarding this question.

I believe Gene was abusive, physically and emotionally to my mother. So many things have been said on the side, regarding him and how he treated her. Though she barely spoke about him. But after my mom died, I did receive a few random letters and cards about them and how mom was not happy with him and how she kind of turned inside herself after they married. Though she never flat out said that he abused her, I know from putting this story together that he probably did, in some ways.

Maybe she was forced to marry because of pregnancy and then she got a gift of some kind when the accident happened, and she was able to divorce him without too much drama or push back. At least that's how I have put these past few years together with the information I have pieced together.

I wanted so badly to get hold of the medical records of my father while he was in the military and why he was in the Naval hospital. Glenn, his cousin, even signed the form for me because he has POA and though I sent in all the paperwork to get those records, they seem to be nowhere to be found. I suppose I will be fine, not knowing all the facts. It doesn't change my day-to-day life, but I guess it might have been nice to see it, read them for myself.

So, I put together what I could about my father and his mental health with just the small conversations I had with my mother along the way and the old papers I received when he died. And any and all conversations I could have with uncles, and old friends of theirs from way back when. My grandfather, before he passed as well, told me a few things. Though as with many men on my mother's side of the family I was not sure how much was trustworthy.

I will say if I had to guess what was going on with my father perhaps, he really was being emotionally and sexually abused by his own mother. It would explain some of his emotional issues and it would explain the one time my mother told me that his mother was raping him.

There were so many tales and lies in my family by my mother, my uncle, my grandfather, my stepfather that all these years later I took what facts I could find, and I placed them in this book.

I wanted to believe that my father was a kind man. A hard-working man. A man of honor and integrity. And perhaps he was all of those things. My brief moments of talking to him only showed me a broken man whose mind, and body had deteriorated from years of being in a wheelchair without proper therapy for his body, mind, speech.

A man whose world stopped, literally that fateful night in 1968 when his friends were killed, and his life would never be as it was just a few moments before.

A man who did not seem to know that the years were passing and that world was changing around him. Everything he talked about, did, or owned, was all still in the year 1968. Even his old typewriter and television in his room in the home were all from 1968 or before.

I was never sure if he really did not understand or if he was hoping that he would get one more redo and that the accident might not actually happen at all.

And he was also a man who had a lot of hate for my mother.

My sweet friend Steve Burrell gave a toast one evening and said "here's to the men our fathers and who they could have been." And I have thought about that a long time. The men they could have been. The man my father could have been. The man his father could have been had he not been killed that night in that car.

I am not one to believe in fate but after writing this book, perhaps in some ways, Genes life began and ended just as it was supposed too so that my life could begin and flow the way it was supposed to.

I do not know what to say about any of it after 55 years. Except I did feel sorry for Gene. His life was stolen from him in one shattered moment.

I wanted to say I'm sorry to him for not being able to share his life with him. But after writing this book I thought maybe Gene was not someone I really wanted to grow up with. And knowing what I know now about my paternal grandparents, I am not sure that I wanted to grow up with them either. And they died when I was quite young, one when I was 9 and one when I was 13, so if I had not been with my mother then I would have been raised by my handicapped father and his nurse, I assume. And maybe it was best that things went they way they did for me. Not for him surely but for me.

Now he is buried next to his parents, (Figure 23 Thomas Robinson grave stone, Figure 22 Dana and Frances gravestone) my grandparents. I hope that if he ever needed peace, he has it now.

NOTE: I have attached most all of the documents that I received in the box after my father died. They will tell you that the stories I tell are true. Court documents, newspaper articles, Birth and Death Certificates, a copy of one of the first albums my father's band released, (Figure 25 The Misfits newspaper article) given to me by John who you see in the poster of the band. (Figure 26 The Misfits band photo) Marriage certificate of my grandparents Dana and Mildred. My father Eugene's birth certificate which shows my grandfather had been a Police officer. Military discharge papers, a letter from the US Naval Hospital dated 1967 regarding my father's mental state and why he could not return to the military. Court papers regarding my mother's attempt to declare my father unfit to care for himself and court documents showing my mother finally got full custody of me.

My father's death certificate and a letter from the Department of Veterans Affairs Signed by the President, Joseph R. Biden thanking him for his service to our country. (Figure 28 Presidential remembrance letter*)*

I also received his military flag which I display in a case along with the letter from the president and a small black and white photo of my father in his fatigues. The only photo I have of him showing him in (Figure 29 Thomas Robinson - Marine Corps*) the military.*

Also, my only photo of my father and I in 1968 after I was born and shortly before the accident. (Figure 31 Thomas and Angela photo 2*) And the first time I met my father as an adult* (Figure 32 Young Thomas Robinson*) And 1967 before he was married to my mother* (Women and Girls*)*

STEVE BURRELL

*"Every new friend is a new adventure... the start of
more memories."*

~ Patrick Lindsay

As the years passed and my mother dies, I still felt so uneasy that I did not
know much about the accident. It still pained me that my mother never
talked about the very thing that would change her life and mine forever.
And it still haunted me a bit. Such a deep tragedy, such a deep loss.

It pained me that she was rarely honest and the she kept so many
secrets. I wondered why? Why did not she just talk it out. Even 40 years
after the accident before she died, she wouldn't talk about it. She asked me
on her death bed if I had any questions, I said I would like to talk about
the accident. All she could say was, I do not remember much.

So, I decided to do my own research. Thank goodness for the internet.
Thank goodness I had one small piece of history, the newspaper article
from 1968 that I first saw when I met my father for the first time.

One of the first things I did was go to *FindAGrave.com*. If you are not
familiar with it you can find most peoples grave sites. Or where their ashes
are stored, if at all. Its not a perfect site, but it is for searches that are not
complicated. Famous people included.

I found the gravesite of Sidney Boyd Burrell, the passenger who was
killed in the accident. And with a hail Mary and crossed fingers I posted
a public message on this page. I said exactly this: *Sidney died in an automobile accident on the 4th of August, 1968. He has a son and a brother who
he was very close too. Though I did not know him personally his death has*

touched my life very deeply for 40 years. You are missed by your family and friends and those who have wished to know you from a distance.

This year will be 40 years since your death, and I know you are thought about daily.

My hope was that someone would see this message and contact me. A friend from his past, a family member. Someone who knew my parents, anyone. I posted this message in 2008. And I waited and waited and waited and in 2017, 11 years later, I received an email from a man named Steve Burrell.

He was Sidney's son. BINGO! Steve had been mentioned in the newspaper article about the accident, but only to say that Sidney had a 4-year-old son at the time of his death. I had been searching for that son for years. As luck had it, Steve's mother Sharon happened to be looking online at the anniversary of Sidney's death and she found my message on the FindAGrave site.

She contacted her son who did some research and then sent me an email. I had zero idea what to expect. Also, my parents last name in the newspaper announcement was not exactly correct so even if he had been searching for me, it would have been difficult to find me. As it turns out, he had been.

I did not know who Steve was, what had happened to him over the years, was he still living in Georgia, was he kind, an asshole, married, divorced, children. I was nervous! What would I say now? I had anticipated this exchange for many years.

His email to me was very kind, short but to the point. Told me his name, his age, where he was living that he was married, and thanked me for the message that I had left on his father's memorial and said he would welcome contact with me.

YES, this is what I had wanted. As luck would have it, I was literally leaving for a family reunion in Georgia in two weeks' time. So, I reached out to Steve and we made arrangements to meet for dinner. He was happy to make reservations at a nearby restaurant and meet up. I would get to meet his mother Sharon, his aunt, Sidney's sister Janette, Steve's wife Amy and his uncle Dale, Sidney's brother, and Dale's wife.

It was nothing as I had pictured, it was actually better. Steve was such a kind man. A soft-spoken man. He welcomed me with open arms, and we have a lot to talk about.

We hugged when we met at the restaurant, and we went to a semi private room for dinner. He brought all kinds of items with him, costumes from the time that our parents were in the band, music, booklets, trinkets, photos. It was amazing, just as I had hoped it would be but was uncertain it would be.

He even had taken the songs of our father's band from an old reel to reel and had them placed on a CD. He had put copies of old photos on the jacket cover, of our dads, the band. Photos I had never seen in my life. Photos that I will now never forget.

He made a beautiful toast at dinner, and he said words that were so kind and made me tear up. "To our fathers and the men, they might have been." (Meaning if the accident had not taken both their lives in different ways) It was very touching. There was much more to the toast, but I was so emotional over it all that I forgot some of it.

I took home a few things from the band that he said I could have. A few shirts they used to wear as costumes. And the music CD that Steve had made. I came home and listened to that CD for hours and days. In my head every time seeing our fathers as young men, living their lives in a very different time. Playing music, seeing their future ahead of them.

At that dinner, Steve's aunt had brought along a photo album and in that album were photos of my parents I had never seen. I was so teary eyed. It was just insane to me that all these years later, here I was looking at photos of my young parents and their friends. At parties, hanging out, with the band. Just being free and young.

You remember I told you that one thing my mother did tell me, once, is that the accident happened because they had all been drinking then got behind the wheel of a car? But then years later she recanted that story and said they were just kids driving too fast.

That evening at dinner I asked Steve's aunt about that because it was the evening of the accident that they were all partying at her house. And in the photos, you see bottles of liquor on the tables. She said, "you mother may not have wanted to remember but they were all drunk when they got into that car." That was all I needed to know. And the death certificates said nothing about liquor but putting it all together, the way the accident happened, the brutal deaths of Sidney and Donna, how fast it happened, and the police report in the paper. There is no doubt in my mind that that accident could have been avoided. But it was also a different time. Not that people do not still drive impaired, drunk, high. We just understand more, and we live in a time of Ubers and Lyft's and taxis and apps. And in a time where there is zero shame in telling your loved ones that it is not ok for them to drive if you think they are impaired.

At that dinner, talking about the past, the deaths of two people, the lives that were changed, there were tears. It was still a very raw event for many of us, for them. I felt touched and pained at the same time.

Even Steve's mother cried. I could still feel the pain in her after all these years of losing her son's father. I believe she still loves Sidney and was pained by him and his loss in many ways.

That dinner, though wonderful and educational, exhausted me. Here I was putting together a 40-year-old mystery. With some of the very people that were affected by it. People that were with our parents just moments before the accident and the death of two of them.

As the years went on Steve and I got to know each other. Our personalities are very different, but our past is a shared tragedy.

I was only 3 months old when the accident happened, but Steve was 4. Old enough to know his father. But he says he has very few memories of his father. Perhaps that is ok. Perhaps that's best. If I recall, he says he also has no memory of being told that his father was dead. Perhaps that too is best.

As I get to know Steve, I see that he is a very sensitive and kind man. I wondered if the accident affected him after all. He has some fears of travel because he doesn't want to leave behind those he loves, just in case there is an accident of some kind. He says that he cannot leave his dog because of these fears but I think perhaps he probably feels this way about all those he loves, not just his pet. He would be so hurt leaving and not coming home to them. He says he couldn't bear the thought of how they would feel if he never returned. Though I did not really understand it at first, my heart ached for these deep emotions he has.

Though I am no therapist I have thought about these words and his emotions regarding them for a while now. And I wonder though he says he has no real memory of his father, if this fear of leaving and never coming back is actually part of his childhood trauma. The trauma of his father leaving one evening and never returning to Steve's world. Steve growing up without a father and then with a step parent just as I did.

And not really being as close to that step father as he may or may not have been with his real father, Sidney. Just as I too was not as close to my step father as I wanted to be. But those were things unanswered as both our fathers were, in different ways, taken from us.

Not to speak ill of the dead, especially the dead I never knew. But in my research, I was told by several people that Sidney was a player when it came to women. Even his ex-wife told me this. He cheated on his wife, perhaps more than once. He was not ready to be tied down with a family, though he had married Steve's mother. He liked pretty ladies and that is one reason he was dating Donna. As you can see from the newspaper photo, she was a lovely young woman. Sidney unfortunately created victims in his short life. I will never weaken the stories that victims told me; but I will keep some of it to myself. And for this book I did my best to use the stories I was told or found and to unravel them to the best of my ability without hurting others or dismissing words of those that were victims of sexual abuse.

I know nothing more than the few details from family and old friends who are still alive today to tell their stories of Sydney, Donna and my parents. I do not have all the details of Sidney's life of course and because he is long dead and some of his friends and family are still alive, I take what they give me as truth because I do not know anything else. All I have had most of my life is a small newspaper article that told me his name, and how he died.

I have also had the pleasure of meeting Steve's wife, Amy. She is such a delightful person. At first, she was quiet, and I was not sure what I thought of her or what she thought of me. But as the years have gone on, we have gotten to know each other, and I simply love her. She is kind, funny, interesting, intelligent and just welcomed me into her life, without question. I love spending time with her. She has actually taught me a lot and opened my eyes to how her life has unfolded.

In some ways Steve and Amy went through similar things as I did, being in a cult that they eventually left. One that left some bitter feelings in their hearts and minds. Sometimes they also had marital issues, or money issues. Things I suppose many people go through. They remained in Georgia, but my family, as you know, moved all the way to the other side of the country. Its interesting to share our stories, some similar but others totally opposite from one another.

Its hard to actually write down my deep emotions over meeting Steve. The stories we tell, the times we spend together getting to know each other. The memories that we share and do not share. We were both just young kids when our worlds were turned upside down.

Perhaps like me he may some days wonder how his life would have been different had it not been for that evening and the death of his father.

I used to wonder about that, but as I wrote this book, I began to realize that I am not sure I would have liked a life with my father and mother together. I felt they had some toxic qualities as a couple and as individuals. And it seems Steve's parents also had some toxic behaviors that left them better off apart.

Though I did not know Steve's father either I believe after writing this book, that perhaps he too had some qualities that were not all together good. Perhaps Steve was better off with the life that he was given after his father's death. Neither of us will ever know that and to be honest, I'm pretty happy with how things turned out for myself.

I feel honored that Steve and his family welcomed me into their home, their life. Two people torn apart and brought together by tragedy.

In my head I had imagined all these scenarios about one day meeting the man that I had been curious about all my life. Where had his life gone? Who was he? How was he?

As it turns out, he just lived his life.

In other people's world he may be just another human. But to me he is a man who grew from tragedy. In my world he was a part of the puzzle piece that needed to be placed to help me become less fractured, less bent, than I believed I always was.

In my world he and his family are now my family.

WOMEN AND GIRLS

"It took me quite a long time to develop a voice, and now that I have it, I am not going to be silent."

~ Madeleine Albright

We all have influences in our life as children and adults. Though my life was never easy, and filled with many toxic humans, there were those that I, at least for a while, considered influential in my life. Some remain, some I have dismissed or have passed. Some dismissed me. Some I dislike, but thank for showing me who I do not want to be, ever.

As you are fully aware by now, I grew up in a cult that taught me that as a girl or a woman you are the least important person, human, that you will be submissive to every man in your life, your brother, your husband, your male children. Or, when you are taught that you are the "weaker vessel" and that all decisions ultimately belong to your male spouse, and that you are rarely allowed to question them, or when you are taught to fear men, literal men because they are always above you in rank. Then your world view of being a woman, is terribly confusing. Not that the world around us doesn't actually have some of these views. But outside the cult, women are allowed to stand on their own feet, make decisions for themselves, and leave relationships if they choose to do so. Thinking for yourself, as a woman. Amazing.

You are taught, inside the cult, that you will most likely not need an education because your duties are to please your man and get bible studies to convert people into the same mind-numbing abusive cult that, unless you make a change, will most likely be how you live and die.

I had and have a deep desire to have strong supportive women in my life. A few I remember challenged me in ways that either helped or hindered by growth. Though many women I remember seemed strong, they were actually quite weak. Their whole worlds were controlled by a cult, run by men.

In the cult even the woman I thought were my role models, once I spent years in the real world, ended up being just sad shells of empty souls, themselves longing for healthy role models.

A few of them I miss. A few I loved deeply. A few challenged me, hurt me, loved me, abused me, helped me fall, or picked me back up. Some stayed, some came back around but many more disappeared into the abyss of the cult never to return to my life. Yet for some there is still time to cut the chains that shackle them.

But there were a few others that along the way influenced me, even to this day. Not always for the good, but it is part of what shaped me. They were either women in my life, or girls that I grew up with along the way.

And though I crossed paths with many inside the cult, these for some reason that I cannot actually pinpoint are ones that have stuck in my head from a very young age. I suppose their existence in my life was for some reason to give me small lessons that I still remember today.

And for some that I mention, I have to admit I miss them sometimes. I considered them friends or even family. But they chose the cult over me. And that is something that we both have to live with.

I am not sure they think about me anymore even though I sadly admit that sometimes I do think about them.

Janice Case

When the accident happened, I was now being raised by both my grandfather and my Step-grandmother, Janice Case Leverette. As well as my mother.

I adored Janice. As a girl I saw her as beautiful and sleek, smart and funny. She dressed to the nines. She showed me how to wear my hair, how to speak properly, how to laugh. She taught me about horses, as we lived on a horse ranch in Georgia. She also showed horses and I kid you not, the entire living room of our tiny house was decorated with every ribbon she won. Every color, ever size, every time she placed. First, second, third. Looking back, it was all she really lived for. She taught me how to ride, how to clean stalls, and how to shoe horses. She taught me how to train them, feed them, brush them, care for them. And how to properly fear them. As a child those huge horses were scary and massive and mysterious. I needed to properly fear them so that I would not get hurt by them. Yet she did not teach me this lesson in regard to humans.

She also taught me, by her very actions, about unhealthy obsessions and habits, like treating horses better than people, alcoholism, narcissism, and complacency.

All my youth she told me stories about being and American Indian. How she grew up on the Reservation and how her heritage was something she was so proud of. She even posts photos of herself to THIS day on Facebook dressed in American Indian apparel. But DNA would prove that she was not American Indian. And with further investigation, she did not grow up on a reservation. Janice was a liar and always has been. And I am not sure if she knew she was lying. I think her brain was so messed up from alcohol and abuse that if she told a story enough times, then surely it must be true.

I absolutely adored this woman. As a matter of fact, I think that if I had had my way, way back then, I would have stayed with this woman as my mother. Janice once told me that right before my mother had begun getting her life back together after the accident and was going to get divorced from my father, that she, Janice had wanted to keep me, adopt me for her own. Of course, my mother was having none of that. But it did feel good thinking that Jan really loved me and wanted me.

My mother, however, did not like Jan. Janice was my mother's age and married my mothers' father. I am not sure if mom was jealous or she knew that her father was an abuser and that this marriage was going to be filled violence and booze, all the time. Just like my grandfather's first marriage had been.

Or that my mother had wanted a relationship so badly with her father and that Janice was getting in the way of that bonding. Hard to read what ever went on in my family.

I think Jan and my mother wanted to like each other, but as the years progressed, I saw and heard less and less of and from Jan.

Though my years with her were very short and I was very young, I had a very young girl's view of who I thought Janice was.

It was not until much later in life that I began to realize that Jan was not who I thought she was.

She was a manipulator and an alcoholic. A liar an abuser and honestly just a downright selfish human with BPD (borderline personality disorder), and a narcissistic Sociopath. Her stories changed all the time. And she is a constant victim. Everything in life was done TO her. No one understood her, she sacrificed everything for others, and she had nothing to show for it. She made everyone who she came in contact with to be her abuser. Yet she never really saw how she was just as much of an abuser as she claimed others to be.

The end of our relationship came in about the early 2000s. I had left the cult and was now living with a man that would eventually become my second husband. Jan seemed to be off her rocker most of the time. I would send her emails, for example about a gathering or party we went to and show her a photo of how we were dressed. She started replying to my emails with the rudest comments. How can you go to parties with a man you are not married to? Why do you always dress in black you look ridiculous, put some color on. No one understands you WA people with your dark colors. Then it was why don't you read more books, why don't you come back home more, why aren't you appreciative of what I did for you.

Mind you at this point I had not lived in or near the state of Georgia for over 30 years. So, my relationship with her, or at least one I was trying to maintain, was a very long distance. And it was getting more and more abusive. In 2008 when Barack Obama was up for election for President, I was on vacation in Italy and there was a long email thread with a ton of people that I did not know, on the thread. It was a racist email about how there is no way a black man should be in the white house and some more nonsense. I replied all to the email and scolded every person on there for their racist and hate filled comments. Janice came unglued with me. She started sending me email about how dare I reply all to an email, though that is what everyone was doing in that thread, how dare I support a black man, how dare I do not understand that a black man was going to ruin America, unhinged, unhinged. UNHINGED.

For a couple of years, I tried to maintain a relationship with Jan. Emails, phone calls, visits to Georgia to see her and her new husband. But she got more and more abusive, and I eventually had to cut ties with her. The final straw for me was an email she sent to me telling me that I had ruined her life because she had to spend so many years raising me after the accident and that I was never grateful for that. And she could never get those years back. I was literally a 3-month-old baby who did not make any choices of her own during that time. She blamed me for something that wasn't even partially my fault.

Imagine if you will, here I am out of the cult, I have lost everyone, including my mother to the cult, and the only woman that I needed at this point, the one woman that I adored and admired, was now turning against me and being my abuser. She was literally telling me that I owed her everything and that if it wasn't for me then she would have had a better life. Though she had already told me that she loved me so much that she had wanted to adopt me.

I was very confused and deeply hurt. Though it had been years of this wishy-washy crazy relationship, one that I deeply wanted to save, one that eventually, with tears and a broken heart, I painfully and yet happily, ended.

I stopped sending emails or calling or sending cards or coming to visit. I sent her a letter letting her know how much she had hurt me but that I could no longer get my heart broken by her. She never responded and that was that.

When my mother was dying, I did try and call her to let her know. She answered the phone and immediately turned the entire situation on herself. How could she possibly be expected to come out to Washington to go to a funeral when no one understood how important her life at home was and that she always made every sacrifice for everyone else, and no one did anything for her. Unhinged.

I said you are welcome to come out if you want but I just wanted to let you know she was dying. Her response was that she did not care and she did not want to hear my tears. Click.

She then called me one more time while I was in the parking lot of the gym and said something to the effect of why no one had called her to tell her when the funeral was and who was going to be paying for her to come out. And she needed Xanax to get on a plane but that she had too much anxiety and would not be coming out after all. And that we were all thankless for everything she had done for us anyway. Unhinged, once again.

There was of course more, way more to talk about my life with her, my years with her, my sad but hopeful attempts to keep this relationship alive. But just like she does to everyone else, I no longer wanted to give her too much space in my head or my book.

This woman that I had once admired and spent years giving my heart to, and deeply loved, was now just another person who I was no longer speaking with, and she doesn't even care. Just another abuser that I left in my past.

She will die alone and because of her selfishness and misplaced anger, it will be no one's fault but her own.

I do not remember why but there came a point when I was being watched by another woman after the accident, as I got older, 5 or 6. She was an older German woman. Today I call her my godmother because of the fond and educational memories I have of her.

She was part of the church as well. She and her husband Bill were some of the kindest people I knew. She treated me with utmost love and respect. And she treated me like an adult, not a child. She was stern but fair, soft but unyielding.

She had a garden and taught me how to plant seeds like corn, green beans, carrots. How to pick the bounty when it was ready. How to prepare it, like snapping beans and washing them for cooking or for freezing.

She taught me how to crack and egg, how to make pie crusts, pies with fresh fruits. How to read a recipe. How to measure ingredients. How to iron handkerchiefs and how to sew things like buttons and darn socks.

She grew huge sunflowers, and we would spend hours picking the seeds to save and plant for later. Or to roast and salt and snack on just for us.

Because we lived in the south, we had fireflies. She would help me get a big Mason jar ready by poking small holes in the top and catching fireflies and waiting until the sun went all the way down to watch them light up that old jar. And to let them go when we were done so as not to harm them.

She taught me to ride a tricycle and to crochet.

She also was tough with me. If I was rude, she would scold me. If I was selfish or needy, she sat me down to talk about changing my attitude. She was also the soap in the mouth if you lie person. That I might proudly say, only happened to me once. I'm not a slow learner but sometimes a painful one.

She never raised her voice, but I knew when things were serious.

She was one tough woman. She had been in a terrible car accident in 1967 and one of her lungs collapsed. As she told it the doctors wanted to remove it and she said, "hell no". And with naturopathic remedies and time she says her lung reinflated and was healthier than ever. She loved her naturopathic medicines. My mother thought she was a bit crazy.

When I was young, I had constant sore throats. CONSTANT. It seemed nothing stopped them. Well Rose was having no more of that so at the non-consent of my mother, Rose decided to take me to her naturopath. I will never forget the disgusting tart taste of this heavy red liquid he gave me. He tilted my head back and slowly dripped it down my throat. It was disgusting. Then he gave us a huge jar of it to take home and to take every day until it was gone.

It was our secret, Rose and I. I was not to tell my mother anything about it. For a whole week we poured that tart sticky cold liquid into my mouth. I cannot tell you what happened next but 50 years later I can tell you that I do not remember a single sore throat after that week. NOT ONE. Except when I had strep back in 2015. Otherwise, I am sore throat free. I call it a miracle or that Rose was magic. Did not matter she was everything to me.

She loved me up to the day she died. She never judged me, never abused me, only had my best interest at heart all the time. She never used the church against me, never said she would only love me if.

I do not remember her being a big hugger, but I do remember her big laugh, her kind heart, her patience and her big smile with one missing tooth on top.

I remember her with nothing but fondness and a large smile on my heart.

Janice Kirby

When we moved to Arizona from WA state, I knew no one. We went to Phoenix, then Phoenix to Tucson. My mother made friends with a few females in the church. One of them being a young woman named Janice.

Janice and her husband Rod were a very young couple. They had no children and they lived in a trailer not far from the one we lived in. I used to walk to and from school every single day alone. I stayed many long afternoons alone. Janice did not really like that much and since she was at home a lot, she offered for me to come to her place after school and she would watch me and or keep me company. That ended up being pretty life changing for me. Her and her husband Rod were literally some of the nicest people I knew. They were young too so they listened to all kinds of cool music, we baked together, we just had a ton of fun. They kind of took me under their wings.

I have these memories that I used to think were from times with my parents, but after many years I was contacted by Janice and we reconnected in Arizona. I stayed with them in their home for a few days. We had many years of things to catch up on. Why we moved, what had happened to us, my mother's death.

And as I walked through my memories with her and her husband and I saw trinkets in their home, and old photos of me, and vinyl's. So many vinyl's. I realized many of the amazing memories I have as child in Arizona were memories I made with Rod and Jan. Not with my own family.

Music, food, laughter, hugs. All memories with them and from them.

I cannot emphasize enough how broken my heart was when we left Arizona, and I did not hear from them again. And it was not the days of social media. Of course, I could have reached out to them. Even if they had still been in the cult, which they were not, I assume they would have still welcomed me with open arms. That's just the kind of wonderful people they were to me, are to me.

When Jan emailed me, she said they still called me "their little Angela". Oh, my heart was so happy to hear from them. I teared up actually thinking about all the years I had wasted not seeing them, talking to them.

It was an amazing few days of getting to know them again. Reminiscing about my family, the time we lived in Arizona and all the bad things as well as the good that we remembered about living there and being with them. My family's dysfunction. The birth of their children and one of my sisters.

They told me stories about how my parents had the reputation of being partiers and drinkers. Yeah, I thought that's pretty much how I remembered them too.

They were still the kind, sweet, people that helped guide and change my life.

Robin Wartman

When we lived in Arizona there were so many older women that became such an influence on me. Mostly because none of my moms' younger friends had kids. I was the only one for many years and so many of them took me under their wing and treated me with such love and kindness. They knew I was with a stepparent, about my mom's past, that we had moved from the south to be in Arizona. I am not sure that they knew everything, but I did not care, these people became everything to me.

Robin, as it turned out, I would consider her one of my best friends. She was 10 years older than me, married. Looking back, I now know that when I was 9, she was only 19 and had been married since she was 16 years old. I did not think much of that then, but years after Robins death I knew that she got married so young because her stepfather, her 2nd stepfather I believe, had been sexually abusing her and her sister Connie. And as she put it, her husband Steve wouldn't leave her alone, he kept begging her to get married. Marriage is what saved her from her homes abuse, but her demons were deeper than that.

Her sister Connie got married when she was 15.5 because she too was being sexually abused by their stepfather and as far as I know they just let these girls get married instead of having the abuser arrested. They too were in the cult.

Robin was kind and funny and beautiful. I loved her so much. She always smelled like coconut hand cream. Anything coconut today reminds me of Robin.

She used to stand up for me when my mother would be rude or abusive. She used to always take my side when things weren't going right. She treated me like an adult, an equal.

Her and her husband and at the time her first child, Wesley, moved to WA state around the same time we did. 1979 or 1980. Things just went downhill for her then. She had a 2nd child, a girl, Jessica.

Looking back on things I remember everything regarding her was awkward. She spent tons of time alone, she never worked, mostly it was because she had two kids to raise, she had no education, and she was in the cult. Her husband was a decent provider and as I recall and good man and a good father.

There seemed to be so many secrets between her and my family and her husband and even those in the congregation.

Though I can look back many years after her death and see what was happening to her, back then all I could tell you is that her friends started abandoning her and so did her husband and so did the congregations.

She ended up getting disfellowshipped from the congregation. I thought it was for fornication. Come to find out years later it was for her drinking problem. So instead of helping a very sick woman they just tossed her aside like yesterday's trash.

Even my own mother, who claimed that Robin was one of her closest friends, in an instant washed her hands of her.

My sweet friend was an alcoholic and struggled most of her life with her drinking. She hid bottles all over the house. She drank and drank and drank. And though I did not see it then looking back it describes her moods, why she did not always drive, why she lived in the dark for many years, or spent her days in bed.

She was miserable and sick. She needed help and did not get it.

My mother once said, "oh Robin has MS and its none of our business how she handles it" But the truth was she was an alcoholic and she was drinking herself to death and NO ONE, as far as I knew, was helping her. They instead were letting her get sicker and sicker and then just cutting the cord and letting her die.

Her own husband just divorced her. The congregations that preach love and kindness and that they will help you no matter what your circumstances, they just let her die.

My own mother just said she needs to just get over it and just serve god. Yes please "just get over" being an alcoholic. That's not actually how it works.

She was an alcoholic and no one seemed to think that she needed help. Immediate help.

Instead, her life was cut short because of her disease.

Right before she died, I remember telling my friend, who happened to be Robins niece, that we needed to go visit her. She was in a sort of nursing home/hospice place because her body was shutting down from her drinking. I had this awful feeling that Robin did not have much time to live and as it turns out I was right.

So, we went to where she was staying in this awful, urine smelling, cold, cold, damp building with a few beds and very sick people. Robin immediately recognized me and we hugged and I told her how much I loved her.

A couple weeks later her boyfriend had snuck a case of wine into her room and she literally drank until she went into a coma. Then a few days later she was taken off life support.

In April of 2004 Robin, at the age of 46 she had literally drunk herself to death. (Figure 34 Angela and Valerie photo)

I felt ashamed for many years after I left the cult because looking back, I did not help her. I too just let her fade into the background as the church dictated, we should do. Instead of encouraging us in the congregation to actually help our fellow friends we just turn our heads the other way and hope we do not get swept up in the storm. The church is NOT equipped to be doctors or nurses or specialists of any kind. It is unacceptable that their only advice for someone who has a disease, is just to pray more, read the bible more, be a better Christian.

Her death is as much on their hands as it is on her own families.

My memories of Robin were of a fun woman who went camping, hiking, taught me to laugh, to treat my skin with great care, always moisturize. She loved music and hair care. She danced, she laughed, she had a beautiful soul, and she was my friend. She was my sweet kind friend. And to this day when I hear her favorite song, or smell a certain smell, all my memories of her come rushing back.

Valerie Aleta

Now here is an interesting one because Valerie and I are the same age. We met when we were around 12 years old. She too was in the cult with me. We attended the same congregation and the same schools.

Her mother was single most of the time. She did have two stepfathers, one that was mentally damaged from being a Vietnam Vet and another that even as I remember him, was a complete blowhard jerk, who as Valerie put it, purposely made her life miserable and who turned out to be an abusive human who treated his wife terribly. And this particular situation, when her mother wanted to divorce, and the elders basically told her that she could not divorce and had to stay with this abusive human, this was when Valerie decided this cult was no longer for her. She could not justify people telling a woman that she had to stay with an abusive man.

But Valerie was much more to me than just a friend. She was someone I truly looked up to. She was smart, funny and independent. Independent, THAT was the key. She did not take shit from anyone. She was paving her own way. At least that's how my young memory remembers her. She left the cult way earlier than I did. I think at age 13 was when she had enough. At least in her mind and heart at 13 but after graduation, she was out.

She talked about going to college as far back as I can remember. And though she was baptized into the church, she just went ahead and went her own way. And for some reason she did not seem to be on the radar of the elders like me or others were so I think her transition out was just easier.

She left for Germany after high school. Got her degree, got married and had a couple kids. She came back to America and though we saw each other a couple of times, it wasn't until I had fully left the cult that we actually began to reconnect.

She came to my 50th birthday party. Has been to my home a few times and now we are starting to really connect. We talk about our youth, our mothers, our time in and outside the cult. I was in the cult for many years longer than she was and sometimes I fear that I talk too much about the things that we all went through. But she is gracious with me.

One memory in my life is one of the very first ones I have of moving to Washington state. I was in the 5th grade. There was going to be a field trip. Now mind you my mother only allowed me to go on field trips if another Jehovah's Witness in my class was going to be going. Mother trusted no one, especially not me.

This trip was a day trip on a boat around Puget Sound. We would get to fish and drag the bottom of the ocean for Mussels. We would cook the mussels on the boat. Learn about boats, geology, water, marine biology and the like.

That trip was a big deal for me because I was new to the area and I had never been on the ocean before. And I loved to socialize.

Valerie was going and so my mother forked over a couple bucks and let me go.

I learned so much on that boat that day, much more than I ever realized until much later in life.

Valerie and I were just talking about it a few weeks ago at lunch. And she said that trip for her too was a big deal because she learned that there was so much more to life than just the isolated cult and its shallow teachings. There were boat captains, fishermen, marine biologists, chefs.

When you grow up in a cult, as I have previously alluded to, you are so isolated as to what goes on in the world. You are even isolated to possibilities when it comes to careers.

Even though it might not seem like a huge deal to mention Valerie in my book and I have certainly done it or her no justice here. Her friendship to me even though it was brief when we were young, it shaped and changed how I looked at life. And though I did not act on those idea until much later, Valerie is a big reason that I did.

I am so honored that she is back in my life, sharing our old age together and making new memories with a shared past that in my opinion helped shape that bond.

When you grow up without hope or love you cling to the smallest things and they can change your life in the end.

Figure 34 Angela and Valerie photo

Sheila Kendrass (name changed)

I almost wrote a whole chapter about this particular "friend" but then I decided I was giving it too much head space. Why? I couldn't tell you. I think it is because in some ways, she broke my young heart.

As with Gina I truly believe that this person was my friend. She even tried to fix me up with her brother who by the way was not a Jehovah's Witness and who in the end became a criminal, spent time in jail, tried to stalk me for years and was sexually aggressive.

Sheila had a very high opinion of herself. But I found her to be smart and beautiful and I thought that our friendship was solid. I thought I could trust her with my deepest secrets. And though she did trust me with a few of her deep dark secrets as kids, she ended up like many in that time of my life, to not be a friend at all.

She wrote me a letter once, I guess we were 13 or so, telling me that we could no longer be friends because she was black and I was white and that she needed to have more black friends because her parents thought she had too many white friends.

Now back then, in a cult, with forced friendships, it did not occur to me that people had different color skin. I mean of course I knew they did but we were not allowed, at least I thought, to dismiss friendships based on skin color. I guess it just did not occur to me that people walk away from friendships because of that. In the real world today, in my 50s I can see this happening over and over again. Not in my actual life, but in the world around me.

But growing up in a cult that tells you that everyone is your friend, inside the cult, no matter what, a letter stating, I was too white to be her friend, baffled me. And deeply hurt me. It is not like I could change that part of myself to suit her needs.

I was enchanted by Sheila. Her confidence, her freedoms that her parents gave her. Her beauty.

Even though I kept her secrets back then like when she snuck out of the house to go to parties with her older brothers' friends, and to attend prom with a boy who was not part of the church, which was a strict no no. Her stories of being raped by her brothers' friends. Her pregnancy out of wedlock that led her to forcibly marry a loser. I literally kept her secrets my entire life. I am not sure if it ever occurred to her that I was keeping them even up to this book writing, a loyal friend. Something she proved not to be to me. Not ever really.

She even made fun of me sometimes. I guess I used to take it because she was my friend. And I was used to being made fun of at home and at school.

Even her mother was rude to me. She told me I was ugly that I needed better clothes that my teeth needed to be fixed. (Lets be clear they did) Her parents also hated my parents. And it was odd I remember her mother defending me when my mother was abusive to me but not liking me on a regular basis. Maybe it was because I was "too white" for her daughter. But let's be clear I did not have a clue what that actually meant.

I was deeply fixated on this girl/woman. I think I put her on a pedestal even though she was far from perfect. I remember some fun times we had, how her independence shaped my thoughts and how in the end she just walked away from me not once, but many times. Until the last time in 2006 when I left the cult for good. I literally have heard nothing from her since.

I supported her through all her trials, her rape, her pregnancy, her marriage, her divorce, her remarriage, her crisis of god, her embarrassing criminal brother.

And she just easily walked away from me.

After I left the church, I thought about Sheila for years. But I am not sure that she and many of those "friends" back then, ever thought about me again. I was deeply touched by my memories of these people and they shaped my life in many ways. But to them I was just another person who left god and will die in a fiery Armageddon.

Karen Brown

This was an unlikely friendship. When I first met Karen, I did not like her and I felt that her friendship was being forced on me. She was a couple years younger than me and I remember that she still liked playing with dolls and I was way to mature for that.

She was awkward. She had asthma and was sick a lot. She lived in a very small town and I mean small, like 100 people, small.

I cannot say that I actually remember how we became friends but, in my head, it seems like it just kind of happened.

She was in the cult with me but her parents were way less strict than mine. Her mother was dealing with deep depression for many years. And it was because of her mother that I began to wonder if women in the cult are just going to all "get" depression and live a terrible life before they die. All due to the abuse of that cult.

Karen and I enjoyed many years of friendship. I used to drive 3 hours from my home to hers most weekends just hang out with her and gossip like most of us did those days.

Karen loved school and she loved to read. Two things I was very bad at. But we shared our love for music and our love for clothes and shopping. Her parents allowed her to go to senior prom. My parents did not.

Her parents adopted her a sister who eventually grew up not being part of the cult and living her own life.

It was because of Karen that I met Delano. The one with (cough) the animal problem.

Karen got married and I did not attend the wedding because at the time I was already having a crisis of religion and it seemed most things in my life were being questioned. And make no mistake no matter how close you were to a friend; you never knew if you could trust them with your deep dark secrets especially if it had to do with the cult.

Karen and I used to pop sparkling cider and ring in the new year at her home most years. I thought it was naughty and fun and something I deeply looked forward to. A secret I thought she might one day not keep.

She was the one who caught Jerry and I one night in her living room while he was sexually assaulting me. BUT instead of asking if I was ok she said that she was so bothered by what she saw that she would probably tell on me if I did not confess my sins.

I of course had done nothing wrong and was assaulted by my boyfriend but because of the views and values of the church, which as I have stated creates victims and does not take the side of a victim, she felt that it was her obligation to tell on me. She in a way was supporting the abuser and not her friend the victim. It is a cult thing.

As far as I know, she never did tell anyone. I never told anyone and my life just kind of moved forward. I wondered if she had known about all the abuse I had been through as a girl if she would have taken my side as an ally or victim blamed like she had that one evening? And to be clear

I needed her as my ally because the sexual abuse from my boyfriend at the time was ramping up, but I decided I could not trust her, so I never did.

I think about Karen often. I do not think she has had any children and I know she lives back in that small town that she grew up in, with her husband.

It has been over 20 years since we have spoken. Though both of her parents are now passed, I did reach out on social media to just tell her how sorry I was for her loss. And to her credit, she thanked me and we shared a couple of memories. But that was all.

Update, these past few days, she and I have now spoken on the phone. She now lives in Florida, has left the cult for similar reasons as I and our conversation was so easy and familiar, and I had forgotten how much I loved this woman. I was very tearful and deeply touched when she told me she missed me and loved me. As with some from my past, I have to give them grace because they too were trapped in an abusive cult and only did or acted the way they were being told to. I look forward to making new memories and sharing our old ones together as older women.

Sherri Krahn

I was living in Phoenix when I met this family. Sherri was the mother, and she had 3 daughters. She was part of the cult but her husband was not.

He was a very mean man. He yelled at his family all the time. He even had a huge room full of fish tanks, with tons of different fish and one was filled with Piranhas. If he did not like something his daughters did, he would even feed their fish to his Piranhas. He would even threaten to stick our hand in the Piranha tank if we did not obey him.

He was obese and disgusting. I hated going to their house when he was home.

One evening I was having dinner with them; it was spaghetti and I used to love spaghetti as a kid. It was not something my mother usually cooked. Anyway, a long noodle in my mouth, I slurped it up and BAM this man started screaming at me.

He was saying how tacky I was and how I would never be allowed over there again and that no one trained me how to eat my food properly. I swear I cried for days.

I was just a kid, maybe 8 or 9. He was terrifying. BUT his wife was not.

She was so kind to me all the time. And she used to do these fun things for the kids in the congregation. Like have afternoons where she would teach us how to sew, or bake. I learned how-to put-on buttons, how to make a basting seam, how to thread a needle, how to use a thimble, how to darn a sock. Actual useful things that to this day, I use. I just loved her.

She was soft spoken and kind, all the time. Especially to me. I remember many summers at her home with her kids. We would swim until we were waterlogged, almost every day. If I remember correctly, it was Sherri who convinced my mother to allow me swim lessons at the local pool so that I was more confident in the water. To my mother's credit, she allowed that, and that was one of the best summers of my life.

I think years later she divorced that abusive man, or he died of a heart attack because of his weight. I lost touch with her and her daughters after we left Arizona. But as small as it seems, her kindness and the things she taught me with love, have left a very deep indent in my heart.

Elizabeth Dolier (name changed)

I met her and her husband in 1974 while living in Arizona. She was actually the sister-in-law of Robin, who I previously mentioned.

She was part of the cult as well. For a while she was friends with my mother and then we all moved and things changed a bit but in the end her and my mother remained friends until my mother's death in 2010.

Elizabeth and her family moved to Washington state as well. I think a bit before us, but I cannot remember exactly.

Elizabeth was an interesting one for me and I almost did not put her in the book, though she was pretty much always a part of my life until I left the cult in 2006.

And to be clear before I write anymore about her, I loved Elizabeth to death. I looked up to her and I adored her. And there were many times in all my years knowing her that she stood up for me and I felt she loved me unconditionally. AND she was one of the ONLY ones at my mother's memorial service that even acknowledged me and hugged me and told me she loved me and how sorry she was for my loss. But as with most it was fake love. Love with conditions. Though I do not want to think that I want to think that her love for me was genuine. Perhaps it was but she was too attached to the cult to see how it was ruining her and her relationships.

To me Elizabeth had such potential in life but she wasted every second of it on that cult. I wasn't sure if she was afraid of what the real world would bring or if she truly, in her heart believed everything she was being taught. To me she seemed way smarter than that.

Once while living in Arizona Elizabeth had picked me up from school and I was so proud to tell her that I did not salute the flag with the other kids that day, but I was allowed to hold the flag while the kids saluted it. Knowing what you now know about the cult, you understand that my behavior too was very bad and something the cult would deeply frown on. To Elizabeth credit, she laughed and laughed at that story and even up to the last time we spoke that was a story that she continued to tell about me with great fondness I think.

My mother claimed they were friends, but I am not sure that my mother liked Elizabeth that much. She certainly did not like Elizabeth's habits. Like not having enough money for food but spending hundreds of dollars on a bottle of wine. Borrowing money from my parents often, though she seemed to have money for things that were unnecessary. Elizabeth got pregnant over and over again because her husband did not think it was necessary to put on a condom. Elizabeth did not believe in vaccinating her children, for whatever reason even my mother was baffled. Elizabeth, consciously or not, treating others as if she was always better than they were. I think it was to cover up the embarrassment of her constant poverty, but I can only guess years later. Though I always thought she was too good for a cult.

My mother certainly had a love hate relationship with Elizabeth's husband, who worked just enough over the years to keep a roof over their heads but keep them impoverished. They eventually had three children they could barely afford.

I was not sure why Elizabeth stayed in the cult and why she stayed with her husband. I loved him deeply, but he was a terrible father, and a terrible husband. He allowed one if not all of his children to be sexually abused and then he would golf with the abuser or welcome him into his home for dinner. I am not sure how long he knew about the abuse, and to be clear, I also am not sure how long Elizabeth knew about it. But they certainly did nothing to stop it.

Though the cult fosters this kind of thinking and behavior I simply, as a parent myself, cannot imagine sweeping sexual abuse under the rug and then allowing the abuser to continue to abuse. This is not new thinking in cults. But let me be clear it is unacceptable and a crime. And when it is someone you know or have grown to know as family, disgusting and baffling.

And their thinking and lack of action also allowed this man to abuse other young girls inside the congregations. Something no one seemed too urgent to do anything about. Cults.

And my mother, she knew what was going on and she too chose not to intervene because her own thinking about sexual abuse was highly toxic.

I lost a lot of respect for Elizabeth after I found out many things about her and her husband. Though they had known me since I was a very young girl, and I have some good memories of them. Their secrets, their lack of protecting their children and their flippant way of treating others who did not suit their financial needs, was simply too much for me in the end.

I do smile sometimes when I remember Elizabeth's interesting wit and all the years we spent together. I guess I thought she might be one of those grow old together humans. Perhaps sitting on the deck gossiping over a glass of wine. Both of us sharing memories of my mother.

But I lost so much respect for her watching her stay in an abusive marriage and letting her kids or at least one of her kids be sexually abused. And she never walked out on that church or the husband who allowed ignored and even, dare I say, encouraged the abuse.

Tess Charles (name changed)

Right before I was about to publish this book, there was a woman who ended her friendship with me. Now do not get me wrong, after 17 years out of the cult it was not the first time that a friend had come and gone. And I am sure it will not be the last. And I have learned that in the real world, friendships can end because we get to make choices about who we want in our lives. Our friendships are not forced, they are in our control.

However, this particular one, when it was over, I felt ashamed of myself for allowing this friendship to last as long as it did. And it is not as if my husband did not warn me, more than once, that this was probably going to end badly.

And her words to me when it ended were pretty hurtful. And most of it was lies, projection, abuse and word salad. Her emails to me were nothing but revisionist history. She was apparently living a completely different friendship than I was living for many years. She threw one of her classic tantrums, that I had seen many times before, and blamed me for things that she herself was doing. I began to see quickly why she had zero real friends in her life and why she could never keep a boyfriend. Did I say zero friends?

I was the boiled frog. I jumped into the water with both feet and as the years went on, the water began to boil, and I was boiling along with it.

Once things ended, I began to see red flags all over this relationship. Wait, I saw red flags along the way, but ignored them. Her stories of abuse, over and over again by one man or another. Her paranoia of everyone and everything. Her lack of friendships. Tess's need to be in control of every situation, from driving, to where we ate or had tea, to music, to conversations, to gatherings.

Even today when I hear a song that I like I think, wow it is nice to listen to this band or song without being told that I was not allowed to because SHE did not like it. Or to talk about a book or a movie or show I like without being told how much she hates all the things that I like.

Everyone else in her life was wrong about everything but she never was. But let me be clear, she was wrong, a lot.

She knew everything there was about money yet made some of the worst decisions regarding finances of anyone I knew. Yet if you brought it up to her, you surely did not know what you were talking about. She was right and you were wrong, again.

Other people sued her because *THEY* were crazy. When the reality was, she was simply unhinged.

She was the smartest and best read of everyone. We are all morons, and she was not. No need to read books, she already knows everything. No need to watch or listen to politics because she already knows everything going on, though she never watched or read the news. I take that back; she did like a conspiracy theory thrown in here and there.

She was the best and brightest in her school. She had the best grades, everyone else was a moron.

She hated all men but loved them at the same time. All men were idiots, unless they wanted to fuck her. And she used sex as a weapon. Luring men into her home and life with promises of unreasonable sexual fantasies, then once she had them hooked, she then began to abuse them and take advantage of them. Then she quickly turned on them and called them abusers.

Anyone who enjoyed happy hour at a bar or restaurant was automatically an alcoholic or cheating on their partners.

She carried a gun everywhere she went, because she was literally afraid and paranoid of everything coming around the corner. Everyone was out to hurt or kill her.

She used to scream at delivery drivers and wait staff, customer support staff and airline employees. She was abusive to her kids with her words and deeds and though it was not until the end that she abused me with her words. Looking back in many ways she was abusing me and using me repeatedly. But she was sly, not unlike the way my mother used to treat me.

I knew and felt that there was dysfunction. Her life stories, some of them made zero sense to me. And though some of her boyfriends were not great people, I am sure that their tales to me about her abuse and tantrums, were not far from the truth. BPD or Manic disorder, she put it on full display as soon as I called her out on some of her behaviors, she was having none of it. And it was I who was the nut, the abuser, not her.

I had some fun times with her. I really did but, in the end, she just used me like she did every man she came across. She used me for money, for connections, for friendship and for control.

She even had the audacity to say that my stories of my abuse and growing up in a cult were not true because they could not be verified. I see so now that you have been called out on your own abusive behaviors you turn your vile abusive talk onto me. Dismissing my life, my past.

I recommended she seek therapy once just an attempt to help her through some of her past trauma. She said she had been to therapy for years. I wanted to say well then, your therapist was not very good at his or her job. It seemed if that was true that she was not actually helped by therapy as many people are. But according to her daughter, she had never actually been to therapy because she knew more than any therapist and therefore no therapist could help her.

Trust me, therapy would have been exactly what she needed.

My lessons from this one are that no matter how many years outside a cult I have been, humans are complicated. And abuse comes in many forms, and we can even fall back into patterns with abusive people, no matter how much therapy we have had or how many great people we have met along the way.

I believed I had full control over making healthy decisions regarding this friend. I failed miserably. I failed my own instincts and warning signs.

And when you grow up with a parent or both parents who are complete narcissists, sometimes you are drawn to those personalities, and you do not even recognize it. Narcissism is a creepy destructive trait. It will creep into your life and will destroy you.

Once it was over, I sat back to contemplate the years and I recognized that her behavior was exactly like my mother's. Yet to hear her tell it, she loathed my mother because of the stories I had told her. Lies, hate, tantrums, very high highs and very low lows. Blame was a very big characteristic she had. Blame me for everything wrong in her life yet not recognizing her problems are her own doing. Blame everyone else for all her woes instead of recognizing her own faults. I still feel a bit sad about not having her in my life, but I recognized, not quickly enough, that she was toxic to me and to everyone she comes around. Everyone.

I actually began to feel a weight lifted off of me when I knew the phone was not going to ring and the emails were not going to come. And that I would not be called upon to bail her out of another financial or relationship situation.

However, I do want to thank her for teaching me another lesson in life. I am sure I was way overdue for it.

~~

As I sit in my beautiful new vacation home and smile at my life, my loves my friendships my memories good and bad, I can only thank people from my past. And there were many more I did not mention in this book.

I used to be so angry at the loss of so many people and things. But as I aged and life moved forward all I could do was give grace to those who hurt me, those who left me, and I feel deep love for those who picked me up along the way and said why don't we walk forward and let the past settle itself.

HEAD OVER HEELS

"At any given moment you have the power to say, this is not how the story is going to end"

~ Christine Mason Miller

In the early fall of 1995, the year I turned 27, my life as I knew it was about to change forever. I met a woman and then.... I met a man.

But the real changes came in the year 2000. That was the year, THE YEAR. My grandfather who I deeply loved, passed away. My mother at the age of 51, told us she had breast cancer. My husband decided he no longer wanted to be a father or a husband, so he packed up and left. One of my closest friends, Nicole, her mother died from cancer. As if this was not enough, I had a heavy bookshelf fall off the wall at work and fractured my skull, getting me fired and putting me on a long path of health issues. And three years of emotional and financial turmoil due to suing this company for unlawful termination along with many sexual harassment complaints and a few other things.

I was now a single mom, with no job, no money, a mother who was literally dying due to her bad and next bad choices and I was also in love with another woman's husband.

I was beginning to see that my life was spinning out of control. And as fun as some of it was, other parts were pure torture.

I was having amazing sex with another man. I was partying and taking pills, prescription pills, I did not really need to take. Getting drunk every night and unfortunately sometimes even driving in that condition. I was getting myself into all kinds of trouble. Well, the kind of trouble that the church considered trouble.

I was throwing parties, running my mouth, flaunting my false arrogance. Getting deeper in debt and falling deeper in love with another man.

Some friends of mine, in the cult, snitched on me and blamed me for things I did not do. They said I was taking drugs, weed, and having sex with them. To be fair I kissed a girl, and I liked it, that's about it. There was not much more to tell. BUT since they were trying to save their own asses in the church they then threw me under the bus. As an engaged couple they had been having tons of sex, a no-no, and doing lots of other no nos. Sex, drugs, threesomes.

This event or non-event led me to being Disfellowshipped from the cult for the first time ever in my life. It was terrifying because one day you are one person and the next day you are another. No family, no friends, no community. THIS particular situation would, as I later understood, be one of the best things to ever happen to me. You see once I got a taste of being out of the church during those lonely months being Disfellowshipped, it was really all I wanted after that. Even though I was eventually allowed to come back to the cult, I knew from that year of being out that I did not really belong anywhere but outside of it.

But all of this was pivotal in my life's transition. All of it and it happened all at once. I do not know how to explain it all or put it onto paper properly but I'm going to do my best.

Being in a cult is deeply toxic. The weight of every decision is based solely on how the cult will feel or react to your decisions. And how you will be judged or perceived by the church and its members. How much gossip will there be, how much of your life will be out in the open. How much will you be able to take.

When I met my now husband in 1995 I knew and yes I knew at that moment, that life was never going to be the same. It took a lot of roads, turns and even some heart break to get here, for both of us but we did it. And to be clear my story is not everyone's story; my end is not how

264

everyone's ends. I understand and respect that. I keep my head clear regarding my own life story. Never forgetting where I came from and how I got here.

As the road was changing so were my views. I was tired. Really tired of pretending to be part of a cult that in retrospect, was killing me. As I mention about my mother, I believe it also had a hand in killing her. It certainly did not save either of us. Cults never save people they just use and abuse them and then toss them aside when they have used them up.

I was tired of pretending my marriage was fine, it was not. I was tired of pretending that I was happy. I was not. I was tired of fake friendships. I was tired of my mother's abuse and control. I was tired of not living my life, at all. I was tired.

Everything about life at this point seemed like a slow run. I wanted so badly to run out of my own skin sometimes and just be something else or believe something else.

I wanted real friends, I wanted to stop being judged, I wanted a real relationship with my mother, my family and I wanted a real companion.

Everything was forced. Everything. Every single day was forced friendships and forced smiles and I was tired. Of. It. All.

I thought I was a bit of a rebel my whole life. My mother used to say I had too much independent thinking. I just had thinking, I guess. And I thought there is no way that this is the end of my life. I did not fit very well in the life I was given so I thought now is the time to make a new life.

But how would I do it, seriously. I had been in a similar place before, as you read, when I left home the first time and got married, like a rebel to my first husband. But that ended poorly and left me with years of poverty and a husband that did anything but take care of his family. In laws who did not like me, more fake friends, less living, more surviving. And endless array of dread.

But I stayed on the fence as far as the church and my family was concerned and that was a problem. *THE* problem.

I wanted out of my home and married a man who was not part of the church, but the church kept pulling me back because it was all I knew. The only life I knew, was the church. The only friends I had, were in the church. I did not know how to live a life without the church and though I had rebelled by marrying a man who was "worldly" as they phrase it, I was not prepared to go full Monty out of the church.

I was young, ignorant and lost in a place where I was supposed to feel whole and welcome.

But as that year came and went, slowly things were changing for me. And I am not sure that I had a tight hold of the steering wheel or if the car was just going where it needed to go.

But after my mother's diagnosis, the family kind of went bat shit crazy. Crazier. No one agreed on how to help mom, cleaning her home, helping with things. My stepfather did not seem to be taking any of it very seriously. And my sisters and I were all at odds. I was now almost a divorced woman; my youngest sister was still living at home and my other sister had only been married a little over a year.

But on the other side of the wall as my family was trying to get closer to god because of my mother's illness, I couldn't wait to actually get out from control of the church. And would my mother die and when and if so how would that affect everything. This family was both kept together and broken apart by this woman. And by the cult.

During this time, I was trying my best to take care of my mother. After her surgery, where mind you she decided to only have the lump removed but not her breast and she refused Chemotherapy. One reason she said was because Chemo kills people not the disease. Her friend Mary had died just this same year from cancer and my mother blamed her death on the Chemotherapy instead of the fact that Mary had both lung and Pancreatic cancer that had taken over her whole body. And in my years of research, I found out that Mary and her husband Larry did not have health insurance and that she did not take care of herself, regular checkups etc. That Larry wasn't a good husband or provider or father. They were always poor and she kept popping out babies but was not being equipped to handle them or her own health properly. And the teachings of the cult about the world ending any day now did not help with this neglect.

Not that Pancreatic cancer is something that people survive. But Mary's cancer had spread to her whole body and even a small amount of health care and care from her husband may have made it so she did not die the brutal lonely death she did.

As it would be with my mother. She knew she had a lump in her breast for over a YEAR and she did nothing about it. I am not sure if she just thought it would go away or some miracle would happen, but it did not go away and it eventually spread, even after the surgery and eventually killed her. The neglect that people have for their own care and their families care because of this "Armageddon any day now" mentality is incredibly abusive and so unnecessary. And honestly deeply sad.

In my life, I was now a single mom working two jobs especially since my Ex-husband was not paying child support.

Oh yes, he was supposed to, but his checks, well they always bounced. ALWAYS.

So now I'm working two jobs, taking care of my child, keeping a home of my own, taking care of my mother and my mother's home, and seeing a married man on the side. All while still attending church services and preaching from door to door. Looking back, it was exhausting and wonderful all at the same time.

I also had a head injury that for years and I mean years, even to this day, has affected me. I lost my job after being injured on the job and it took me years to even get back to work. I had to sue the company that fired me. And I had to learn to do things like use my right hand again. I started wearing glasses because the injury had ruined some of the vision in my left eye. I used to put sticky notes all over my house to just remind me to do simple things, like brush my teeth, take out the trash.

And this so-called loving cult I was in, did nothing to help me, nothing. They did not reach out, they did not call, they did not offer food or even a shoulder to cry on. They did what they always do, leave you behind.

It was at least 5 years after my injury that I started to get back to some normalcy. All while working two jobs, and now my main job was an 11.00 an hour job instead of my well-paying tech job. I had no health insurance. I ran out of unemployment. I spent three years suing the corporation for firing me after my injury and even then, the payout was nothing as it should have been. Especially considering the way things ended and the abuse I also sustained while working at that company. When I sued them for unlawful termination I went ahead and sued them for sexual harassment as well. I had been going to HR for years about the abuse I was receiving at the company, and they did nothing to stop it. And then when I was injured, they thought it proper to just fire me because to them I was worthless. They protected and still do abusers of all kinds. Not that this is the first or only company that does that, but I was taken back by the sheer nonchalant attitude they have towards their employees. Especially those that are the lowest paid inside the corporation.

And being tossed aside without concern of my serious injury or everything I had been through those particular years. I was astonished. But looking back I remember thinking this company has treated me exactly as a cult treats its members. Toss me aside as soon as I do something or say something or think something that they do not like.

The years were ticking by and my relationship with a married man continued. But it was beginning to boil over. Its hard to keep these kinds of things secret, especially in a cult when everyone is up in your business 24/7.

His wife knew, for how long I cannot be totally sure, that her husband was cheating on her. I think she was absolutely sure in 2004 when she happened upon an email exchange that he and I had going while he was on vacation once.

We, him and I were also having an additional relationship with another woman in the congregation. That went on for over 3 years. She eventually left us and went back to the cult. Though she was fine being with us if she was getting the sex she wanted and gifts and vacations. But as soon as things started getting real, she crawled back to the cult. THEN she "confessed" her sins to the elders and my understanding is that she told them we forced her in a relationship and basically held her hostage for 3 years. Give me a fucking break. She was so happy if it was a secret. But as soon as she thought people were going to find out, then she wanted nothing to do with us. And she was also happy to play the victim and make it seem as if we somehow abused her.

Let me be clear, she knew I was having an affair with him, and she couldn't stand not being part of something like that, so she seduced him. And she was young and pretty and a virgin. I mean who wouldn't want to have that. But then she used her relationship with him to abuse and taunt me. She would tell me that her relationship with him was none of my business. She would flaunt the time she spent with him in my face. She would do just about anything to make sure that I did not have him. But in the end, she did not want him anyway, she just wanted power over me. And she loved secrecy and since she had been sexually abused for years and was in a cult that treated sex as a crime, but never actually reported sex crimes. She even moved in with me so she could have more access to him and have more sex with him without anyone being the wiser. I, looking back, cannot really blame her for acting the way she did.

But once she used us both, she was out. Then she tried to change her story to make it seem as if we somehow forced her to do things she did not want to do. That we as a couple somehow abused her, seduced her, coerced her. Sit. The. Fuck. Down.

I cannot believe anyone who knew her believed that. Even one of my sisters who was, still is, her best friend. I am sure though they have had many a laugh at our expense over the years.

She ended up not getting Disfellowshipped for her behaviors. Then a few years later married a man she had been having sex with, just so she wouldn't get disfellowshipped this time either. And that marriage ended just a few years after it started. That did not shock me one bit. She knew how to play the system and she did it over and over again.

My lover at the time, things with his marriage were coming to an end. Let me add that he had been asking his wife for a divorce for over 7 years, but she was having none of it. So instead, she stayed in the marriage, making his life as miserable as she could. She would say things like she was never leaving him, that god put them together, she did not care if he was miserable, she was never letting him go. And she once said to me that as long as she could keep living her extravagant lifestyle that she would be ok with him and I having an affair, but she was never giving up her money or her home.

In the end she ended up losing all three. Her husband, her money and her home.

But she took plenty of pills and washed them down with vodka in the early mornings. She cried a lot and got angry a lot. She tried to pull people to her side so that she could make sure she humiliated her husband as much as possible. She had a way of trying to make him feel guilty about his behaviors and decisions, but he was like me, he was out. How he would fully pull that trigger would be another matter.

Those years of him wanting a divorce many of them had zero to do with me. Honestly, he just wanted out of this marriage. And if in the end, it hadn't had been me, it would have been someone else. He was that miserable. Not only with her but with the cult as well.

So one evening in a fit of anger, he lost his temper, she called the cops, and he spent a night in jail. She immediately filed for divorce and boy what a laughable mess that was.

In her papers she was demanding that he come back to her. BUT that she would tell him who he was allowed to be friends with. What kind of car he was allowed to drive. What he was allowed to spend his money on.

She also demanded that he come back to the church and the he serves god the proper way and the way she insisted that he serve.

I am not sure who was more delusional, her or the lawyers that helped her write this nonsense.

The back and forth did not last very long because the cult was already aware of how things were playing out. Its not like she could keep her mouth shut about the matter. Victims love the spotlight.

The divorce was final in 2006. Everything ended with an explosion. As it does in a cult. In the real world, well people get divorced for all kinds of reasons. And though, yes, sometimes its messy, divorce inside the cult is as dramatic and messy as it comes.

And the gossip! What's the old Mark Twain saying, a lie gets halfway around the world before the truth puts on its shoes.

Even if you want to take a side, you always have to take the side of the person who remains in the cult. Who remains with god, their god, period.

She got the house, 1.427 million dollars, and most of the assets.

And just like we predicted she was bankrupt 18 months later. She made nothing but poor decisions regarding anything financial. She was flashy and fake and arrogant and honestly just plain dumb when it came to money management. She was having no one tell her how to manage her life or her money not even a professional. She bought condos and cars, houses and first-class tickets for herself and her friends. She did not work and the money was hemorrhaging out. Before she knew it, it was gone.

He on the other hand, though he lost most of his fortune in the divorce, had his career, his freedom and his whole future ahead of him.

Cult free. Bad marriage, over.

Because our secret or not so secret was now out in the open, we had some decisions to make. I was done with the cult and all its fake friendships and false promises. I was done with cult lies, coverups and abuse. He was done with the cult in different ways and for different reasons. But no matter, we were both free.

However, freedom comes at a cost. Freedom from a cult comes at a huge cost. The loss of your entire community, including family.

He and I had spoken many times over the years about what our lives together, cult free, would look like. We knew our community would abandon us and perhaps our families. Which mine did but his actually did not. His parents at least. They stayed faithful to the church but still loved their son very much. And though they did not approve of how things ended with his wife and that he and I were and had been together, one thing I can say for certain, they absolutely disapproved of how his wife had treated him, put him in jail and then tried to get everyone on her side by lying and building hysteria everywhere she went.

Trying to get his parents on her side. Let's be clear he was their only son, their only child, they were not going to turn their back on him and take her side regarding any of this.

And his father adored me. And as the years went on it was apparent by many conversations that his parents did not like or approve of his wife. They tolerated her for all those years because she was the wife of their only son. But his mother and father told me many a story about the things they disapproved of regarding her. Her disrespect of him, her flippant attitude regarding their relationship and her arrogant know it all attitude. That frankly is always a turn off.

The elders in the church tried to get us to talk to them about what had happened, and I said sure why not. But my partner did not feel the need to talk to them even when they came to our house to tell him that he had NO choice but to speak to them. They handed him a letter telling him the time and place he had to meet with them. And it was, as he puts it, in that moment that he realized that these men, this church only had control over him, if he allowed it. And from that moment on he was not going to allow it. He would take full control of his own life, his own decisions, period.

I went and spoke to 3 elders, and I sang like a canary about my relationship with this married man, threesomes, drinking, whatever they wanted to hear I was ready to spill. I no longer cared about the cult; I had already stayed in it too long.

However, I had an agreement with the woman we were having a sex tryst with that I would not mention what we had been doing for 3 years if she also agreed not to speak to the elders about it. We would just go our separate ways and she could just slide back into the cult and back in with her family, no harm done. This agreement was an assurance that if we ever wanted to come back to the church, we could without bringing her into it, or her bringing us into it. She, as you previously read, did not keep her end of the bargain, she tossed us under the bus the first chance she got. As if we would not be in enough trouble having an affair, a polyamorous relationship would have been too much for the cult to handle. Typical cult friendships, zero loyalty. Always cover your own ass, and do not give a shit about who you leave behind or how.

In my interrogation I think I gave these elders more than they bargained for. I simply did not know that they did not know things. And my partners now Ex wife wasn't exactly being forthright with the elders either. She told them a very different story than the one I told. Mostly because she wanted to save her ass in this whole fiasco. And honestly, she was still hoping to save her marriage.

And she loved being a victim, and I mean loved it, so she was ready to tell a story of years of abuse, how she knew nothing about her husband's affair and how she was being spiritually traumatized by it all. How embarrassed she was that people found out about his affair and how could she show herself in the congregations anymore.

Gurl please. You loved every single second of humiliating your husband and playing the victim. This was an Oscar worthy role that she was heavily invested in.

I told the elders she knew about the affair; she had known for years and she even encouraged it by inviting me over to her house frequently, going on vacations with me, treating me as a friend day in and day out.

And that I had saved chats and emails to prove that she knew. I had years of written verification. And I was more than happy to share those verifications with them if they needed or wanted me to.

They seemed shocked by this revelation because apparently, they had already spoken with her and she told them a sob story that simply put, was lies.

They wanted to disfellowship us from the congregation but on the other hand insisted that they were torn because we had finally just spilled the beans. We received no confirmation regarding their decision but when I was recently going through old paperwork, divorce papers, letters etc. there was a letter from the organization saying they had reversed their decision regarding our punishment because of new information that had come forward.

My guess was that that new information was that his Ex had lied and so had the other woman who had been part of our sexual life for a few years. They both lied, and we were once again free to live our lives.

And that was that. My family spoke to me for a while but shortly after all this blew up, my mothers cancer came back and then she died and the family went into holy roller status and the relationships would never be the same. My family, my friends, his friends, chose the cult over us. And it was as simple as that. Cut and dry. They shed no tears for us and though I did shed a few tears for losing the only life I knew, I was ready to actually live my life.

And to be clear my mother hated my boyfriend, partner at the time. She couldn't stand to be in a room with him for more than a few seconds and she loved to tell me on a regular basis how awful he was and how she couldn't believe I had done what I had done. How I embarrassed her and humiliated her on a regular basis. It was the same old conversation just a different subject.

Like everything with her, it did not matter who my partner was, how much I served her god, how many times I went to church, she would in the end never approve of or love me the way I needed her too.

Then we just moved forward with our lives. Not without a lot of learning along the way. We had now left our community and lives of 37 years. We had made enemies along the way but honestly these people had never been our friends. They never truly had our best interests at heart. They were only concerned about the cult and their own reputations. They did not want the stink of our decisions on them.

When we truly needed their support, they were, as is typical of Jehovah's Witnesses, nowhere to be found. No phone calls, no emails, no texts, nothing. To be fair, my partner did get a couple of phone calls and an email or two asking what was going on. But other than that, they all disappeared when things got tough. We knew they would, but it was still a shock.

Imagine if you will, waking up one day to a silent world. Your phone doesn't ring, your emails do not come, your relationships, all severed. Even your HVAC guy, or your Eye Dr. if they were Jehovah's Witnesses, they severe their ties, their business dealings with you.

He was divorced, I had been divorced for a few years. We lived together in a rental house while we let the dust settle on what had just transpired and talked about what tomorrow would bring. We were sure the fireworks inside the congregations, with our friends and family, not just here but all over the world were still hot to the touch. But for us it was just silent.

Though the blowback for us was both losing our community and the shock of the silence, we had each other. And for many who leave or are kicked out, they have no one, nothing. They are left dead in the water with no resources, no money, no real-world experience. So how will they make it without the toxic cult that they left? What will their tomorrow bring?

And this is the point. The cruelty is the point. Keep people trapped, uneducated, no friends outside the cult. Keep them poor, depressed, hopeless and scared. Then if they ever leave, they have very few choices so they either kill themselves or crawl back to the vile abusive cult that they have no idea to live without. And they will most likely be depressed and miserable until their dying day. Many of them dying penniless.

As the years went on, we watched our old friends and Ex spouse's crater. Bankruptcies, divorces, depression. With the help of the internet and a few people inside the cult who were on their way out themselves we could easily watch what was going on with those that threw us under the bus.

And yet while they floundered and took more prescription pills, we created a whole new life for ourselves. We bought a home, we married, we traveled the world. Little by little we began to build a new community for ourselves.

We joined clubs, met people with similar interests. My new husband's career began to take off and he was becoming more successful than ever.

We went to therapy, separately for different reasons. And we both say how powerful that was not just for us as individuals but for us as a couple.

We have buried all 4 of our parents, together. We have gained friends and lost friends along the way. But that in the real world is normal. We have learned, loved, laughed, and honestly never looked back.

For me the thought of shunning your family and friends because of a difference in belief, or difference of opinion doesn't make much sense. It is absolutely foreign to many people in the real world. I call it emotional terrorism because that's exactly what it is. Its deeply psychotic.

Yet as I have become more involved in politics for example, I have seen these kinds of behaviors in regards to sides. People will simply cut you off or stop speaking to you because your views are different.

This behavior is preposterous. It separates us, it divides us, it creates long lasting emotional damage. It breaks down the human bond and spirit. It is no different than leaving a cult because sometimes even politics can be a cult or have cult like behaviors. We see it everyday in America.

We have voted, celebrated holidays and birthdays. We have been welcomed into our friends' homes to build traditions. We get involved in politics, we have taken college courses, we have been part of hobbies and clubs, we think for ourselves, and we read continually. We keep up on local and world news and we offer opinions and views about everything and anything. We are now allowed to be who we want and think what we want. We are allowed to be ourselves and we make no apologies for it. Nor do we have to.

I had more gaps to fill in educationally than my husband did. He actually was better read than I. Some of that being that his parents did not really restrict many of his decisions. My parents, at least my mother, she restricted everything I was allowed to do. Especially if it would benefit me later in life. She restricted my education, my reading, the movies I watched, the music I listened to and the friends I chose. The clothes I wore and the opinions I had. In my family we never talked about politics or what was going on in the world. We never watched local news and we never traveled. My husbands' parents were at least a bit more balanced when it came to keeping up with what was happening in the world, local news and books.

Looking back on these last few years I think I forget sometimes how hard it all was at first. But how rewarding it all was in the end. Things you are not prepared for like making new friends, trusting people and telling your story. How you got somewhere, how much it hurt sometimes, the challenges, the loss of people and rebuilding your life when you are already half way through it.

I get asked what I regret or if I regret or what would I change. Nothing. I would change nothing.

I had hoped by this time that both of my sisters would have woken up from the cult. Perhaps they would see with their own eyes and with the help of unlimited information how destructive cults are. Especially the one they still cling to. It is easy, just a click of the keyboard to research the abuse this particular cult creates and allows. How it ruined our family and, in my opinion, had a role in killing our mother.

Living in the real world outside the abuse and mind-numbing conversations of cult members is fucking refreshing. And so liberating. It was amazing the things I had to learn and relearn once I started living my life thinking for myself and once, I realized all the nonsense the cult had filled my mind with. Not just the relationships but the actual information that they fed us each and every week. Absolute nonsense. Wrapped in their own thinking and their own misinformation. And their clever way of controlling people, dangling their salvation over their heads to keep control of them. Day after day, year after year.

As the years roll on and the cult is farther and farther behind me I can say how refreshing it is to just wake up, live my life with zero worries, zero stress and have the ultimate peace in my days. I never worry the phone is going to ring because I have offended someone or the elders want to tell me what a terrible Christian I am and how I need to come talk to them in their tiny room filled with bibles and cult literature. I never worry that someone I think is a friend will end up being someone I cannot trust. (though this has happened its just different outside a cult) I never worry that a song I like or a movie I watched is going to put the congregation into hysteria leading me down a path of abusive speech regarding my personal choices. Or that my car is too expensive or my home too extravagant. Or I have had too many glasses of wine, said the wrong thing. Or, or, or. I never worry that in the blink of a eye my community can be torn from me simply because I was human and made human choices.

My community now, knows who I am, where I came from and what I stand for. And they never ask anything of me but to be me. They love me and accept me for who I am. And they have empathy for the things that got left behind in my world, like family and so-called friends.

Though sometimes they find it hard to truly understand how my life was, our life was. They never dismiss us. And sometimes even say they cannot believe how well rounded we are for going through and coming out the other side.

There are days that I still grieve those that are living that were left behind or that left us behind. Grieving the living as I have once stated, is very hard. Almost harder than any actual death I have grieved. But we only get one life, one chance to make our mark. One chance, period. Live your life the way you choose, love those you choose to love and let others live their lives.

Never discount what someone has been through to get to the place they are. We all drop into this world with our life being chosen for us. But there then comes a time when that choice becomes ours. Take that choice and make your life your own. Do not let anyone tell you who you cannot be, who you must be, or why you are not good enough.

NOT QUITE THE END

"In the end, we only regret the chances we did not take"

Once again sitting in the salon of a Dive boat in Indonesia. Finishing many years of work, research, and sometimes uneasiness.

This book has taken me 10 years to write. I had a lot of research to do and I started with almost nothing. A small newspaper clipping, a few words and I was off.

Thankful for the internet and thankful for those who did not even know me, but helped me along this path anyway.

Old friends of family, some family and even law enforcement, the military and many many others.

When I started writing this book, I was still so angry at my mother, the sham friendships, the fake love of a community I had spent more than half my life in, the lost years of my life.

This book helped me to grow and to understand myself and those that were left behind and those that came after.

The years of research, my travels, my friends and new community that I made along the way, saved my life.

Along with the absolute best partner, friend and husband I could have ever imagined.

The support from my offspring has been deeply touching as well. They understanding me, my past, my abuse. And loving me without conditions. They never questioned me or my desire to write this book.

I learned grace, was given hope and became more grounded than I ever thought possible.

Did my years of research, anger, sweat and dead ends answer my questions or satisfy me?

I can only say that some of the puzzle was complicated. Some of my questions were answered. Some holes still exist. But they are no longer holes that are too big to jump over. They are simply small holes, no longer too large to walk over.

Along this journey, I could not decide if it was harder to leave my cult and my community or leave the abuse of friends, family and schoolmates. Was it harder to pick myself up from abuse or pick myself up from shunning? Was it harder to wake up one day and have my whole world gone? Or harder to understand that those that I loved, abused me without regret and without remorse. That those who should have protected me, did not and chose willingly not to protect me. It was no accident.

That those that are or were supposed to love you, whether it is in family or a cult, know absolutely nothing of love.

I understand my mother only slightly more. My anger towards her no longer consumes me.

I understand humans only to my personal breaking point. Learning and experiencing what a difference human beings inside a cult and humans in the real world are, sometimes overwhelmed me.

Some of the best advice I received while writing this book came from those within my new community. Three solid friends, Cheryl, Mary and Diana. All three different personalities, education, humor and backgrounds. But all three gave me something solid to hold onto. And not once were they anything but supportive of my passion to write this book. I cherish each of them and feel honored that they share my journey every day.

Did I get release? Perhaps.

What I learned along the way and dredging up some of my painful past, was that you do not have to like or approve of people, period. Its ok to say no and no thank you and fuck you. It's ok to walk away from abusers.

And that there will be those in your life that will hurt you. That you cannot trust and that will always do what they can to make your life miserable.

Just because someone is your parent it does not mean that they will love you or you them.

A parent is not always suited to be a parent. A parent does not always have the best interest of the child at heart.

A parent can be toxic and even use that toxicity to ruin their children's lives, intentionally or not.

Even if our past had abusive parents, family or friends. We can still find ourselves drawn to people like that. People with alcoholism, BPD, Depression, manic behaviors, toxic, abusive, controlling, liars.

Cults are bad, period. They rob you of your identity, youth, education, experiences, and in the end, they steal those you love away.

Thank you everyone and I mean *everyone*. Everyone who loved me. Everyone who abused me. Everyone who took me and in and everyone who tossed me aside. Everyone who laughed at me and everyone who dismissed my stories as false. Thank you for my tears, my laughter and my lessons. Thank you for letting me know I was no longer part of your journey and for some, choosing a destructive cult over me. Thank you.

I take zero of my life for granted. Nor do I dismiss that one wrong turn by everyone and anyone from my past would have sent me on another journey. So, thank you also for all your bad decisions as well.

To everyone who is part of my new community. I cannot emphasize enough how much you mean to me.

To those who came and went in the few years that I have changed my life, thank you for teaching me lessons that were new to me.

To those who helped me grow, gave me the strength to be confident, taught me about life, real life, who taught me love and loved me, who held my hand, who pulled me up, who gave me and allowed me my voice as I grew outside a cult and into the world around me.

My life has a before and after the cult. Before and after abuse. Before and after education, lessons, travels and love.

Before meet after.

DEDICATIONS

First and foremost, I dedicate this book to my husband Brad. Literally the one person who saw me, saved me and loved me better than anyone ever has. His love, patience, kindness and sometimes a little push, are exactly what I needed in my life. Thank you for showing me the world and letting me know that I too am worthy.

To my child. You certainly keep me on my toes, and your support and unconditional love make my heart sing. I deeply love your beautiful soul.

To all my old friends, the ones who abandoned me when I needed them, thank you, without your *conditional* love I would never have found a world where true love trumps all your bullshit.

To my new friends, you helped me build a whole new community. You welcomed me with open arms and though you did not always under-stand my past, you embraced my stories, and you helped me grow into a whole new, better, smarter, humbler human.

To my mother, see I told you I would do something important one day, with or without you.

APPENDIX

MASS OF WRECKAGE IS ALL THAT REMAINS OF CAR
Carried Donna Schulten and Sidney Burrell to Their Deaths

Crash Kills Cobb Be

By LYNDA BARRON
Journal Staff Writer

Three Cobb Countians, one of them Miss Cobb County of 1967, were killed in traffic mishaps over the weekend.

The dead were identified as 20-year-old Donna Ray Schulten, of 1025 Spring Street, Smyrna; Sidney Boyd Burrell, 24, of 819 Cherokee Road, Smyrna, and Ruby J. Lawrence, 59, of Route 2, Acworth.

Miss Schulten and Burrell were killed in the same wreck that critically injured 24-year-old Thomas Eugene Robertson, of 137 Stewart Street.

Robertson's 19-year-old wife, Dixie, was also injured in the crash of the 1964 sports coupe.

Both the injured are in Kennestone Hospital, where his condition Monday was listed as critical and hers as satisfactory.

The four were all in the

DONNA SCHULTEN
Cobb Beauty...

small coupe headed north on North Cooper Lake Drive near the Higavie's Drive intersection in Smyrna. Miss

Schulten was driving, officers said.

The car apparently attempted to pass another vehicle when she lost control of the car, went off the left side of the road, traveled 76 feet and struck a large tree. There were no skid marks, officers said.

The accident was reported to Smyrna police at 11:47 p.m.

Burrell was pronounced dead on arrival at Kennestone, and Miss Schulten died a few hours later of multiple injuries.

The car was left only a twisted mass of fiberglass and metal.

Miss Schulten was chosen Miss Cobb County of 1967 and was currently in Miss Atlanta competition. Burrell, with his brother Dale, operated Burrellco Machine Shop.

SIDNEY BURRELL
... Killed in Crash

Figure 1 Crash newspaper article

285

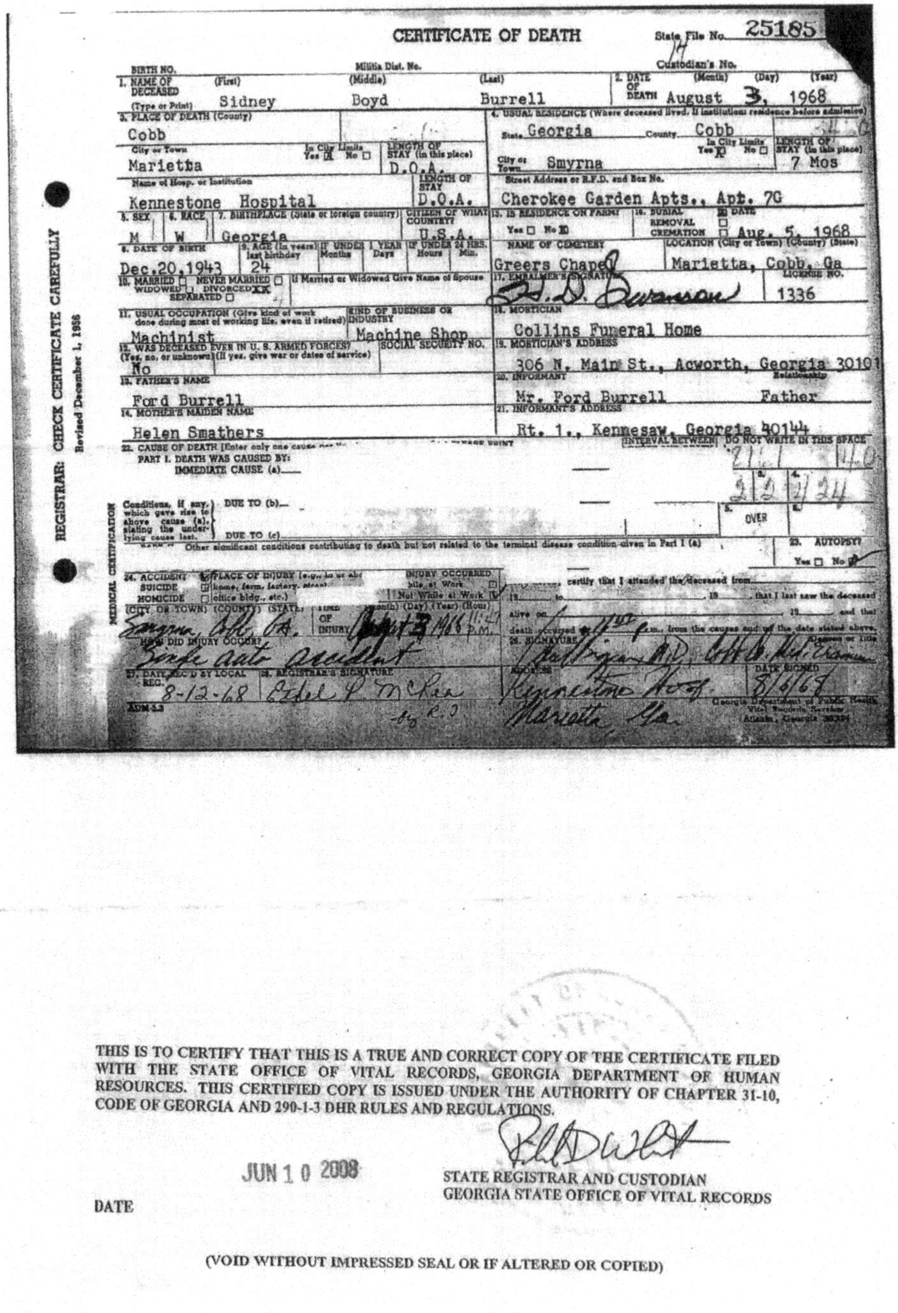

REGISTRAR: CHECK CERTIFICATE CAREFULLY

Revised December 1, 1956

CERTIFICATE OF DEATH

State File No. 25185

Custodian's No. 14

BIRTH NO.

Militia Dist. No.

1. NAME OF DECEASED (Type or Print): (First) Sidney (Middle) Boyd (Last) Burrell

2. DATE OF DEATH: (Month) August (Day) 3, (Year) 1968

3. PLACE OF DEATH (County): Cobb

City or Town: Marietta. In City Limits: Yes ☒ No ☐. LENGTH OF STAY (in this place): D.O.A.

Name of Hosp. or Institution: Kennestone Hospital. LENGTH OF STAY: D.O.A.

4. USUAL RESIDENCE (Where deceased lived. If institution: residence before admission): State: Georgia. County: Cobb

City or Town: Smyrna. In City Limits: Yes ☒ No ☐. LENGTH OF STAY (in this place): 7 Mos

Street Address or R.F.D. and Box No.: Cherokee Garden Apts., Apt. 7G

5. SEX: M. 6. RACE: W. 7. BIRTHPLACE (State or foreign country): Georgia. CITIZEN OF WHAT COUNTRY?: U.S.A.

8. DATE OF BIRTH: Dec.20,1943. 9. AGE (In years last birthday): 24. IF UNDER 1 YEAR: Months / Days. IF UNDER 24 HRS.: Hours / Min.

10. MARRIED ☐ NEVER MARRIED ☐ WIDOWED ☐ DIVORCED XX SEPARATED ☐. If Married or Widowed Give Name of Spouse:

11. USUAL OCCUPATION (Give kind of work done during most of working life, even if retired): Machinist. KIND OF BUSINESS OR INDUSTRY: Machine Shop

12. WAS DECEASED EVER IN U. S. ARMED FORCES? (Yes, no, or unknown) (If yes, give war or dates of service): No. SOCIAL SECURITY NO.:

13. FATHER'S NAME: Ford Burrell

14. MOTHER'S MAIDEN NAME: Helen Smathers

15. IS RESIDENCE ON FARM?: Yes ☐ No ☒

16. BURIAL ☒ REMOVAL ☐ CREMATION ☐. DATE: Aug. 5, 1968

NAME OF CEMETERY: Greers Chapel. LOCATION (City or Town) (County) (State): Marietta, Cobb, Ga

17. EMBALMER'S SIGNATURE: H. D. Swanson. LICENSE NO.: 1336

18. MORTICIAN: Collins Funeral Home

19. MORTICIAN'S ADDRESS: 306 N. Main St., Acworth, Georgia 30101

20. INFORMANT: Mr. Ford Burrell. Relationship: Father

21. INFORMANT'S ADDRESS: Rt. 1., Kennesaw, Georgia 40144

22. CAUSE OF DEATH [Enter only one cause per line for (a), (b), and (c).] INTERVAL BETWEEN ONSET AND DEATH. DO NOT WRITE IN THIS SPACE

PART I. DEATH WAS CAUSED BY: IMMEDIATE CAUSE (a)

Conditions, if any, which gave rise to above cause (a), stating the underlying cause last. DUE TO (b) DUE TO (c)

PART II. Other significant conditions contributing to death but not related to the terminal disease condition given in Part I (a)

OVER

23. AUTOPSY?: Yes ☐ No ☒

MEDICAL CERTIFICATION

24. ACCIDENT ☒ SUICIDE ☐ HOMICIDE ☐. PLACE OF INJURY (e.g., in or about home, farm, factory, street, office bldg., etc.). INJURY OCCURRED While at Work ☐ Not While at Work ☒

(CITY OR TOWN) (COUNTY) (STATE): Smyrna, Cobb, GA. TIME OF INJURY (Month) (Day) (Year) (Hour): August 3 1968 11:40 P.M.

HOW DID INJURY OCCUR?: Single auto accident

25. I hereby certify that I attended the deceased from ____, 19__, to ____, 19__, that I last saw the deceased alive on ____, 19__, and that death occurred at 11:40 p.m., from the causes and on the date stated above.

26. SIGNATURE: [signature] M.D., Cobb Co. Medical Examiner. Degree or title

ADDRESS: Kennestone Hosp. Marietta, Ga. DATE SIGNED: 8/6/68

27. DATE REC'D BY LOCAL REG.: 8-12-68. 28. REGISTRAR'S SIGNATURE: Ethel P. McClain

ADM-53

Georgia Department of Public Health, Vital Records Service, Atlanta, Georgia 30334

THIS IS TO CERTIFY THAT THIS IS A TRUE AND CORRECT COPY OF THE CERTIFICATE FILED WITH THE STATE OFFICE OF VITAL RECORDS, GEORGIA DEPARTMENT OF HUMAN RESOURCES. THIS CERTIFIED COPY IS ISSUED UNDER THE AUTHORITY OF CHAPTER 31-10, CODE OF GEORGIA AND 290-1-3 DHR RULES AND REGULATIONS.

JUN 10 2008

DATE

STATE REGISTRAR AND CUSTODIAN
GEORGIA STATE OFFICE OF VITAL RECORDS

(VOID WITHOUT IMPRESSED SEAL OR IF ALTERED OR COPIED)

Figure 2 Sidney Burrell certificate of death

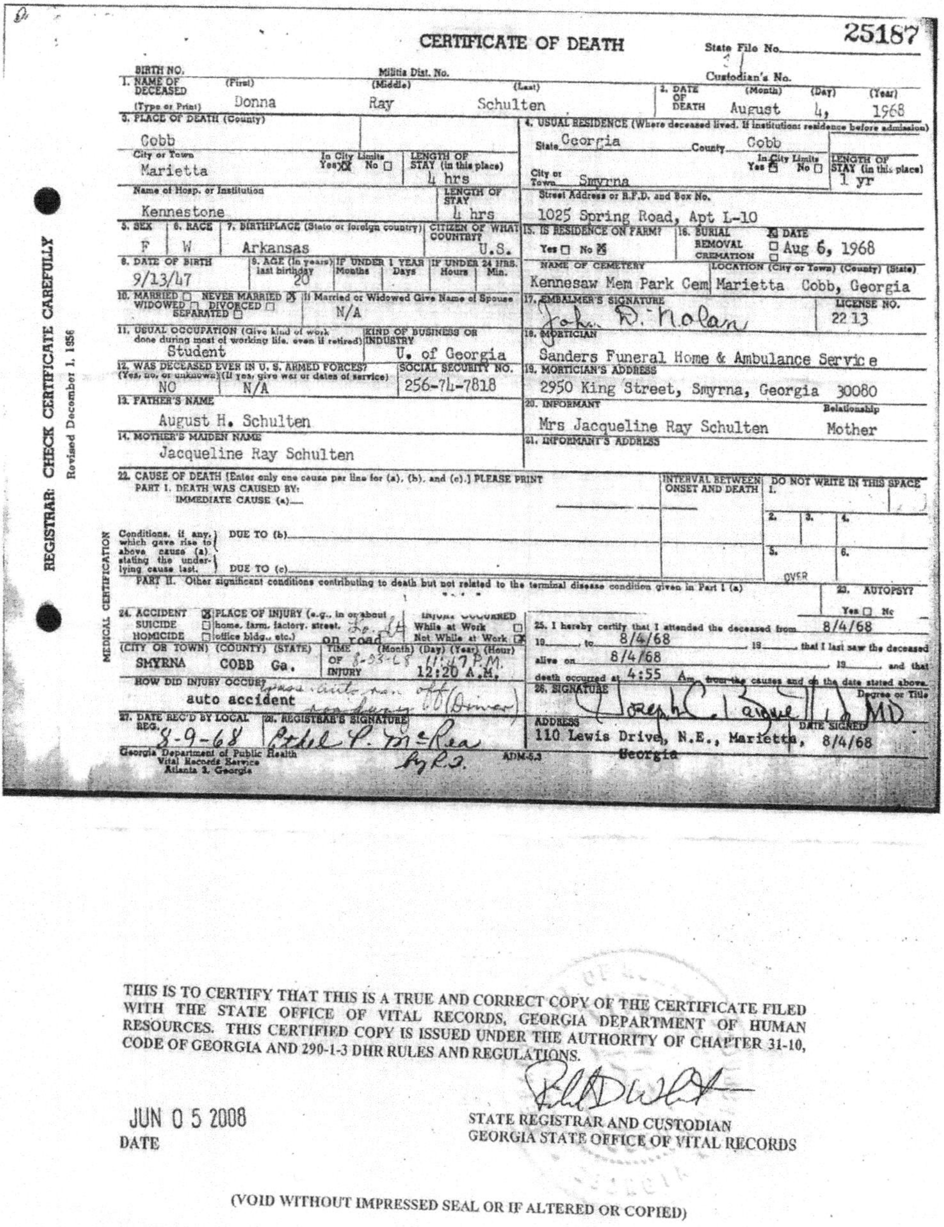

CERTIFICATE OF DEATH

State File No. 25187

BIRTH NO.

Militia Dist. No.

Custodian's No.

1. NAME OF DECEASED (Type or Print) (First) Donna (Middle) Ray (Last) Schulten

2. DATE OF DEATH (Month) August (Day) 4, (Year) 1968

3. PLACE OF DEATH (County) Cobb

City or Town: Marietta — In City Limits: Yes XX No ☐ — LENGTH OF STAY (in this place): 4 hrs

Name of Hosp. or Institution: Kennestone — LENGTH OF STAY: 4 hrs

4. USUAL RESIDENCE (Where deceased lived. If institution: residence before admission)

State: Georgia — County: Cobb

City or Town: Smyrna — In City Limits: Yes ☒ No ☐ — LENGTH OF STAY (in this place): 1 yr

Street Address or R.F.D. and Box No.: 1025 Spring Road, Apt L-10

5. SEX: F — 6. RACE: W — 7. BIRTHPLACE (State or foreign country): Arkansas — CITIZEN OF WHAT COUNTRY?: U.S.

8. DATE OF BIRTH: 9/13/47 — 9. AGE (In years last birthday): 20 — IF UNDER 1 YEAR: Months, Days — IF UNDER 24 HRS.: Hours, Min.

10. MARRIED ☐ NEVER MARRIED ☒ WIDOWED ☐ DIVORCED ☐ SEPARATED ☐ — If Married or Widowed Give Name of Spouse: N/A

11. USUAL OCCUPATION (Give kind of work done during most of working life, even if retired): Student — KIND OF BUSINESS OR INDUSTRY: U. of Georgia

12. WAS DECEASED EVER IN U. S. ARMED FORCES? (Yes, no, or unknown): NO — (If yes, give war or dates of service): N/A — SOCIAL SECURITY NO.: 256-74-7818

13. FATHER'S NAME: August H. Schulten

14. MOTHER'S MAIDEN NAME: Jacqueline Ray Schulten

15. IS RESIDENCE ON FARM? Yes ☐ No ☒

16. BURIAL ☒ REMOVAL ☐ CREMATION ☐ — DATE: Aug 6, 1968

NAME OF CEMETERY: Kennesaw Mem Park Cem — LOCATION (City or Town) (County) (State): Marietta Cobb, Georgia

17. EMBALMER'S SIGNATURE: John D. Nolan — LICENSE NO. 2213

18. MORTICIAN: Sanders Funeral Home & Ambulance Service

19. MORTICIAN'S ADDRESS: 2950 King Street, Smyrna, Georgia 30080

20. INFORMANT: Mrs Jacqueline Ray Schulten — Relationship: Mother

21. INFORMANT'S ADDRESS

REGISTRAR: CHECK CERTIFICATE CAREFULLY

Revised December 1, 1956

MEDICAL CERTIFICATION

22. CAUSE OF DEATH [Enter only one cause per line for (a), (b), and (c).] PLEASE PRINT

PART I. DEATH WAS CAUSED BY: IMMEDIATE CAUSE (a)

Conditions, if any, which gave rise to above cause (a) stating the underlying cause last. DUE TO (b) — DUE TO (c)

INTERVAL BETWEEN ONSET AND DEATH

DO NOT WRITE IN THIS SPACE 1. 2. 3. 4. 5. 6. OVER

PART II. Other significant conditions contributing to death but not related to the terminal disease condition given in Part I (a)

23. AUTOPSY? Yes ☐ No

24. ACCIDENT ☒ SUICIDE ☐ HOMICIDE ☐ — PLACE OF INJURY (e.g., in or about home, farm, factory, street, office bldg., etc.): on road — INJURY OCCURRED While at Work ☐ Not While at Work ☒

(CITY OR TOWN) (COUNTY) (STATE): SMYRNA COBB Ga. — TIME OF INJURY (Month) (Day) (Year) (Hour): 8-03-68 11:47 P.M. 12:20 A.M.

HOW DID INJURY OCCUR? auto accident

25. I hereby certify that I attended the deceased from 8/4/68 19__, to 8/4/68 19__, that I last saw the deceased alive on 8/4/68 19__, and that death occurred at 4:55 A.m. from the causes and on the date stated above.

26. SIGNATURE: Joseph C. Bague MD — Degree or Title

ADDRESS: 110 Lewis Drive, N.E., Marietta, Georgia — DATE SIGNED: 8/4/68

27. DATE REC'D BY LOCAL REG.: 8-9-68 — 28. REGISTRAR'S SIGNATURE: Ethel P. McRea

Georgia Department of Public Health Vital Records Service Atlanta 3, Georgia — ADM-5.3

THIS IS TO CERTIFY THAT THIS IS A TRUE AND CORRECT COPY OF THE CERTIFICATE FILED WITH THE STATE OFFICE OF VITAL RECORDS, GEORGIA DEPARTMENT OF HUMAN RESOURCES. THIS CERTIFIED COPY IS ISSUED UNDER THE AUTHORITY OF CHAPTER 31-10, CODE OF GEORGIA AND 290-1-3 DHR RULES AND REGULATIONS.

JUN 0 5 2008

DATE

STATE REGISTRAR AND CUSTODIAN

GEORGIA STATE OFFICE OF VITAL RECORDS

(VOID WITHOUT IMPRESSED SEAL OR IF ALTERED OR COPIED)

Figure 3 Donna Schulten certificate of death

Donna Ray Schulten

Photo added by N S Ferguson

Added by N S Ferguson

BIRTH 13 Sep 1947

DEATH 4 Aug 1968 (aged 20)

BURIAL Kennesaw Memorial Park
Marietta, Cobb County, Georgia, USA

MEMORIAL ID 21600040

Obituary - Marietta Daily Journal - Monday, August 5, 1968

Donna Ray Schulten, 20, of Smyrna, died early Sunday in Kennestone Hospital from injuries suffered in an automobile accident.

Survivors in clude parents, Mr. and Mrs. August H. Schulten Jr. of Smyrna; one sister, Jacqueline Esther Schulten of Smyrna, paternal grandmother, Mrs. A. H. Schulten Sr. of North Little Rock, Ark.

Miss Schulten was a native of Little Rock, Ark. She moved to Smyrna 11 years ago from Memphis, Tenn. She was a 1965 graduate of Campbell High School where she was active in school clubs and other activities.

She was chosen Miss Cobb County in 1967 and was first runner-up in the 1968 Miss Independence Day of Cobb County. Miss Schulten was a junior at the University of Georgia, where she was majoring in education. She was an officer in Delta Gamma Sorority and was elected to the court of two University of Georgia fraternities. She was homecoming representative from Oglethorpe Dormitory at the University and was an entrant in the forthcoming Miss Atlanta Contest.

Inscription

Our Darling - Delta Gamma Sorority

Created by: N S Ferguson
Added: 17 Sep 2007
Find a Grave Memorial ID: **21600040**
SPONSORED BY Gigi M. Jackson (Jerry)

Figure 4 Donna Schulten grave site

Photo added by Wendell Way

Sidney Boyd Burrell

BIRTH 20 Dec 1943

DEATH 4 Aug 1968 (aged 24)
Georgia, USA

BURIAL Greers Chapel Cemetery
Kennesaw, Cobb County, Georgia, USA

PLOT Row 10, Lot 3, Grave 4

MEMORIAL ID 28282502

Sidney died in an automobile accident on the 4th of August, 1968. He has a son and an a brother who he was very close too. Though i did not know him personally his death has touched my life very deeply for 40 years.

You are missed by your family and friends and those who have wished to know you from a distance.

This year will be 40 years since your death and I know you are thought about daily.

▲

Figure 5 Sidney Burrell grave site

Randall Wilkins

Death • United States Social Security Death Index

Name	**Randall Wilkins**
State	**Georgia**
Residence Place	**Georgia**
Last Place of Residence	**Hall, Georgia**
Previous Residence Postal Code	**30501**
Age	**23**
Birth Date	**17 Jan 1953**
Death Date	**Nov 1976**

Document Information ⌃

Collection Information

United States Social Security ⓘ
Death Index

Cite This Record

"United States Social Security Death Index," database, *FamilySearch* (https://familysearch.org/ark:/6190 3/1:1:V9MP-X4Q : 8 January 2021), Randall Wilkins, Nov 1976; citing U.S. Social Security Administration, *Death Master File*, database (Alexandria, Virginia: National Technical Information Service, ongoing).

Family Tree

Sign in or create a free account to discover even more information in our shared Family Tree.

SIGN IN   CREATE ACCOUNT

Similar Records

Randall A. Wilkins
Find A Grave Index

https://www.familysearch.org/ark:/61903/1:1:V9MP-X4Q

Figure 6 Randall Wilkins death record

Mr Leverne Lee Leverette

Obituary • United States, GenealogyBank Obituaries, Births, and Marriages 1980-2014

Name	**Mr Leverne Lee Leverette**
Sex	**Male**
Age	**79**
Residence Date	**27 Dec 2000**
Residence Place	**Acworth**
Death Date	**27 Dec 2000**
Birth Year (Estimated)	**1921**
Occupation	**Treasurer**
Event Type	**Obituary**
Event Date	**28 Dec 2000**
Event Place	**Georgia, United States**
Newspaper	**Marietta Daily Journal**

This record was indexed by a computer. If you find an error,

CLICK HERE TO REP...

Possible Family Tree Match

Levern...
• L7KO-RFL

ATTACH TO F...

DISMISS MATCH

Similar Records

Leverne Leverett
United States, Social Security Numerical Identification Files (NUMIDENT), 1936-2007

Leverne Lee Leverette
United States, GenealogyBank Obituaries, Births, and Marriages 1980-2014

Leverne Lee Leverette
Find A Grave Index

L L Leverette
United States Social Security Death Index

Document Information ⌄

Collection Information
United States, GenealogyBank Obituaries, Births, and Marriages 1980-2014

Cite This Record
"United States, GenealogyBank Obituaries, Births, and Marriages 1980-2014," database with images, *FamilySearch* (https://familysearch.org/ark:/6190

Mr Leverne Lee Leverette's Spouses and Children

Janice Leverette	Wife	F	⌄
Lance Leverette	Son	M	⌄
Dixie Lee Coffey	Daughter	F	⌄

Figure 7 Leverne Leverette death record

Dorothy Dix Davis Leverette

Death • Find A Grave Index

View on
www.findagrave.co

Name	**Dorothy Dix Davis Leverette**
Death Date	**26 Oct 1984**
Birth Date	**07 Mar 1918**
Event Type	**Burial**
Event Place	**Roswell, Fulton, Georgia, United States of America**
Cemetery	**Old Roswell Cemetery**
Photograph Included	**Y**

Document Information

Collection Information
Find A Grave Index

Cite This Record

"Find A Grave Index," database, *FamilySearch* (https://www.familysearch.org/ark:/61903/1:1:QVK3-CKB8 : 10 September 2021), Dorothy Dix Davis Leverette, ; Burial, Roswell, Fulton, Georgia, United States of America, Old

Attached in Family Tree to
Dorothy D...
• GDML-FGN

Similar Records

Dorothy Leverette
United States Social Security Death Index

Dorothy D Leverette
Georgia Death Index, 1933-1998

Attached To:
Dorothy Dix ...
1.. • GDML-FGN

Figure 8 Dorothy Leverette death record

Figure 9 Dorothy Leverette grave site

Figure 10 Henry Hull obituary

DEPARTMENT OF COMMERCE
BUREAU OF THE CENSUS

CERTIFICATE OF BIRTH
GEORGIA DEPARTMENT OF PUBLIC HEALTH

State File No. 8434

Register's No. 346

1. Place of Birth

(a) County Muscogee   MIN&
                               Dist. No.

(b) City or Town Columbus
(If Outside City or Town Limits, Write Rural)

(c) Name of Hosp. or St. Address City Hospital

(d) Length of Mother's Stay Before Delivery: In Hosp. ___ In This Community ___

2. Usual Residence of Mother

(a) State Georgia   (b) County Muscogee

(c) City or Town Columbus
(If Outside City or Town Limits, Write Rural)

(d) House No. & St. or R.F.D. & Box 2213 12th Avenue

Hour of Birth 7:10 A. M.

2. Full Name of Child Thomas Eugene Robinson

4. Date of Birth February 3, 19 44

5. Sex Male   6. Twin or Triplet ___   Born 1st 2nd or 3rd ___   7. Full Term Pregnancy If Not Give Months Gestation ___

8. Is Mother Married 9. To Father of This Child? Yes

FATHER OF CHILD

9. Full Name Dana Titus Robinson

10. Color White   11. Age at Time of This Birth 32

12. Birth Place of Father Chattahoochee County, Georgia

13. Usual Occupation Police

14. Industry or Business ___

15. Social Security No. 260-102606

MOTHER OF CHILD

16. Maiden Name Frances Mildred Harden

17. Color White   18. Age at Time of This Birth 27

19. Birth Place of Mother Columbus, Muscogee County, Georgia

20. Usual Occupation Housewife

21. Industry or Business ___

21. Social Security No. 260-101047

23. Was This Child Born Alive? Yes   24. Total No. of Children Born to This Mother 1

Born Alive (a) Now Living 1   (b) Now Dead 0   Born Dead (c) Dead 0

25. L.R.'s Own Signature J. A. Thrash

26. Date Filed March 3, 1944   Date of Supplemental Report ___

SUPPLEMENTARY DATA NOT A PART OF LEGAL CERTIFICATE

Give Complications of Preg. or Labor ___

Was This an Operative Delivery? ___

Was There a Birth Injury? Describe ___

Congenital Deformity? ___

27. I hereby certify that I attended the birth of this child who was born on the date stated above. The personal information as given on this certificate was furnished by Mr. & Mrs. Dana Titus Robinson

Related to the child as Parents

Was 1% Silver Nitrate Solution Used in This Child's Eyes? Yes

Attendant's Own Signature W. P. Jordan M. D.

Attendant's P. O. Address Columbus, Georgia   Date Signed 2-21-44

Figure 11 Thomas Robinson birth certificate

295

GEORGIA DEATH CERTIFICATE

State File Number 2021GA000011978

1. DECEDENT'S LEGAL FULL NAME (First, Middle, Last) THOMAS EUGENE ROBINSON	1a. IF FEMALE, ENTER LAST NAME AT BIRTH	2. SEX MALE	2a. DATE OF DEATH (Mo., Day, Year) ACTUAL DATE OF DEATH 02/02/2021

3. SOCIAL SECURITY NUMBER 256-82-2401	4a. AGE (Years) 76	4b. UNDER 1 YEAR Mos. Days	4c. UNDER 1 DAY Hours Mins.	5. DATE OF BIRTH (Mo., Day, Year) 02/03/1944

6. BIRTHPLACE GEORGIA	7a. RESIDENCE - STATE GEORGIA	7b. COUNTY MUSCOGEE	7c. CITY, TOWN COLUMBUS

7d. STREET AND NUMBER 8414 WHITESVILLE ROAD		7e. ZIP CODE 31904	7f. INSIDE CITY LIMITS? YES	8. ARMED FORCES? YES

9a. USUAL OCCUPATION U.S. MARINES	9b. KIND OF INDUSTRY OR BUSINESS MILITARY	

9. MARITAL STATUS DIVORCED	10. SPOUSE NAME	

12. MOTHER'S MAIDEN NAME (First, Middle, Last) MILDRED FRANCES HARDIN	13a. INFORMANT'S NAME (First, Middle, Last) JOHN G. ROBINSON	11. FATHER'S FULL NAME (First, Middle, Last) DANA TITUS ROBINSON

13b. RELATIONSHIP TO DECEDENT COUSIN

13c. MAILING ADDRESS 609 MOSS DRIVE HAMILTON GEORGIA 31811	14. DECEDENT'S EDUCATION HIGH SCHOOL GRADUATE OR GED COMPLETED

15. ORIGIN OF DECEDENT(Spanish/Hispanic/Latino) NO, NOT SPANISH/HISPANIC/LATINO	16. DECEDENT'S RACE (White, Black, American Indian, etc.) (Specify) WHITE

17a. IF DEATH OCCURRED IN HOSPITAL	17b. IF DEATH OCCURRED OTHER THAN HOSPITAL (Specify) NURSING HOME-LONG TERM CARE FACILITY

18. HOSPITAL OR OTHER INSTITUTION NAME (If not in either give street and no.) ORCHARD VIEW ASSISTED LIVING	19. CITY, TOWN or LOCATION OF DEATH COLUMBUS	20. COUNTY OF DEATH MUSCOGEE

21. METHOD OF DISPOSITION (specify) BURIAL	22. PLACE OF DISPOSITION KENNESAW MEMORIAL PARK 1306 WHITLOCK AVENUE MARIETTA GEORGIA 30064	23. DISPOSITION DATE (Mo., Day, Year) 02/09/2021

24a. EMBALMER'S NAME MARK ROUGHTON	24b. EMBALMER LICENSE NO. 4701	25. FUNERAL HOME NAME STRIFFLER HAMBY MORTUARY COLUMBUS

25a. FUNERAL HOME ADDRESS 4071 MACON RD COLUMBUS GEORGIA 31907	

29a. SIGNATURE OF FUNERAL DIRECTOR GARY HERBERT MURPHY	26b. FUN. DIR. LICENSE NO. 5647	AMENDMENTS

27. DATE PRONOUNCED DEAD (Mo., Day, Year) 02/02/2021	28. HOUR PRONOUNCED DEAD 09:25 AM

29a. PRONOUNCER'S NAME Mira LADON MURPHY Austin	29b. LICENSE NUMBER RN074493	29c. DATE SIGNED 02/02/2021

30. TIME OF DEATH 09:25 AM	31. WAS CASE REFERRED TO MEDICAL EXAMINER NO

32. Part I. Enter the chain of events-diseases, injuries, or complications that directly caused the death. DO NOT enter terminal events such as cardiac arrest, respiratory arrest. Or ventricular fibrillation without showing the etiology. DO NOT ABBREVIATE.

Approximate interval between onset and death

IMMEDIATE CAUSE (Final disease or condition resulting in death)	A. COVID 19	UNKNOWN
	Due to, or as a consequence of	
	B. MUSCLE WEAKNESS	UNKNOWN
	Due to, or as a consequence of	
	C. MYONEURAL DISORDER	UNKNOWN
	Due to, or as a consequence of	

Part II. Enter significant conditions contributing to death but not related to cause given in Part 1A. If female, indicate if pregnant or birth occurred within 90 days of death.

D.

33. WAS AUTOPSY PERFORMED? UNKNOWN	34. WERE AUTOPSY FINDINGS AVAILABLE TO COMPLETE THE CAUSE OF DEATH?

35. TOBACCO USE CONTRIBUTED TO DEATH UNKNOWN	36. IF FEMALE (range 10-54) PREGNANT NOT APPLICABLE	37. ACCIDENT, SUICIDE, HOMICIDE, UNDETERMINED (Specify) NATURAL

38. DATE OF INJURY (Mo., Day, Year)	39. TIME OF INJURY	40. PLACE OF INJURY (Home, Farm, Street, Factory, Office, Etc.) (Specify)	41. INJURY AT WORK? (Yes or No)

42. LOCATION OF INJURY (Street, Apartment Number, City or Town, State, Zip, County)	

43. DESCRIBE HOW INJURY OCCURRED	44. IF TRANSPORTATION INJURY

45. To the best of my knowledge death occurred at the time, date and place and due to the cause(s) stated. Medical Certifier (Name, Title, License No.) PIYUSH B. PATEL, MD, 056625	46. On the basis of examination and/or investigation, in my opinion death occurred at the time and place and due to the cause(s) stated. Medical Examiner/Coroner (Name, Title, License No.)

45a. DATE SIGNED (Mo., Day, Year) 02/15/2021	45b. HOUR OF DEATH 09:25 AM	46a. DATE SIGNED (Mo., Day, Year)	46b. HOUR OF DEATH

47. NAME, ADDRESS, AND ZIP CODE OF PERSON COMPLETING CAUSE OF DEATH PIYUSH B. PATEL, 6363 VETERANS PARKWAY COLUMBUS GEORGIA 31901	

48. REGISTRAR (Signature) /S/ CHRISTOPHER JP HARRISON	49. DATE FILED - REGISTRAR (Mo., Day, Year) 02/15/2021

Form 3909 (Rev. 04/2012), GEORGIA DEPARTMENT OF PUBLIC HEALTH

Figure 12 Thomas Robinson death certificate

LEGEND: Insert N/A in the items below which are not applicable.

PERSONAL DATA	1. LAST NAME - FIRST NAME - MIDDLE NAME	2. SERVICE NUMBER

1. LAST NAME - FIRST NAME - MIDDLE NAME		2. SERVICE NUMBER		2a. GRADE, RATE OR RANK	3. DATE OF RANK (Day, Month, Year)
ROBINSON, Thomas Eugene		2208855		PFC	10ct66

PERSONAL DATA

4. DEPARTMENT, COMPONENT & BRANCH OR CLASS: U. S. Marine Corps

5. PLACE OF BIRTH (City and State or Country): Columbus, Georgia

7a. RACE: b. SEX: Male

		6. DATE OF BIRTH	DAY	MONTH	YEAR
c. COLOR HAIR d. COLOR EYES e. HEIGHT f. WEIGHT 8. U. S. CITIZEN			3	Feb	44

8. U. S. CITIZEN: ☒ YES ☐ NO

10a. HIGHEST CIVILIAN EDUCATION LEVEL ATTAINED: N/A   b. MAJOR COURSE OR FIELD   9. MARITAL STATUS: Single

High School   4

TRANSFER OR DISCHARGE DATA

11a. TYPE OF TRANSFER OR DISCHARGE: Discharge   Academic

b. STATION OR INSTALLATION AT WHICH EFFECTED: MAD, NATTC, NAS, Memphis, Tennessee 38115

c. REASON AND AUTHORITY: #260 - Paragraph 13265.1a Marine Corps Personnel Manual & BUMEDINST 1910.2D

12. LAST DUTY ASSIGNMENT AND MAJOR COMMAND	13. EFFECTIVE DATE	DAY	MONTH	YEAR
Student MAD, NATTC, NAS, Memphis, Tennessee		23	Mar	67

13a. CHARACTER OF SERVICE: HONORABLE

b. TYPE OF CERTIFICATE ISSUED: DD 256 MC

SELECTIVE SERVICE DATA

14. SELECTIVE SERVICE NUMBER: N/A

15. SELECTIVE SERVICE LOCAL BOARD NUMBER, CITY, COUNTY AND STATE

16. DATE INDUCTED: DAY MONTH YEAR   N/A

17. DISTRICT OR AREA COMMAND TO WHICH RESERVIST TRANSFERRED: N/A

SERVICE DATA

18. TERMINAL DATE OF RESERVE OBLIGATION			19. CURRENT ACTIVE SERVICE OTHER THAN BY INDUCTION: None
DAY	MONTH	YEAR	a. SOURCE OF ENTRY
	None		☐ ENLISTED (First Enlistment) ☐ ENLISTED (Prior Service) ☐ REENLISTED ☐ OTHER:

20. PRIOR REGULAR ENLISTMENTS: None

b. TERM OF SERVICE (Years): 4

c. DATE OF ENTRY		
DAY	MONTH	YEAR
9	May	66

21. GRADE, RATE OR RANK AT TIME OF ENTRY INTO CURRENT ACTIVE SERVICE: PRIVATE

22. PLACE OF ENTRY INTO CURRENT ACTIVE SERVICE (City and State): Atlanta, Georgia

23. HOME OF RECORD AT TIME OF ENTRY INTO ACTIVE SERVICE (Street, RFD, City, County and State): 663 Barnes Mill Road, Marietta, Cobb, Georgia

25a. SPECIALTY NO. AND TITLE: 6600   b. RELATED CIVILIAN OCCUPATION AND D. O. T. NUMBER: N/A

24. STATEMENT OF SERVICE

24. STATEMENT OF SERVICE		YEARS	MONTHS	DAYS
a. CREDITABLE FOR BASIC PAY PURPOSE	(1) NET SERVICE THIS PERIOD	00	10	15
	(2) OTHER SERVICE	00	03	20
	(3) TOTAL (Line (1)+line (2))	01	02	05
b. TOTAL ACTIVE SERVICE		00	10	15
c. FOREIGN AND/OR SEA SERVICE		00	00	00

25. DECORATIONS, MEDALS, BADGES, COMMENDATIONS, CITATIONS AND CAMPAIGN RIBBONS AWARDED OR AUTHORIZED: Basic A/OElecTech

27. WOUNDS RECEIVED AS A RESULT OF ACTION WITH ENEMY FORCES (Place and date, if known): National Defense Service Medal; Marksmanship Rifle Badge

28. Service Schools or Colleges, College Training, Courses and/or Post-Graduate Courses Successfully Completed: None

SCHOOL OR COURSE a	DATES (From - To) b	MAJOR COURSES c	29. OTHER SERVICE TRAINING COURSES SUCCESSFULLY COMPLETED
None	None	None	None

VA DATA

30a. GOVERNMENT LIFE INSURANCE IN FORCE: ☐ YES ☐ NO

b. AMOUNT OF ALLOTMENT

c. MONTH ALLOTMENT DISCONTINUED: N/A

31a. VA BENEFITS PREVIOUSLY APPLIED FOR (Specify type): N/A

b. VA CLAIM NUMBER: C- N/A

AUTHENTICATION

32. REMARKS

Recommended for reenlistment
No time lost current active duty
Good Conduct Medal period commences 9May66
Period in an excess leave status: From 18Dec66 To 27Dec66
Check Excess leave for 10 days advance

33. PERMANENT ADDRESS FOR MAILING PURPOSES AFTER TRANSFER OR DISCHARGE (Street, RFD, City, County and State): 210 Carolyn Street Marietta, Georgia

34. SIGNATURE OF PERSON BEING TRANSFERRED OR DISCHARGED

Social Security Number 427-76-4199

35a. TYPED NAME, GRADE AND TITLE OF AUTHORIZING OFFICER: D. T. MANN, 2ndLt., USMC, AsstAdminO

b. SIGNATURE OF OFFICER AUTHORIZED TO SIGN

DD FORM 214 1 NOV 55   REPLACES EDITION OF 1 JUL 52, WHICH IS OBSOLETE.

ARMED FORCES OF THE UNITED STATES REPORT OF TRANSFER OR DISCHARGE

SR/OQR OR HQMC-2

S M C

Figure 13 Thomas Robinson Marine Discharge

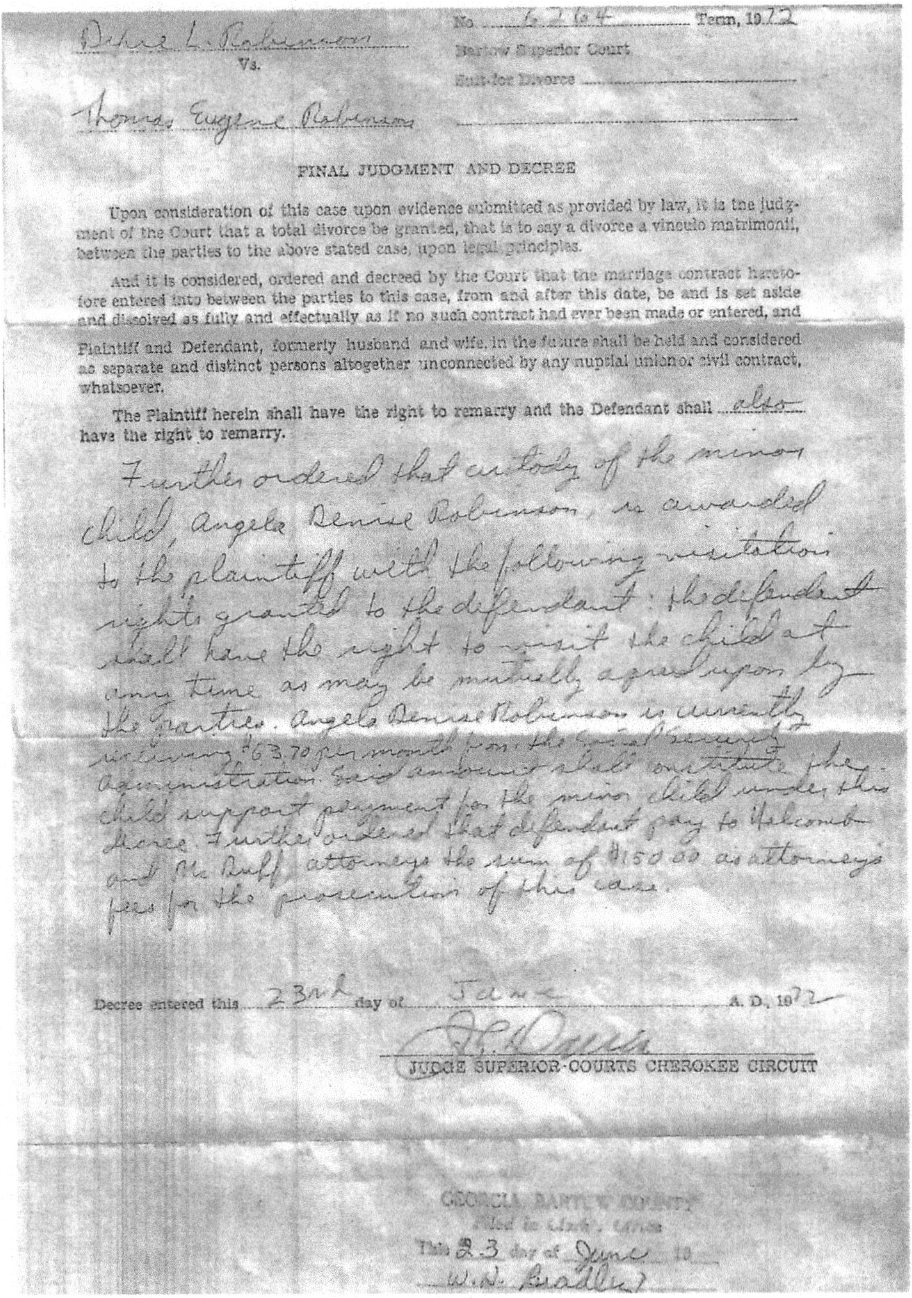

Dixie L. Robinson

Vs.

Thomas Eugene Robinson

No. 6264 Term, 19 72

Bartow Superior Court

Suit for Divorce

FINAL JUDGMENT AND DECREE

Upon consideration of this case upon evidence submitted as provided by law, it is the judgment of the Court that a total divorce be granted, that is to say a divorce a vinculo matrimonii, between the parties to the above stated case, upon legal principles.

And it is considered, ordered and decreed by the Court that the marriage contract heretofore entered into between the parties to this case, from and after this date, be and is set aside and dissolved as fully and effectually as if no such contract had ever been made or entered, and

Plaintiff and Defendant, formerly husband and wife, in the future shall be held and considered as separate and distinct persons altogether unconnected by any nuptial union or civil contract, whatsoever.

The Plaintiff herein shall have the right to remarry and the Defendant shall _also_ have the right to remarry.

Further ordered that custody of the minor child, Angela Denise Robinson, is awarded to the plaintiff with the following visitation rights granted to the defendant. The defendant shall have the right to visit the child at any time as may be mutually agreed upon by the parties. Angela Denise Robinson is currently receiving $63.70 per month from the Social Security administration. Said amount shall constitute the child support payment for the minor child under this decree. Further ordered that defendant pay to Holcomb and McDuff, attorneys the sum of $150.00 as attorney's fees for the prosecution of this case.

Decree entered this 23rd day of June A. D., 1972

JUDGE SUPERIOR COURTS CHEROKEE CIRCUIT

GEORGIA BARTOW COUNTY
Filed in Clerk's Office
This 23 day of June 19
W. N. Bradley

Figure 14 Dixie and Thomas divorce judgement

U. S. NAVAL HOSPITAL (74)

MEMPHIS, TENN., 38115

IN REPLY REFER TO:

NHMfs/18/fb
6320/1/J:X60401
10 March 1967

Mr. D. T. Robinson
210 Carolyn Street
Marietta, Georgia

Dear Mr. Robinson:

You no doubt are aware that your son, Thomas, has been a patient in this hospital for diagnostic study and evaluation. Probably he has already indicated to you through private correspondence that he has been upset to such a degree as to affect his emotional health and interfere with his military duties. The purpose of his admission to the hospital was to attempt to determine the causes for his distress and do whatever possible to help him overcome or correct them.

After considerable study and testing, our doctors have recommended that your son be released from the Marine Corps. It is most difficult to eliminate the various causes of his trouble and although he is somewhat improved, treatment for this disorder is of long duration and difficult. His return to civilian life, scheduled for the near future, will be to his best interests and to the best interests of the service.

I am sorry that I have to report this unfavorable news about your son, but am hopeful that his future endeavors will be more successful and that he will further improve. Should you desire any further information concerning your son's hospitalization here, please communicate with the Patient Affairs Officer at this hospital.

Very truly yours,

H. F. LENHARDT
CAPTAIN MC USN
COMMANDING OFFICER

Figure 15 medical eval for discharge Thomas Robinson

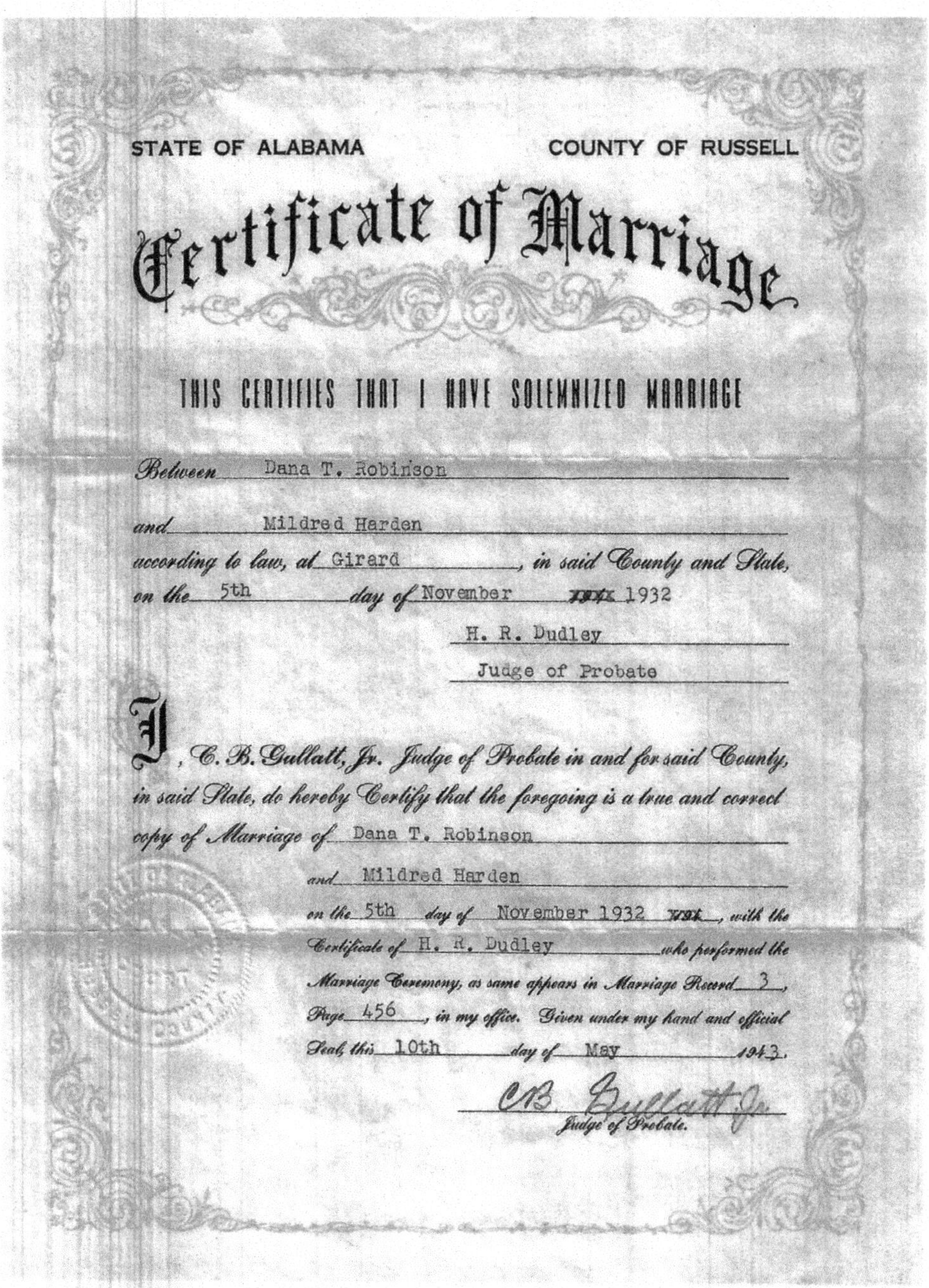

STATE OF ALABAMA   COUNTY OF RUSSELL

Certificate of Marriage

THIS CERTIFIES THAT I HAVE SOLEMNIZED MARRIAGE

Between   Dana T. Robinson

and   Mildred Harden

according to law, at Girard , *in said County and State,*

on the 5th *day of* November ~~19~~ 1932

H. R. Dudley

Judge of Probate

I, C. B. Gullatt, Jr. *Judge of Probate in and for said County, in said State, do hereby Certify that the foregoing is a true and correct copy of Marriage of* Dana T. Robinson

and Mildred Harden

on the 5th *day of* November 1932 , *with the Certificate of* H. R. Dudley *who performed the Marriage Ceremony, as same appears in Marriage Record* 3 , *Page* 456 , *in my office. Given under my hand and official Seal, this* 10th *day of* May 1943.

CB Gullatt Jr.
Judge of Probate.

Figure 16 Dana and Mildred marriage certificate

Dana T Robinson

Death • Find A Grave Index

Name	**Dana T Robinson**
Death Date	**Jan 1981**
Birth Date	**24 Sep 1911**
Event Type	**Burial**
Event Place	**Marietta, Cobb, Georgia, United States of America**
Cemetery	**Kennesaw Memorial Park**
Photograph Included	**Y**

Family Tree

ATTACH ...

Similar Records

Dana Robinson
United States
Social Security
Death Index

Dana T Robinson
Georgia Death Index, 1933-1998

Mr Dana T Robinson
United States, GenealogyBank Historical Newspaper Obituaries, 1815-2011

w.familysea rch.org/ark: /61903/1:1 :QV21-DD54 : 10 September 2021), Dana T Robinson, ; Burial, Marietta, Cobb, Georgia, United States of America, Kennesaw Memorial Park; citing record ID 84133492, *Find a Grave*, http://www .findagrave. com.

https://www.familysearch.org/ark:/61903/1:1:QV21-DD54

Figure 17 Dana Robinson death report

Georgia Department of Human Resources
Vital Records Unit

CERTIFICATE OF DEATH

State File No. ______

BIRTH NO. Militia Dist. No. Custodian's No.

1. NAME OF DECEASED (Type or Print) (First) Mildred (Middle) F. (Last) Robinson
2. DATE OF DEATH (Month) Aug. (Day) 9, (Year) 1976
3. PLACE OF DEATH (County) Bartow
City or Town: Acworth — In City Limits Yes ☐ No ☒ — LENGTH OF STAY (in this place) 7 yrs.
Name of Hosp. or Institution: Residence — LENGTH OF STAY 7 yrs.
4. USUAL RESIDENCE (Where deceased lived. If institution: residence before admission)
State Georgia County Bartow
City or Town Acworth — In City Limits Yes ☐ No ☒ — LENGTH OF STAY (in this place) 7 yrs.
Street Address or R.F.D. and Box No.: Rt. 1, Grover Landing Road
5. SEX F
6. RACE W
7. BIRTHPLACE (State or foreign country) Georgia
CITIZEN OF WHAT COUNTRY? USA
8. DATE OF BIRTH Dec. 23, 1916
9. AGE (in years) last birthday 59 — IF UNDER 1 YEAR Months Days — IF UNDER 24 HRS. Hours Min.
10. MARRIED ☒ NEVER MARRIED ☐ WIDOWED ☐ DIVORCED ☐ SEPARATED ☐
If Married or Widowed Give Name of Spouse: Dana T. Robinson
11. USUAL OCCUPATION (Give kind of work done during most of working life, even if retired) Cosmeticion
KIND OF BUSINESS OR INDUSTRY: Drug
12. WAS DECEASED EVER IN U. S. ARMED FORCES? (Yes, no, or unknown) (If yes, give war or dates of service) No
SOCIAL SECURITY NO.
13. FATHER'S NAME Tom Hardin
14. MOTHER'S MAIDEN NAME Anna B. Yelverton
15. IS RESIDENCE ON FARM? Yes ☐ No ☒
16. BURIAL ☒ REMOVAL ☐ CREMATION ☐ DATE Aug. 11, 1976
NAME OF CEMETERY Kennesaw Memo. Park — LOCATION (City or Town) (County) (State) Marietta, Cobb, Ga.
17. EMBALMER'S SIGNATURE [signature] — LICENSE NO. 2341
18. MORTICIAN Collins Funeral Home, Inc.
19. MORTICIAN'S ADDRESS 4947 North Main St., Acworth, Ga. 30101
20. INFORMANT Mr. Dana C. Robinson — Relationship Husband
21. INFORMANT'S ADDRESS Rt. 1, Grover Landing Road, Acworth, Ga. 30101

MEDICAL CERTIFICATION

22. CAUSE OF DEATH (Enter only one cause per line for (a), (b), and (c).) PLEASE PRINT
PART I. DEATH WAS CAUSED BY:
IMMEDIATE CAUSE (a) Ventricular arrhythmia — INTERVAL BETWEEN ONSET AND DEATH: Seconds
Conditions, if any, which gave rise to above cause (a), stating the underlying cause last.
DUE TO (b) Coronary atherosclerotic heart disease — Years
DUE TO (c)
DO NOT WRITE IN THIS SPACE 1. 2. 3. 4. 5. 6.
PART II. Other significant conditions contributing to death but not related to the terminal disease condition given in Part I (a)
23. AUTOPSY? Yes ☐ No ☒
24. ACCIDENT ☐ SUICIDE ☐ HOMICIDE ☐ — PLACE OF INJURY (e.g., in or about home, farm, factory, street, office bldg., etc.) — INJURY OCCURRED While at Work ☐ Not While at Work ☐
(CITY OR TOWN) (COUNTY) (STATE) — TIME OF INJURY (Month) (Day) (Year) (Hour)
HOW DID INJURY OCCUR?
25. I hereby certify that I attended the deceased from 1/31 19 76, to 8-9 19 76, that I last saw the deceased alive on 8-9-76, 19 76, and that death occurred at ____ m., from the causes and on the date stated above.
26. SIGNATURE Richard A Barlach, MD — Degree or Title
ADDRESS Richard Barlach 50 Plaza Way Marietta, GA — DATE SIGNED 8/12/76
27. DATE REC'D BY LOCAL REG. 8/19/76
28. REGISTRAR'S SIGNATURE Robert L. Owen

OAS(5)-3

"Certificate of Record"

"This is an exact copy of the death certificate received for filing in Bartow County, Georgia."

Signed by ______ Local Custodian Office

Figure 18 Mildred Robinson certificate of death

STATE OF GEORGIA, ____Cobb_____COUNTY.

To the Sheriff of said County or His Deputies:

You are hereby commanded to summon a commission of three men named in the annexed Commission (two of whom must be physicians and one an attorney) and cause them to assemble at the office of the Ordinary of the County aforesaid at ___9:00___ o'clock on the ___8th___ day of ___January_____, 19_70_, then and there to execute said commission and make return thereof.

This ___8th___ day of ___January_____, 19_70_

_____, Ordinary.

GEORGIA, ____Cobb_____COUNTY.

We, and each of us, do swear that we will well and truly execute this commission to the best of our skill and ability.

_____, Physician.

_____, Physician.

_____, Attorney.

Sworn to and subscribed before me, this ___8th___ day of ___January_____, 19_70_

_____, Ordinary.

GEORGIA, ____Cobb_____COUNTY.

By virtue of the annexed commission to us directed we, the undersigned, first being sworn, and having made such examination by inspection and proof as the law requires, report that we do find the said ___Thomas Eugene Robinson___ to be a person of sound mind and capable of managing ___his___ affairs.

_____, Physician.

_____, Physician.

_____, Attorney.

Cobb County _____COURT OF ORDINARY.

Chambers ___Jan. 7_____, 19_670_

Whereupon it is considered, ordered and adjudged that the said ___Thomas Eugene Robinson___ is a person of sound mind; and that as such ___he___ be restored to sanity and capacity.

_____, Ordinary.

ACKNOWLEDGMENT OF SERVICE

We, Dana Titus Robinson ,

and Mildred Robinson , hereby acknowledge service of the within and foregoing petition and order. All other notice and service are hereby waived.

This 10th day of November, 19 69

Dana Titus Robinson

Mildred R

Guardian Ad Litem

Cobb COURT OF ORDINARY, 19

Upon reading the foregoing petition, duly filed and it appearing that the notice of the same required by law has been given and no reason being offered to the contrary, it is ordered that the usual commission issue, directed according to law.

, Ordinary.

I hereby appoint Attorney to set in my stead

on the lunacy commission of

This , 19

County Attorney, Cobb County.

GEORGIA, Cobb COUNTY.

TO 1 E. A. Musarra , Physician.

TO 2 Bill Wallace , Physician.

TO 3 Jerry Gentry , Attorney.

GREETING:

Thomas Eugene Robinson having made petition on oath, to the Ordinary of said County alleging that he is a person of sound mind, you are hereby required, after first being sworn well and truly to execute the commission to the best of your skill and ability, to have the said Thomas Eugene Robinson personally brought before you, to examine him by inspection, and to hear and examine witnesses on oath, if necessary,

under which claim you find the said Thomas Eugene Robinson to come.

Witness my hand and seal, this 9th day of January, 19

Ordinary.

304

STATE OF GEORGIA, ____Cobb_____COUNTY.

To the Court of Ordinary of Said County:

The petition of_____Thomas Eugene Robinson_____respectfully shows to the Court as follows:

That on the ____6th__ day of ____February_____, 19__69_ your petitioner was adjudged a person of unsound mind by the Court of Ordinary of_____Cobb_____County, Georgia, ~~xxxx xxxxxxxxxxxxx xxx xxx~~ ~~xMotheigxxxxxxxxxxxxxxxxxxx~~

Petitioner further shows that____Dixie L. Robinson, petitioner's wife_____,

~~xxxxxxxxxxxxxxxxxxxxxxxxxxxxxxxxxxxxxxxxxxxxxx~~, residing in the State of Georgia, ~~xxxxxxxxxx~~

~~xxxxxxxxxxxxxxxxxxxxxxxxxxxxxxxxxxxxxxxxxxxxxxxxxxxxxxxxxx~~.was appointed Guardian ~~xxxxxxxx~~ to represent said petitioner.

Petitioner shows that_____he____ ~~xxxxxxxxxxxxxxxxxxxxxxxxxxxxxxxxxxxxxxxxxxxxxxxxxxxxxxxxx~~ is capable of managing____his_____own affairs.

WHEREFORE, Petitioner prays that this Honorable Court summon a commission to try this case in accordance with the Acts of Legislature of 1947, and that an order and judgment be entered declaring petitioner to be sane and that __he____ be restored to____his_____sanity and legal capacity.

Greene and Smith
by Jack M. Smith
Attorney for Petitioner
Address_510 Cobb Federal Bldg._
Marietta, Georgia

GEORGIA, ____Cobb_____COUNTY.

Personally appeared before the undersigned officer duly authorized to administer oaths _Thomas_

_Eugene Robinson_____, who after being duly sworn deposes and says that the facts set forth in the foregoing petition are true and correct.

Sworn to and subscribed before me, this

_November___ 10_, 19_69_

H. Horrell Greene

Thomas Eugene Robinson

_Dixie L. Robinson_____   ____Cobb_____COURT OF ORDINARY AT CHAMBERS

_Dana Titus Robinson_____   As the Three Nearest Adult Relatives of

_Mildred Robinson_____   _Thomas Eugene Robinson_

You are hereby notified that on the____1st___day of____December_____, 19_69_, the case of

_Thomas Eugene Robinson_____for restoration to sanity and capacity, will be heard by a commission selected in said cause.

This ___13th___ day of____November_____, 19_69_

_____   _____
_____   Ordinary.

Figure 19 Certificate of Restoration of Sanity

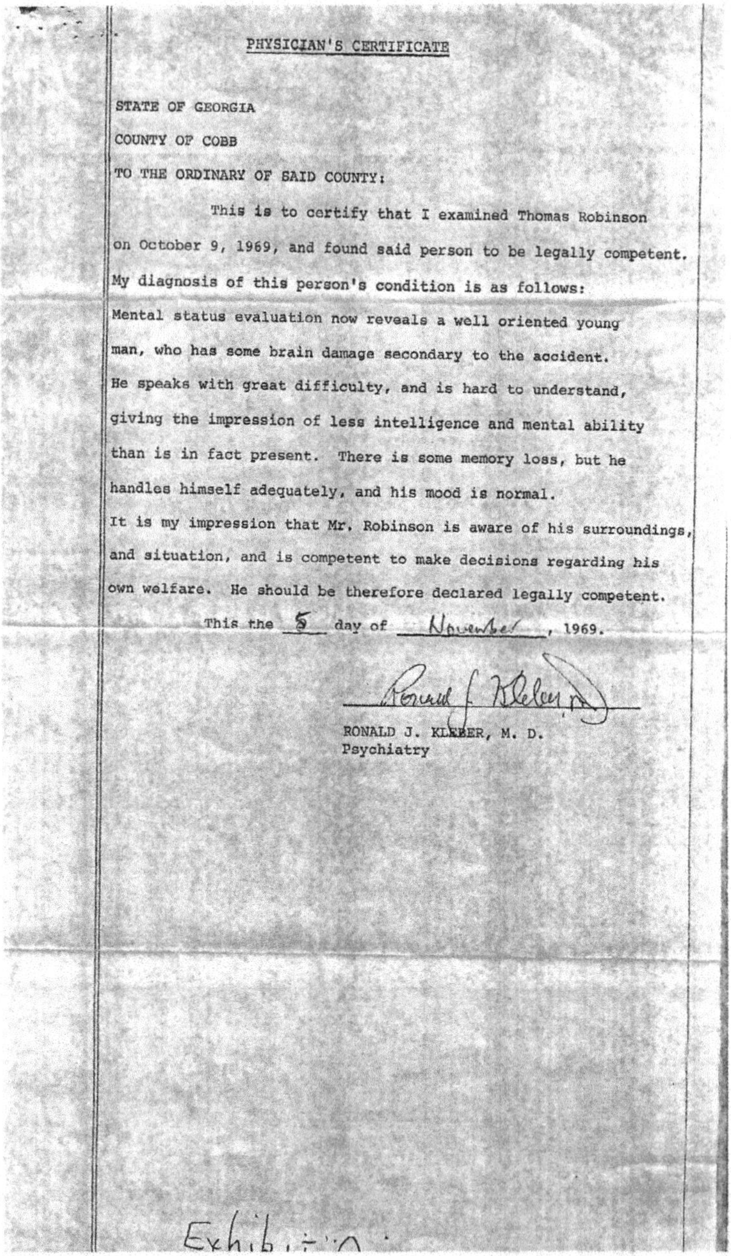

PHYSICIAN'S CERTIFICATE

STATE OF GEORGIA

COUNTY OF COBB

TO THE ORDINARY OF SAID COUNTY:

This is to certify that I examined Thomas Robinson on October 9, 1969, and found said person to be legally competent. My diagnosis of this person's condition is as follows:

Mental status evaluation now reveals a well oriented young man, who has some brain damage secondary to the accident. He speaks with great difficulty, and is hard to understand, giving the impression of less intelligence and mental ability than is in fact present. There is some memory loss, but he handles himself adequately, and his mood is normal.

It is my impression that Mr. Robinson is aware of his surroundings, and situation, and is competent to make decisions regarding his own welfare. He should be therefore declared legally competent.

This the 5 day of November, 1969.

RONALD J. KLEBER, M. D.
Psychiatry

Exhibit "A"

Figure 20 Physician certificate of competency

306

STATE OF GEORGIA

COUNTY OF COBB

IN THE COURT OF ORDINARY OF SAID STATE AND COUNTY:

The foregoing petition of THOMAS EUGENE ROBINSON for a full and perfect accounting of the property, both real and personal, of said THOMAS EUGENE ROBINSON, to be held on the _1st_ day of _DECEMBER_, 19_69_, having been filed, and it appearing to be just and proper, it is ordered that a citation issue to the said DIXIE L. ROBINSON, as such Guarding, to be and appear at the _DECEMBER_ Term, 19_69_, of said court and make a full and perfect accounting of the property, both real and personal, of THOMAS EUGENE ROBINSON, and that a copy of said petition and this order be personally served upon the said DIXIE L. ROBINSON at least ten (10) days before said term of court of Ordinary.

This the _10th_ day of _November_, 19_69_.

_____
ORDINARY, COBB COUNTY, GEORGIA

Figure 21 Thomas Robinson property disposition

Figure 22 Dana and Frances gravestone

Figure 23 Thomas Robinson grave stone

Figure 24 Album - Misfits

THE MISFITS

The Misfits are a new band group to play around the county at various school and club parties and dances. The two in back L-R are Randy Wilkie and Larry Hensley; the two in front L-R are John Faulkner and Gene Robinson. Randy and John both attend Sprayberry High School. Larry goes to East Cobb and Gene graduated from Sprayberry last year and is presently employed at Rich's. The group will play for an Elks sponsored dance, Saturday night for the Pinetree Country Club Teen dance, December 29.

Figure 25 The Misfits newspaper article

311

Figure 26 The Misfits band photo

Figure 27 Onyx Blu's Band poster

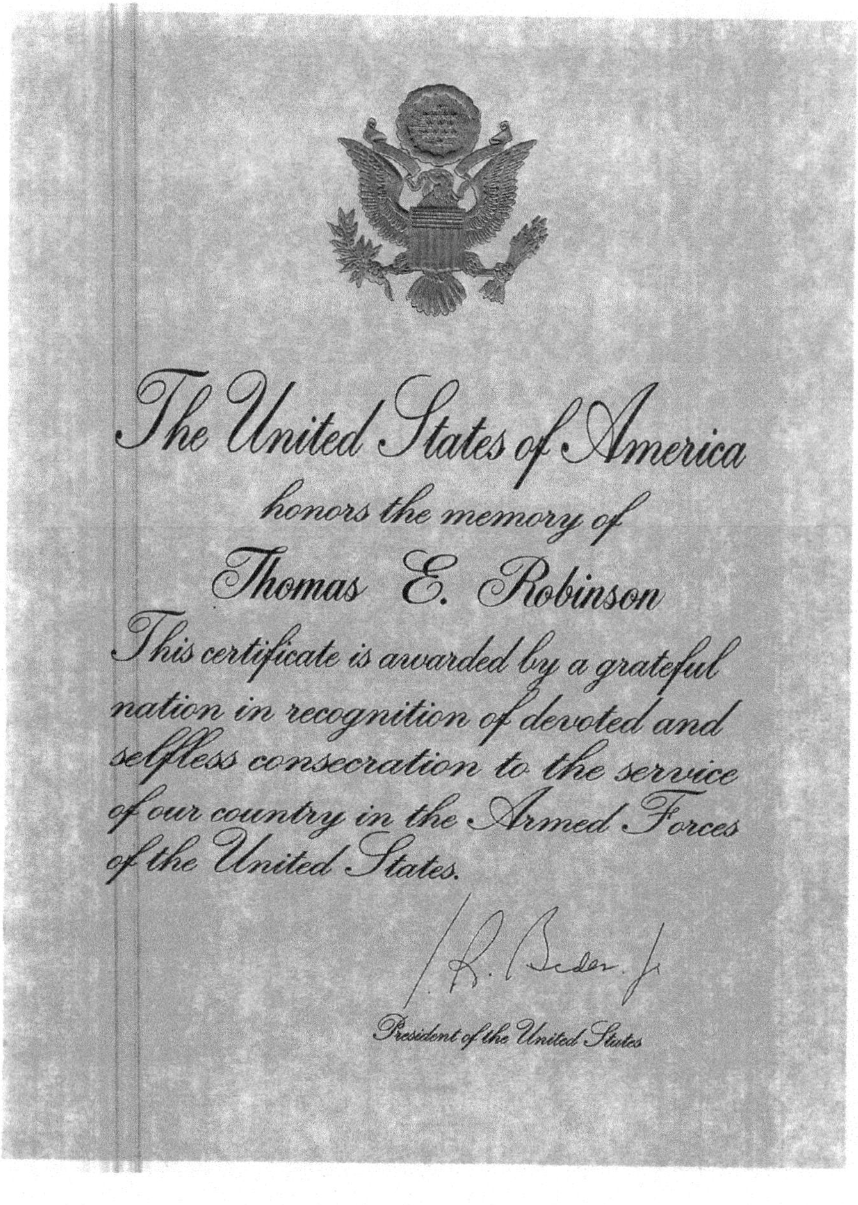

The United States of America

honors the memory of

Thomas E. Robinson

This certificate is awarded by a grateful nation in recognition of devoted and selfless consecration to the service of our country in the Armed Forces of the United States.

President of the United States

Figure 28 Presidential remembrance letter

Figure 29 Thomas Robinson - Marine Corps

Figure 30 Thomas and Angela photo

Figure 31 Thomas and Angela photo 2

Figure 32 Young Thomas Robinson

Robin Naneen Bracken

Social Program Document • United States, Social Security Numerical Identification
Files (NUMIDENT), 1936-2007

No Image Available

**Document
Information** ⌄

**Collection
Information**
United States,
Social Security
Numerical
Identification
Files
(NUMIDENT),
1936-2007

Cite This Record

"United States,
Social Security
Numerical
Identification Files
(NUMIDENT),
1936-2007",
database,
FamilySearch
(https://www.fam
ilysearch.org/ark:
/61903/1:1:6KW
N-HBQN : 10
February 2023),
Robin Naneen
Bracken, .

Name	**Robin Naneen Bracken**
Name Note	**Name and form dates: Application: ROBIN NANEEN BRACKEN (Jun 1972), Application: ROBIN NANEEN WARTMAN (May 1974), Death: ROBIN N WARTMAN (08 Apr 2004)**
Alias	**Robin Naneen Wartman**
Second Alias	**Robin N Wartman**
Sex	**Female**
Social Program Application Date	**Jun 1972**
Previous Residence	**Woodinville, King, Washington, United States**
Previous Residence Postal Code	**98072**
Death Date	**8 Apr 2004**

Family Tree

ATTACH TO FA...

Similar Records

Robin N Wartman
United States Social
Security Death Index

Robin N Wartman
Washington Death Index,
1965-2014

Birth Date	**12 Sep 1957**
Birthplace	**Tucson Pima, Arizona, United States**
Race	**White**
Father's Name	**John H Bracken**
Father's Sex	**Male**
Mother's Name	**Jane A Livingston**
Mother's Sex	**Female**
Event Type	**Social Program Correspondence**

Robin Naneen Bracken's Parents and Siblings

John H Bracken	Father	M	⌄
Jane A Livingston	Mother	F	⌄

https://www.familysearch.org/ark:/61903/1:1:6KWN-HBQN

Figure 33 Robin Wartman death report

Figure 34 Angela and Valerie photo